Essays on
Cuban Music

North American
and Cuban Perspectives

Edited by **Peter Manuel**

UNIVERSITY
PRESS OF
AMERICA

Lanham • New York • London

Copyright © 1991 by
University Press of America®, Inc.
4720 Boston Way
Lanham, Maryland 20706

3 Henrietta Street
London WC2E 8LU England

Library of Congress Cataloging-in-Publication Data
Essays on Cuban Music : North American and
Cuban Perspectives / edited by Peter Manuel.
p.   cm.
Includes bibliographical references and index.
1. Music—Cuba—History and criticism.
2. Cuban Americans—New York (N.Y.)—Music
—History and criticism.   I. Manuel, Peter Lamarche.
ML480.E88   1991
780' .97291—dc20   91-27250 CIP   MN

ISBN 0-8191-8430-6 (cloth : alk. paper)

The paper used in this publication meets the minimum requirements of
American National Standard for Information Sciences—Permanence
of Paper for Printed Library Materials, ANSI Z39.48–1984.

The scorn of our formidable neighbor who does not know us is our America's greatest danger. . . Through ignorance it might even come to lay hands upon us. Once it does know us, it will remove its hands out of respect. One must have faith in the best in men and distrust the worst.

José Martí

Table of Contents

Socialism, Nationalism, and Music in Cuba

Introduction

This volume is a collection of essays written by contemporary Cuban and North American scholars on various aspects of Cuban music, dealing primarily with music in Cuba proper, but also with contemporary derivative genres that flourish in New York City. It constitutes an attempt to respond to the growing Euro-American interest in Cuban music and its offshoots, and, in general, to recognize, through scholarly attention, the extraordinary richness, vitality, and international influence of that music over the last two centuries. Indeed, with the possible exception of certain former colonial powers, there is probably no country on earth whose music has had such extensive foreign impact, relative to its size, as has that of Cuba.

Despite Cuban music's international influence, and the increased attention to Latin American music on the part of North American scholars and musicians, very little has been published in English on Cuban music. Fortunately, Cuban writers themselves have produced a substantial body of scholarly literature -- impressive both in quantity and quality --, but most of their publications have remained untranslated and generally unavailable, for various reasons, not only abroad but often even within Cuba itself. Part of the problem has been the ephemerality of Cuban scholarly books and journals, which, although inexpensive, often run out of print within weeks of their appearance. A more serious problem which confronts any North American who is seriously, or even casually interested in viii

exploring Cuban music, has been the information blockade which has existed between Cuba and the USA since the early years of the Revolution. Cuban censorship of the mass media has contributed to this lack of communication, but, on the whole, Cuban scholars, musicians, and others, with official encouragement, have avidly welcomed interaction and exchange with interested and open-minded foreigners, including North Americans. Rather, it has been the United States government which has imposed tight (and arguably unconstitutional) restrictions on travel to Cuba, importation of publications, and visits by Cubans to the USA; the intent of these restrictions has evidently been to better depersonalize Cubans as faceless enemies, and to prevent public anti-communism from being diluted by a balanced understanding of the Cuban Revolution, with its positive as well as negative achievements. The subsequent obstacles limiting information exchange and communication have, on the one hand, further isolated Cuban scholars from developments in American academia; on the other hand, and more significantly for interested North Americans, they have inhibited understanding and appreciation of the heritage of a country which has contributed significantly to our own culture (as well as demography), and which remains, despite the wishes of successive White House occupants, a mere ninety miles from the tip of Florida.

Hence, it is an explicit goal of this volume to challenge and surmount, in however tentative and limited a manner, this information blockade which has inhibited Cuban studies and mutual understanding in both countries. This book attempts to familiarize interested readers with some of the directions in Cuban music research undertaken in Cuba itself since 1959, by presenting a representative selection of the work of contemporary Cuban music scholars. These articles are complemented by five essays by North American researchers, addressing aspects of music in Cuba and derivative genres in New York.

The inclusion of articles by Cuban scholars is also intended as an attempt to overcome some of the limitations inherent to traditional monologic ethnography in general. In recent years, scholars of ethnography and its sub-disciplines, including ethnomusicology, have become increasingly skeptical of the ability of the Western researcher to represent "the Other." Such considerations have been reinforced by post-structuralist questioning of language's potential neutrality and objectivity and, by extension, of the premises of empirical positivism as a whole. Meanwhile, ethnologists themselves have grown increasingly sensitive to the unavoidable subjectivities and distortions involved in attempting to describe and speak for subjects with whom they are often in an unequal neo-colonial relationship. If Cuba is not as "exotic" or remote as tribal New Guinea, the intense antagonism of diplomatic relations between the USA and Cuba renders any attempt at representation politically charged and sensitive. Some aspects of musical studies, such as those concerning formalistic analysis, may gingerly skirt thorny socio-political controversies. However, it should be clear that both in my own writings and my selection of articles here, far from avoiding such sensitive issues, I have tended to focus on them as the most significant and interesting subjects, especially for their potentially polemical nature. Hence several articles in this volume (especially chapters 8-13) confront, from different perspectives, the ways that socio-political climates in the US and Cuba have conditioned the evolution, dissemination, and meaning of Cuban and Cuban-derived music therein.

While I do not claim to endorse every argument and sentiment expressed in this volume, it would be disingenuous of me to pretend that my own writing and choice of selections are not reflective of my own interests and biases, however "balanced" I may try to be. It may not be irrelevant, in this regard, to state explicitly that I am in sympathy with many of the basic goals and achievements of the Cuban Revolution, that I am ashamed of my government's repeated acts of aggression against the Cuban people, but, that at the same time, I am not uncritical of certain Cuban domestic policies. I am also well aware of the sensitivity felt by many Cubans toward North American commentaries on Cuban affairs. Such sensitivity is quite natural given the arrogant chauvinism characterizing so much North American discourse on Cuba, whether coming from imperialist government ideologues or from radical Yankee visitors who lecture their Cuban hosts on how they should be running their revolution. While such concerns have not prevented me from putting my own thoughts into print, they have motivated me to balance them, in the context of this text, with perspectives allowing Cuban "others" to speak for themselves. Although the plural authorship of this volume does not pretend to constitute an innovative exercise in dialogic intersubjectivity, it does reflect my own commitment to confront the special problems of ethnographic representation inherent to Cuban studies.

Musicology in Cuba

Since 1959, Cuban researchers, funded primarily by branches of the state Ministry of Culture, have produced a considerable amount of music scholarship, most of which has naturally concentrated on the island's own heritage of traditional, classical, and contemporary popular musics, rather than on musics abroad (although projects have also been undertaken in Angola and Grenada). Much research has been conducted under the auspices of the Centro de Investigación y Desarrollo de la Música Cubana (CIDMUC), a research and planning institution in Havana. Other scholars have been variously connected with universities, the mass media, or with the Casa de las Américas, which generates publications, conferences, and other activities relating to Latin American culture as a whole.

Cuban writing on music can be grouped into a number of categories, distinguished by intended readership, effects, and the like. As elsewhere, perhaps the largest body of literature is journalistic, appearing in magazines, newspapers, and books aimed at the general reader; although not scholarly in intent, Cuban music journalism (especially as published in relatively highbrow magazines like *Revolución y Cultura* and the now-defunct *Clave*) is generally sophisticated in quality and quite useful as a source for academic research.

Constituting a quite different kind of literature are the more directly functional studies and surveys which are written, if not commissioned, to comment upon various aspects of music and its management in Cuba. Several of the reports produced by the "Desarrollo" (development) wing of CIDMUC fall into this category, which would cover anything from a critique of the operation of record stores, to an assessment of how many violinists can or should be employed in the eastern provinces. In this volume, Leonardo Acosta's article "The Problem of Music and its Dissemination in Cuba" could be also classified alongside such studies, as it is clearly intended to have an impact not only on casual readers, but, in an applied sense, on those involved in various aspects of the state music industry.

The growing body of Cuban music literature written in a more purely scholarly vein could itself be classified in two or three groups. Most of the research published by modern Cuban scholars has consisted of rather straightforward descriptive studies, covering basic musicological, textual, and organological data, with relatively cursory treatment of ethnological background. Given the ongoing decline of several Cuban folk music traditions, native scholars tend to see the emphasis on descriptive documentation as appropriate, if not urgent. Further, many Cuban music scholars, like musicologists elsewhere, have been trained in an academic tradition which has emphasized formal analysis rather than the humanistic study of music in its socio-cultural context. Linguistic, economic, and political barriers have also tended to isolate Cuban musicologists from developments in English-medium ethnomusicology, and especially from the influence of cultural anthropology thereupon. As a result, in comparison with contemporary Western ethnomusicology, much Cuban musicology has exhibited a relatively heavy emphasis on organology, collection, technical analysis, documentation of neo-Africanisms and the like, rather than on humanistic, interpretive research. In this volume, the articles by Linares and Alen, on the *décima* and *tumba francesa*, respectively, and León's introductory chapter are in this essentially descriptive vein.

Alongside such straightforward empirical documentation, however, Cuban scholars have in fact produced a significant amount of more interpretive studies. These include a number of theoretical works (e.g., on musical enculturation, the evolution of rhythms, or music and cultural colonialism), which relate only tangentially to Cuban music *per se*. Of greater interest here are those studies which focus on a given aspect of Cuban music from a particular conceptual framework. Given the prevailing ideological orientation of the Revolution, Marxism and anti-imperialism color many such works in one way or another; considerably more pronounced, however, are a healthy nationalism and a trenchant anti-racism, which, while wholly congruent with Revolutionary ideology, also characterized the better pre-Revolutionary writing. Perhaps the most inspired contemporary writing on Cuban music combines these underlying themes with an appreciative interest in urban popular music styles. In this volume, Leonardo Acosta's "The Rumba, the Guaguancó, and Tío Tom" introduces the reader to the traditional rumba and one of its most venerable exponents. Rogelio Martínez Furé's widely-read "Tambor" is a more poetic, metaphorical expression of the Cubanization of African musical retentions, while his "Regarding Folklore" combines a cursory overview of Afro-Cuban music with what may be taken as a representative statement of the prevailing Cuban Marxist policy toward folklore in general. A second article by Argeliers León -- "Of the Axle and the Hinge" -- explores the ways in which developments in Cuban art music since 1850 have been shaped by nationalism.

North American perspectives

Any holistic study of Cuban music must acknowledge the extent to which Cuban popular, light-classical, and in some cases, even traditional folk musics have become international phenomena. Cuban-style dance music, from the bolero to con-

temporary salsa, has flourished in Spain, Africa, greater Latin
America, and even such remote places as urban Vietnam, but
its greatest contemporary impact has been in New York City,
where the Cuban *son* and rumba came to form the stylistic basis for salsa, which has served as the dominant popular music
for area Latinos since the late 1960s. John Murphy's "The
Charanga in New York and the Persistence of the *Típico* Style"
situates the popular *charanga* dance ensemble and its music in
the New York context; similarly, Steve Cornelius discusses the
transplanting of music of the Afro-Cuban *santería* religion in
his essay "Drumming for the Orishas: Reconstruction of
Tradition in New York City." Meanwhile, my own article, "Salsa
and the Music Industry: Corporate Control or Grassroots
Expression?" explores how the commercial mass media have
actively influenced the evolution, dissemination, and meaning
of salsa in the city. As an examination of the efficiency and responsiveness of the music industry, this essay also constitutes a
kind of companion piece to two subsequent articles, Acosta's
aforementioned "The Problem of Music and its Dissemination in
Cuba," and an essay by James Robbins, "Institutions, Incentives,
and Evaluation in Cuban Music-Making." It is hoped that these
three articles together may illuminate some of the distinct
ways in which both the Cuban socialist music industry and its
capitalist counterpart in the USA tend actively to shape the
music they disseminate, rather than serving as neutral vehicles
of transmission. Finally, the volume concludes with another
article of my own, which attempts to explore how Cuban
Marxism seeks to accommodate the aesthetic pluralism implicit
in the wide variety of musics flourishing on the island.

Sources and Acknowledgements

Due to the different backgrounds and approaches of the authors represented in this volume, and the variety of topics
dealt with, the essays presented here reflect considerable diversity in terms of content, style, depth, length, and, to some
extent, quality. Whether welcome or not, this diversity reflects
the nature of the extant research on Cuban music, including the

fact that Cuban and North American scholarly communities have operated in relative isolation from each other. Indeed, in compiling this text I have deliberately sought to represent some of the breadth and variety of perspectives extant on Cuban music, rather than selecting a set of homogeneous essays written, say, by North American scholars of similar backgrounds and training. While individual readers will inevitably find certain essays to be more useful and interesting than others, it is hoped that the compilation as a whole may give some idea of the breadth of Cuban musical genres, of significant relevant socio-cultural issues, and of the kinds of conceptual approaches reflected in research to date.

The translated articles and their sources are as follows: "La décima y el punto en el folclor de Cuba" (María Teresa Linares), "Notas para un panorama de la música popular," and "Del eje y la bisagra" (Argeliers León) are all from the out-of-print volume *Ensayos de música latinoamericana: selección del boletín de música de la Casa de las Américas* (Havana: Casa de la Américas, 1982). Leonardo Acosta's two articles were reprinted from obscure journals in his hard-to-find collection *Del tambor al sintetizador* (Havana: Editorial Letras Cubanas, 1983). Olavo Alen's "The Tumba Francesa" is from an unpublished manuscript in English. Rogelio Martínez Furé's "Tambor" and "Diálogo imaginario sobre folklore" (here presented as "Regarding Folklore") originally appeared in *Diálogos Imaginarios* (Havana, 1979), whose first edition was sold out within weeks of its original publication, and which not been reprinted since. The latter article was translated into English and adapted into standard prose format (rather than a dialogue) by Sandra Levinson and Jerome Nickel, and published in that form in *Canto Libre*, a pamphlet produced by the Center for Cuban Studies. The translation employed here is essentially the same, with some minor revisions. The articles by Steve Cornelius and James Robbins are revised forms of chapters in their Ph.D. dissertations, while John Murphy's piece derives from material in his M.A. thesis "The Charanga in New York, 1987-88." My own "Musical Pluralism in Revolutionary Cuba" was previously published as "Music and Ideology in Revolutionary Cuba" in *Journal of Politics and Culture* (3/3, Spring 1990), while my "Salsa and the Music Industry: Corporate Control or Grassroots Expression?" appeared, in edited form, as "Salsa and the Mass Media in the United States" in *Journal of Communication* (41/1, Winter 1991).

León's "Del eje y la bisagra" ("Of the Axle and the Hinge") was translated by Terence Sweeny, and the poetry in chapter V was translated by Elena Manitzas; I have made editorial and stylistic changes in each -- including appending an explanatory phrase to León's title. Aside from these, and Martínez Furé's "Regarding Folklore," all translations from the Spanish are by myself. In the process of translation I have added explanatory footnotes and made minor editorial revisions where appropriate, while trying to preserve the sense of the original. In some cases -- and particularly with León's rather convoluted and taxing style -- I have taken syntactical liberties, but always with the intent of clarifying rather than altering the author's evident meaning; moreover, the Cuban authors have all had opportunities to comment on my translations. I have further added introductory remarks to each of the essays, regarding the background of the works and their authors, and, in some cases, their relation to the other essays and to Cuban music research as a whole. The subdivisions by which I have grouped the articles in the table of contents should not be regarded as airtight, since there is a certain amount of overlap between them. Finally, I have appended a glossary to clarify the numerous Cuban Spanish terms found throughout the text.

I would like to acknowledge the warm assistance and cooperation provided by the Cuban scholars whose work is included here, as well as the hospitality and support of numerous other Cuban acquaintances and informants. Olavo Alen and his colleagues at CIDMUC have been particularly helpful. Roberta Singer provided useful comments on the first draft of the manuscript. Further thanks are due to the Center for Cuban

Studies, and to Michael Krinsky for facilititating research and correspondence.

P.M.

New York, 1991

I

Cuban   Perspectives

on Traditional Folk and Popular Musics

1

Notes toward a Panorama of Popular and Folk Musics

It is fitting that a volume such as this should commence with a general survey of Cuban music, and the following essay by Argeliers León suits this purpose quite well, although it is somewhat idiosyncratic in style and approach, and covers popular music trends only up to the 1960s. León himself, the author of two books and several articles on Cuban music, was Cuba's seniormost musicologist, and served as a teacher, if not mentor, to most of the younger generation of Cuban music scholars. He was also one of the nation's leading art music composers, and served for several years as director of the Music Department of the Casa de las Américas in Havana. León's death in 1991 marked the end of an extraordinarily productive and creative musical and scholarly career.

Naturally, it is difficult to survey a field as vast as Cuban music without introducing a plethora of terms, and the thorough reader may wish to consult the glossary for further explanation of some of the names introduced. Some commentary is also due regarding León's taxonomy of folk (or "people's") music genres, which groups them as (1) archaic peasant or ritual genres, (2) the "urban primary element," and (3) the "urban elaborated element." The latter category is intended to comprise genres characterized, on the whole, by various degrees of professionalism, middle-class patronage, art music influence, and of dissemination via the mass media (sheet music, recordings, etc.) -- in a word, the type of music that otherswriters might refer to as "urban popular," as opposed to the more informal, secular "urban folk" musics which León has called "urban primary elements." In translating this essay I have taken the liberty of substituting these less ambiguous terms for León's original nomenclature. I have also adopted a somewhat liberal, rather than literal approach to translating León's occasionally difficult prose.

1

Notes toward a Panorama of Popular and Folk Musics

Argeliers León

Cuban folk and popular musics, as opposed to art music, originated in the cultural contributions of the two great migratory currents -- namely, the Spanish and the African -- which forged our nationality. By contrast, the classical music created in Cuba has derived from a number of European musical currents, sometimes proceeding in tandem with a movement generated in Europe, and in some instances borrowing liberally from the music of our own people.

In the realm of folk and popular music we may distinguish three broad categories: first is that music which remains closely allied to its original, pre-Cuban sources or antecedents, represented by campesino songs and the ritual music of Afro-Cuban societies. A second category of people's music is the cultivated popular music conditioned by the exigencies of the urban environment, and which is generally known as Cuban popular music. Between these two realms lies a third category of genres, comprising the secular, primarily urban folk musics which, relatively free from influences of ritual and rural ambiences, constitute, as it were, primary sources from which urban popular musics have liberally borrowed.

Of these three categories, the best known, and that with which we are most associated by tourists, is the "cultivated" urban popular music, including such genres as the traditional *contradanza, danza, vals tropical, habanera, romanza, canción, guajira, criolla, clave, bolero, guaracha, danzón, son,* and *pregón,* along with other less familiar genres, such as the *lament* and the *afro,* and certain professional and stylized forms of the rumbas and *comparsa* songs which, in their original forms, we would categorize as urban folk.   Today we would have to add the *mambo,* the *chachachá,* the *guapachá,* the *mozambique,* the *pilón,* the *pa-cá,* the *simalé,* the *mongolés,* and others.[1]

The realm of urban folk music would encompass the original forms of the *yambú, guaguancó, columbia* [i.e., the three major kinds of rumba], *chambelona, changüí, comparsa* songs, and other more regional genres.   In this category also existed choral groups of diverse types of social and musical organization.   In the urban folk realm a great variety of manners of sound production have been employed, from the sonorities which can be extracted from a wooden door, to the blare of a *trompeta* bought in the Chinese barrio.[2]   Indeed, enterprising Cubans have used every conceivable method to accompany their songs. A door has often been used to produce different sounds with a variety of strokes, e.g., by tapping some fingers on the central panel and others on the frame, or striking with the flesh of the index finger, the side of the thumb, the tips of the fingers, the hypothenar, wrist, or with the open hand or palm, whether damping the sound or letting it resonate.   To this range of percussive techniques can be added those performed on a skillet, using stove tongs, or with a pair of spoons struck on the palm, or on a table.   In ensembles in some parts of Oriente, big brass

---

[1] The latter four genres and the *guapachá* were ephemeral pop genres of the 1950s-60s; the *mozambique* enjoyed brief popularity as a *comparsa* and popular dance genre in the 1960s. All notes in this article are added by the editor.

[2] That is, the Chinese oboe, *sona,* used in carnival music in Santiago de Cuba.   Note also that León has classified the rumba (in the form of *guaguancó, columbia,* and *yambú*) as essentially urban genres.

containers are used as resonating vessels for vocalizations made near an open hole in one of the sides of the container; bottles are also used as resonators; and the *mocha*, a small campesino machete, is played as a rasp by scraping its dull edge against a kitchen- or work-knife.

Similar sonorities are sought with other objects. In urban cafes one can hear groups of men performing an informal *guaguancó*, beating on the side of a chair (especially the old "Vienna" chairs) and a marble table, and scraping a key on an inlaid soda bottle, or blowing a bass note across its aperture to sustain the harmony of the group. Such effects could also be used to back up a singer improvising *décimas*.[3] When greater timbral richness and variety were desired, a "*quintico*" could be formed, using a *tumbadora* [conga], an old *cornetín*, with its strident tone, the jawbone of a burro, or diverse sets of cow-bells, for which could be substituted the bars of a plow, spokes of a broken wheel, or a hollowed cylinder of wood.

This simple *quintico* ensemble could be heard in the *chambelonas* which used to be formed for festivals or for the fanfare of some corrupt politician. Formerly these ensembles also used to pass through the capital, incorporating a portable organ as well, to publicize circuses. Similarly, in Manzanillo, Bayamo, and Oriente [since subdivided], one can still encounter dances accompanied by an odd ensemble consisting of a small crank organ, two *timbales*, and a *guayo* [tin rasp]. The old ensembles of accordion, mouth organ, *claves*, *güiro* or some other rasp, and guitar, although rare now, can still be found in rural Camagüey and Las Villas provinces. Still heard in Guantánamo are the groups called *changüí*, consisting of guitar, *tres, claves*, bongo, and occasionally a *güiro* [with singing].

One can speak, in a word, of a range of sound-producing techniques, used by certain social classes and conditioned by a given socio-economic setting, typical of urban folk music. The repertoire of such music, then, is characterized by such tech-

---

[3]Ten-line verse forms; see chapter 5.

niques, together with a set of stylistic norms, which can be summarized as:

> (a) the usage of instrumental timbres which can be seen to occupy a given set of planes or levels, according to pitch, with contrasting timbres superimposed in ongoing rhythmic lines;

> (b) usage of the voice in a more instrumental than strictly vocal manner (in contrast, for example, to the stress on fluid melody in the *canción*);

> (c) alternating solo-choral format;

> (d) association with couple dance or mimetic group dance (as in Carnival *comparsas*).

Such features also characterize African-derived religious music, to which we may now turn. The particular organization of the sugar industry brought whites and blacks together in the mills. The blacks continued to practice African rituals and to believe in old, though not precisely African practices of black magic. Many of the groups practicing the neo-African rituals which still survive were perpetuated and spread precisely by the slaves brought to old sugar mills, by the change of masters, or by the sale of mills or their slaves. Even the surnames of many black families derive from this bitter aspect of our sugar. Thus proceeded the geographical dispersion of these musical repertoires and practices in accordance with the structure of the country's economic base in the different periods of our history.

The presence of African slaves acted in several ways as a catalyst, at times unnoticed, in the formation of our national character. The blacks recreated, along with their ritual practices, their full traditional repertoire of accompanying songs, while reconstructing their traditional musical instruments and, eventually, altering them, readapting them, abandoning some and creating new ones with different woods and metals, in accordance with new possibilities and circumstances. The freed blacks either remained closely tied to these ancestral traditions, or distanced themselves from such customs and adopted, as much as was possible, the life-styles of the more Europeanized (albeit in a provincial rather than courtly sense) citizens. Several freed Africans or creolized first-generation blacks participated in salon ensembles, playing minuets, polkas, "gallops," old lanceros, quadrilles, *rigodones, contradanzas*, and the entire repertoire of slightly out-of-date European salon music. Such musicians also played or sang in churches and Santa Cruz festivals, participated in Corpus Christi theatrical presentations, performed in orchestras accompanying itinerant opera troupes, and joined military bands. In many cases, the black performer, in the capacity of an ensemble member, could even penetrate white society to lend a touch of "mestizo-ness," of "color" with his music as well as his blood. Indeed, just as the degrees and kinds of mixture were diverse, so were the musical influences and results equally varied, changing through the course of normal development and being molded into the forms which became the antecedents of the urban folk and popular genres mentioned above.

The musics associated with African-derived rites differ in terms of the uses and customs of the associated ritual. Today, many of these traditions are disappearing, along with the original groups, or else they are being assimilated into other ritual practices. The most widespread of those Afro-Cuban musics still surviving are: the musics associated with *lucumí* or Yoruba-derived rituals; those of the Calabar-derived *abakuá* society; and music of Congo (Bantu) origin. The *lucumí* and *abakuá* societies flourish primarily in Havana and Matanzas provinces, while Congo traditions are found mostly in the northern part of Pinar del Río, in Havana province, and to a lesser extent, in northern Las Villas. In eastern Cuba, especially Santiago de Cuba and Guantánamo, groups deriving from remote, transculturated Dahomeyan roots, with colonial French influences, can be found in the form of the *tumba francesa* societies. Informants in El Perico, in Matanzas province, recall another old *cabildo francés* [Afro-Cuban mutual aid society], of which only two or three former members remain, along with three dessicated drums and assorted anecdotes about the Afro-French ancestors, who spoke patois and "Parisian." Similarly, elder residents of the village of Placetas, Las Villas province, remember an *arará cabildo*, of Dahomeyan ancestry, while such a *cabildo* still functions in the city of Matanzas.

Spread throughout these general areas mentioned are some musical practices not associated with any particular isolated area, but which appear in certain occasions or opportunities; the same people who participate in some rituals on occasion can be found integrating others, such that they may even be members of Catholic brotherhoods, or be Rosacrucians, Masons, or university graduates, whether white, black, Chinese, or of any degree of mixture.

The Yoruba or *lucumí* musics comprise *toques* [lit., rhythms, strokes] played on the *batá* drums with *güiro* or *abwe* scapers, or on *bembé* or *iyesá* drums. The *lucumí* also adopted *olokum* drums, although their use has long since disappeared. The songs of these groups include invocations to spirits used to precipitate possession of the believer (who is then referred to as possessed, risen, "mounted," or "having a song"). Other songs are imprecations challenging the deity to prove his or her power, or they may be *puya* songs attacking or provoking another singer, or referring to defects in order to force him to respond. These songs are used when the *toque* is performed with *güiros*, or is associated with a *bembé* or *iyesá* event. It would be difficult to describe all the slight variants in the dances, songs, and ritual customs of each group. The texts of these songs are generally in what remains in Cuba of the Yoruba language, although it appears that only corrupted phrases of the *oyó* and *iyesá* dialects remain. In regions distant from the capital, *lucumí* songs have incorporated Spanish words -- a practice more common in Bantu- or Congo-derived musics.

The Bantu-derived rituals are practiced in various societies or *reglas* known by the names *quimbisa, malombe* [*mayombe*], and *briyumba*. They are found in more or less remote rural areas as well as in towns and even in Havana itself. Their songs, which are quite distinct from the *lucumí* ones, are accompanied by various instruments, of which perhaps the most distinctive are the large *makuta* barrel drums and the cylindrical *ngoma* drums. The former is the ancestor of the familiar conga drums, whose use has become standard in *comparsas* [Carnival processions] as well as internationally. These conga drums come in three sizes, the largest of which is the "conga" proper, followed by the *tumbadora*, and the smaller *quinto*. The traditional use of *requintos* (fifes) in military bands appears to be the source of the use of the term *quinto* for the higher-pitched drum, as well as of expressions like "*quintico,*" "*¡fulano quintea que se paso!,*" and "*¡responder a un buen quinteo!*" The two larger drums are also both occasionally referred to as *tumbadores*.

The *abakuá* or *ñáñigo* groups or *potencias* use three types of instruments. One type symbolically represents hierarchic dignities in the societies' organization; these instruments, the *seseribó, empegó, ekueñón,* and *enkríkamo*, are not used for playing music [but rather for ceremonial calls]. The second type consists of only one instrument, the sacred *ekué* drum, which may not be seen. It is used to produce a "howling" friction sound while pressing a *güin* (central rib of the crest of a palm leaf) over the top of the drum skin. In the third group of instruments, which actually accompany songs, are the *bonkó-enche-miyá*, the *obí-apá*, the *kuchí-yeremá*, the *biankomé* (two sticks or *itones* used to play rhythms on the *bonkó-enche-miyá*) and the *ekón*, or cowbell made of two leaves of iron riveted together to form a bell without a tongue. Also used are two *erikunde*, which are basket-like rattles with a base made of the cap of a calabash covered and adorned with a collar of fibers of raffia palm or sisal (made from the cords of these materials sold in the market). These uncovered baskets, by the name *cha-chá*, can be heard in the ensembles which accompany some *comparsas* of Santiago de Cuba.

In the *tumba francesa* are used four large, decoratively painted trunk drums, with skins attached by pegs inserted, with the use of wedges, in holes in the body. Along with the drums, a log is also played [idiophonically], mounted on a wooden base and set on a bench. Our studies have found that this log, called *catá*, is also used in *lucumí* music in Santa Clara, Palmira, Placetas, and Sancti Spíritus. It is interesting to note that *tumba francesa* used to exist in this same area; by contrast, this form is not found in the area represented by the plains of Colón, between Matanzas and Santa Clara, in spite of the fact that old people still recall the *tambor francés* ["French drum"], as they call the drums of the now extinct *tumbas* in that region; thus, they speak of, for example, "so-and-so who knows how to play French," or they recall past fiestas and say, "In my house they used to play *tambor francés*, but not any more." In this region, the old *catá* lost the rack on which it is lain in Oriente, as well as its name; instead, one speaks of "playing the sticks (*palos*)", or "So-and-so, do it with the sticks" (*"dale tú a los palos"*), and when the musician is improvising brilliantly, they say "How about those *palos, mi madre!"* In such cases the other drummers play softer and less intensely so that the *catá* player may stand out.

The *arará* drums, derived, like those of the *tumba francesa*, from old Dahomey instruments, are used in groups of three, to which are added a cowbell, while another musician beats two sticks on the side of the *caja* or largest drum. The system of affixing the heads is different from that of the *tumbas*, and the body of the drum is cylindrical and slightly bulbous. In an opening in the rounded part, at the other end from the skin, another small cylinder is inserted, which serves as a foot, although the drum is played reclining on a chair or on a large wooden fork. The *arará* drums are decorated with pictures and geometric designs, forming trimmings around its entire body.

The original groups in Oriente formerly used a large, conical drum, the *bacú*, to accompany *comparsa* songs and certain *misas espirituales* ["spiritist masses"], practiced along with the most curious amalgams of customs and mystifications, which illustrate how various popular, transcendental, mystical, and religious concepts spread among the public.

From all these currents, with their complex mutual influences, one can perceive a set of stylistic features, whose study and documentation should be reserved for a more specialized work than this one. These stylistic elements, which can be regarded as "cells" assimilated in such an idiosyncratic way as to become distinctly Cuban, evolved and developed over the course of generations, and were combined and recombined; mixing with foreign elements and associated with cult practices ingenuously introduced from other musics, they gave place to folk genres appearing in the cities. These latter came to be further influenced by urban musicians who, having some formal, albeit tenuous, musical education and technique, lent these musics a new character; alternately, such musics were influenced by professional arrangers who injected their own clichés and commercial conventions.

In this social context appears the presence of the *composer*, ever more wrapped up in authorial organizations and even legal controversies regarding cases of copyright and plagiarism, in which, however, all was ultimately plagiarism -- except for whatever was not Cuban -- and where the ingenuity of the self-styled "creators" of this or that genre was limited to the more or less successful mixture of the ingredients already extant in our musical culture.

Thus appeared the *danzas habaneras* which evolved into the *habaneras, contradanzas, guarachas,* and *boleros* of the nineteenth century. The diverse minuets, according to an announcement of a Havana dance school in 1832, were characterized variously as "serious," "common," "pastoral," "courtly," "with allegro of gavotte," *"alemandado," "escoses," "nuevo afandangado," "campestre,"* and even a *dengue* minuet, composed in that city. Other dances announced by this academy were the "national" [i.e., Spanish] ones: *fandango, gaditano, rondeña, seguidillas, malagueñas, olé, guaracha*, and again, the *dengue*.[4]

The historian Serafín Ramírez (1833-1907), in his work *La Habana artística*, relates, along with such announcements from the contemporary press, the great public fondness for dance; he laments the extent to which the "most beautiful creole *contradanza*" has been forgotten, replaced by "this degeneration of our *contradanza* called *danzón*," with its "revolting and risque" rhythm.[5] "It is not the *danzón* [i.e., the dance itself] which must be corrected," says Ramírez, "but rather its music, as it is the latter which provokes such romping about." Earlier he writes:

> Drop this music from the *danzón*, and substitute for it any of the old *contradanzas* of Saumell, Muños, Estrada, Buelta y Flores, Hilarión [which were archaic even by the mid-1800s] or of any old author, in whom are found neither these foreign melodies which now seem to titillate our ears, nor this disgraceful braying of the trumpet, nor the silly scratching of the *guayo* [scraper], nor the bewildering racket made by the drums [i.e., the *timbales*]; eliminate, once and for all, the names of many of these, and those which others bring in foreign tongues, and then we will have eliminated much that is improper and grotesque.

Around 1893, the musician Laureano Fuentes Matons (1825-98) of Santiago de Cuba published his book *Las artes in Santiago de Cuba* and referred to a musical panorama analo-

---

[4]The *fandango* is the most popular folk song-type of southern Spain. *Gaditano, rondeña,* and *malagueña* are characteristic folk song-types of Cádiz, Ronda, and Málaga, respectively; the *guaracha*, although evidently originating in the New World, enjoyed some popularity in colonial Spain, although it has since died out there, flourishing instead in Cuba as a dance song genre.

[5]In the 1880s, the popularity of the *contradanza*, or *habanera*, was supplanted by that of the *danzón*, which is more rhythmic in character and features the isorhythmic ostinato called *cinquillo*.

gous to that described by Ramírez in Havana. Fuentes Matons mentions some "street bands which form on the feast of San Juan and Santiago" and other groups comprising "guitars, *bandolas* [mandolins], flutes, and keyless fifes which are much in use"; after relating the influence of the French immigration in his city, he observes that the ensembles of the city, "consisting of people of color," play *contradanza, passpied, gavota,* sung waltz, and the minuet. Such ensembles would include one or two clarinets, two or three violins, two horns, a bass viol, and a "military-type drum which they call *tambora.*"

The *dengue*, despite the denunciations of some, went on flourishing and generating other genres ever more risque and provocative. While these genres remained largely confined to somewhat disreputable dance salons, such establishments were frequented by aristocratic young men who came to enjoy the music and fraternize with "mulatto party girls"; similarly, daughters of the elite would sing such popular songs beyond earshot of their upright and stern fathers. Meanwhile, the common people, white and black, went on singing and dancing the ardent rumba -- a name which, although specifically denoting a music and dance genre, connotes a general attitude and ambience as well. Thus, rumba as a specific genre was more commonly referred to by the more precise names of its predominant variants, namely, *yambú, guaguancó,* or *columbia.* Chroniclers and poets of the sixteenth and seventeenth centuries have mentioned genres like *ñandú, paracumbé, gurrumbé, yeyé, gayumbas, gurujú,* and *zumbé,* which were described as erotic, lascivious, frenetic, or provocative dances, evidently not far from the rumba styles. Mimetic movements characterized some of these sub-genres, like the *papalote, cariaco, sígueme-pollo, tumba-Antonio,* and the *tornillo.* Shortly before, the *boteo* had been introduced, and after that, several mimetic movements were introduced into salon dances like the *pilón.* Many old rumbas were also of this type. Among those, which we now refer to as rumbas of the "Spanish period," are recalled the *Tus condiciones*, the rumba of *Lala no sabe hacer ná, Pa' la escuela, Tumbar la botella*, and so on, where the dancer tries to evoke, with his actions, the given situation inspired by the solo singer.

The term *yambú* refers to a slower form of rumba or dance style, with lighter, suaver movements, executed in a more bent-over posture; although the *yambú* is an erotic couple dance, the male dancer, unlike in the *guaguancó*, never performs the pelvic thrust movement called *vacunao*, from *vacunar* [lit., to vaccinate], a symbolization of the moment of sexual domination. We may suggest in a purely hypothetical vein that perhaps the unhurriedly lascivious gestures of the *yambú* referred in some epoch to the pre-climactic moments of the sexual act. As the eminent scholar Fernando Ortiz has noted, a possible antecedent of the rumba may be the dances of certain rites in which mimetic representation occurred, and that when the primogenic significance of these disappeared, the movements remained as archaic vestiges. The dancer must be very familiar with the rumba's aesthetic to know just when to do the *vacunao*. Its usage in Cuba finds parallels in other dances in Africa and Latin America using [what elsewhere, e.g., in Brazil, is called] the *ombligada*, wherein dancers touch their navels together. The *rumba columbia* itself, a solo male dance with ostentatious acrobatics and great agility, could well have originated as an initial scene of one of the fertility rites mentioned above. In urban folk genres like the *rumba guaguancó* we invariably find a solo singer and chorus, the soloist improvising or "raising" (*levantar*) the song, and after a while indicating the refrain, or *capetillo*, to the chorus. At that moment, a couple may emerge from the circle and start to dance, each partner proceeding to take the initiative or "seize" (*arrebatar*) the dance; the male eventually manages to dominate his partner with a *vacunao*, at which point the woman, after a few more dance steps, may let herself be replaced by some other woman who has sufficient agility to gracefully dodge the man's *vacunao*. At times, the male may make a demonstrative gesture with his hands, at a point where he could have executed a *vacunao*, as if to say, "Just think what could have happened!"; alternately, he may execute a kick in the air [in the direction of the woman's groin] or a pelvic thrust to indicate his macho domination of the woman, who has been managing to evade him. In the *columbia*, these gestures are made by the solo male dancer in front of the *quinto*, establishing a dialogue between the aggressive and exuberant rhythms executed by the drummer and the dancer. The texts used in the *yambú* are short and ordered in couplets, whether assonant, completely free, octosyllabic, or of irregular meter. In contrast, the text of *guaguancó* is narrative, or relating a sequence of events, or in the form of a *puya* (provocative challenge or duel). In previous times, ten-line *décimas* were used, and certain individuals were renowned for their skill at improvising in this framework. Still today one speaks of "décima-ing" (*décimar*) or "inspiring" or "raising" a *guaguancó*, even when *décimas* are not used, but rather a simple prose punctuated by melodic phrases.

The instrumentation of the rumba can consist of the informal ensembles we described in the beginning of this article, from the frame of a door to an old *bacalao* [codfish] box serving as a *tumbadora*, along with a little box of the type formerly used for candles, here substituting for a *quinto*, being played by a pair of spoons, and, finally, *claves* [two wooden sticks struck together] played by the singer. A more elaborate ensemble would include two conga drums.

The more affluent dance salons of the upper classes eventually came to foster more sophisticated, stylized and elegant forms of rumba and *conga* [genre]; such genres had been popularized through vernacular theater, in which they served as extravagant finales danced by the entire company. It was indeed in the contexts of such theaters and exclusive salons that foreigners were initially exposed to the image -- soon to become a promotional item -- of the friendly and curvaceous *mulata* seductively exhibiting her bust under a palm tree.

The *conga* [genre] has followed a similar path. While it continues to be used in its original context as a song in *comparsas*, it has crossed boundaries of prejudice to fuse, in some contexts, with the rumba in stylized   reincarnations quite remote from the original forms of either genre.[6]

We have mentioned the urban folk music which reflects some influence of art music.   In this category we may place the *guajira*, *criolla*, and *clave* [genre].   From the late nineteenth to early twentieth centuries, Cubans increasingly sought modes of artistic expression which would be sufficiently distant from those of Spain as to identify us as distinct. Such aesthetic nationalism conditioned the coalescence of the stylistic elements which are today heard in campesino music.   This music also served as a refuge for whites who sought a genre which was at once distinctively Cuban and yet devoid of African-derived elements.   Such was the significance of this music in the wretched context of slavery, linked with colonial despotism, and in the ambience of the intense racism that was particularly virulent among white urban youths (especially in Havana).   But the process of coalescence, of course, involved much more than this, comprising other socio-political and stylistic recombinations and developments.

From the eighteenth century on, new dances were continually being introduced into our salons, especially with the advent of French immigrants from Haiti and New Orleans.   While the *contradanza* and the waltz were perhaps the most prominent of these imports, in the dance academy announcement referred to above, we also find mention of the "figured waltz" (*vals figurado*), the *ruso, francés,* and *mousarrina*, along with *contradanzas* in Spanish, Russian, .and English styles.

The waltz, instead of going the way of the *dengue* or incorporating the "bewildering racket of rasps and drums," became slower and acquired a text.   This *vals tropical,* with its three clearly designated tempi in 3/4 and its fluid melody in equal note values, gave birth to many *canciones*.   In these song-ori-

---

[6]Note again, that the rumba and *conga* remain predominantly Afro-Cuban genres, performed, like the *comparsa* processions, primarily by blacks.

ented waltzes (less associated with dance), the melody was treated syllabically and generally lacked the regular upbeats which intensifed the rhythm of the typical waltz.   Instead, this kind of waltz progressed soon to a second tempo (such as appears in the accompaniment to *guajiro* songs), whose text, as we have pointed out, referred to the beauty of our island, or to distant laments of Siboney, or consisted of expressions of nostalgia for imaginary lands, and the like.

Aside from the waltz, the *contradanza* [*habanera*] introduced other stylistic elements.   Many *contradanzas* of Saumell use an accompaniment with the figure quarter-note, two eight notes, quarter-note, in which the central eight-notes form an independent unit from the quarter-notes; this effect was transmitted to the *criolla*, while the accompanying rhythm of other *c o n t r a d a n z a s* tended to reiterate the figure in 6/8: ♩♪♩ ♪ . ♩ ♩ ♩ exhibiting elements found later in the *guajira*. Many of these *guajiras* were published and recorded under the label *punto* [otherwise designating campesino settings of *décimas*].   The *criolla* differed little from the old *canciones*, while adopting a 6/8 meter which in the *canción* had been replaced by a 3/4 time, and adapting a standard Cuban-style accompaniment.

Under the same name *guajira* was produced another genre in duple meter, incorporating many stylistic features of the *son*, and whose text and melodic line refer to campesino music.   The semi-cadence [i.e., on the "dominant"] in these genres remains as the last vestige of the modality of campesino music; within this genre, slight differences in the ambience and character of the accompaniment enable us to distinguish sub-genres like the *guajira-son*.

The same process occurred with the *clave*.   Black Cubans had come to cultivate a secular song performed by different sorts of choral groups, in which they would rehearse, in an informal and self-taught way, the harmonizing of various vocal lines, choosing texts and polishing their language; also popular were smaller groups called *claves*, accompanied by guitars and an unstrung banjo struck [like a frame drum] and called *viola* (Cf. the Brazilian *violao*), along with the *clave* sticks themselves. These *clave* groups often used *décimas* as texts, or else simple sequences of verses with some sort of rhyme. Many white youths imitated these groups, forming *estudiantinas* [strolling student bands], singing in different parts of the city, and brawling amongst each other, as in the case of the old *clave* groups "La Yaya" and "El Jiqui." Also known as *clave* was an ephemeral type of song sung, like the *criolla* and *guajira*, in 6/8, appearing in Cuban *zarzuelas* [light operas], and other lesser vernacular theatrical dramas.

Within this orbit of urban folk music, we must mention, on one hand, the colonial *canción*, in the polished *salonnier* [salon] style, and, on the other hand, the popular version of the same genre. In both cases, *canción* connotes a song in which the vocal text predominates, and which, unlike most of our music, does not accompany dance.

On the whole, the texts of the salon *canciones*, although sentimental and amorous, were not surcharged with social problems or insoluble tragedies, but rather with an ingenuous innocence. In this they resembled the entire range of Hispano-American *canciones* which were inspired by colonial romanticism and, in our case, reinvigorated by the influence of the diverse nationalistic currents of the emerging South American countries. However, it was not in the elite salons, but in the realm of popular music that the explicitly patriotic *canción* flourished, capturing the intensity of our own independence struggle. Alongside this genre thrived the picaresque *canción*, which, although arising in the colonial period, sometimes parodied its salon counterpart and generated a variety of graceful *guarachas*. Only the text distinguishes this genre from the popular *canción* in general.

The Cuban *canción* varies from the simplest and most spontaneous, in both music and text, to the flowery coloratura songs with elaborate texts by Nervo or Darío. This sub-genre has not been cultivated since the last compositions of Sánchez de

Fuentes, or of Guillermo Tomás, whose songs aspired to imitate the lied.

The bolero and *guaracha*, in their current versions, are types of *canción*, thoroughly popular, that is, less sophisticated than salon music, but with greater public appeal. During the nineteenth century, they were songs of popular *trovadores*, of men of the people, who were never invited to perform in the elegant salons or the private concerts of someone like the Countess of Merlín. Nevertheless, their songs passed from mouth to mouth, and were heard as serenades through colonial windows; they were the lyric expression of a Cuban identity which continued to develop from Spanish couplets and other genres. They were sung with guitar accompaniment, generally by two voices. The bolero was more romantic, and the *guaracha* more saucy, but both were fraternal products of this "uncultured" yet musical people.

In its present form, the bolero has been richly influenced by the *son*. It is no longer solely a sung, i.e., non-danceable genre, but rather, basing its style on the rhythm of the *montuno* of the *son*,[7] it now serves as a slow and lilting dance, replacing, at the beginning of the twentieth century, the danceable form of the *habanera* and the traditional-style *son* itself, which eventually declined.

Similarly, the *guaracha* has ceased to be an intimate vocal duet with guitars, and is now performed by a large dance band, and is perhaps the most popular dance genre today. Although similar in style to the *son*, its tempo is faster and its associated dance styles are particularly flashy. It retains its traditional, characteristically Cuban satirical text, while incorporating the *montuno* of the *son* which lets the dancers sing along with the refrain.

---

[7]The *son* can be regarded as consisting of two formal sections: a "song"-like *canto*, followed by an indefinitely long *montuno*, in which responsorial vocals, and sometimes instrumental improvisations, are performed over a simple harmonic ostinato.

The *danzón*, regardless of Serafín Ramírez's comments and criticisms quoted above [i.e., denouncing the alleged foreign influences of black popular music], has completed its life cycle wholly within the realm of our own folklore. It was a predominantly instrumental dance genre, emerging with elements taken from the declining *contradanza* and *danza*, and invigorating these features with a louder, livelier instrumentation taken from Spanish bands. The use of clarinet, ophicleide, and *timbales* outraged the *contradanza* lovers, but these instruments subsequently gave way to others -- piano, two violins, and five-keyed flute -- which were more suitable, and occupied the discrete timbral planes typical of so much of our music. The *timbal* was replaced by *palitas*, forming a more balanced ensemble, namely, the *charanga francesa*, which later made itself even more familiar via the contemporary *chachachá*.

The first factor distinguishing the *danzón* from its antecedents was its form, which developed from an ABA structure to an ABAC. Later, being influenced, like other genres, by the *son*, it came to incorporate a ["vamp"-like] *montuno*, and changed anew into the form ABACAD, the D part itself being in the form of a short rondo: *abacadae*, etc. Since its appearance in 1879, the *danzón* would continue to evolve and be revitalized, just when its decline seemed imminent. Thus, for example, "El bombín de Barreto" introduced a *montuno*, while "Las tres bellas cubanas," of A.M. Romeu, included a virtuoso piano part. As late as 1920 it was the only genre played in many dances, which generally continued until midnight, with dance couples listening as they strolled about the dance floor. Then in 1929, facing a new impasse, the *danzonete* appeared, as a symbol of its open decline, changing the instrumental *montuno* of the third style of *danzón* to a vocal *montuno*, like that of the *son*, that is, adding a vocal text, and eliminating one of the formal sections. Thus did the *danzón* complete its full cycle, evolving from decadent European classical music of the Romantic period, and then, descending from its aristocratic origins, wandering through its musical life, generating new derivatives and eventually stylizing itself to the point where it became a symbol of our musical past.

The *son* is the Cuban musical genre *par excellence*. Vocal and danceable, it is of mixed Spanish and African descent, evolving from a rural ambience free from the classical influences of the elite salons. The *son* adopted from Spanish custom the sonority of the plucked string, but created its own instrument, the *tres*.[8]   It generally uses the cuartet as a text, although some primitive *sones* used *décimas*. But it added to the plucked string the percussive, African-derived rhythms and a formal structure derived from Afro-Cuban music, *viz.*, the open-ended alternation of solo and chorus [i.e., as in the *montuno* of the rumba].

The *son* emerged from its campesino context in the early twentieth century. It was at once a dance genre and the lyrical expression of the most sincere and unpretentious man of the people. From the lowest social strata it has proceeded to ascend and strengthen its style, influencing other genres in the process. Its appearance in the cities revolutionized other genres like the *criolla, clave*, and bolero, which were saved from decline when composers revitalized them by incorporating the *son's* rhythm, calling them *criolla-son, bolero-son*, and *guajira-son*. Similarly, one can see that ternary rhythm disappeared completely from these genres. The *son*, while hastening the decline of the *danzón*, went on to inspire new forms of the danceable bolero and the modern dance-oriented *guaracha*. The original *son* ensembles of *tres, claves,* and maracas were expanded to include bongos, keyed cornets or trumpets, and *marimbula* (or later, contrabass), forming the sextets and septets of the 1920s. Later these *conjuntos* added piano, other percussion instruments, more trumpets, and even dance orchestra instruments in the style of jazz big bands.

---

[8] The *tres* is a guitar-like instrument of three double or triple courses, typically tuned D-G-B.

At present the [traditional-style] *son* is seldom heard, but has been assimilated into other genres and is present in them. Thus, using the essential style of the *son* are the *pregón*, whose text recalls the cries of street vendors, the *son guajiro*, which sings of the virtues, idylls, or journeys of the campesino, and the so-called *afro,* which captures the colloquial speech of the black Cuban.

Also worth mentioning are "laments" and other genres created by popular composers seeking fashionable commercial success, taking stylistic elements from different genres and restructuring them anew, but always in short-lived manners and of little significance in public culture. Thus one finds self-styled "creators" or "inventors" of genres which are in fact nothing but recombinations of elements taken from the pre-existing public patrimony. From such re-orderings emerged, for example, the mambo and the *chachachá*. The former took from the *guaguancó* the short, intermittent, oratorical riffs, adding to them a sometimes nonsensical text arranged in the form of an antecedent and commentary, or consequent. The instrumentation also changed. The text is used in a more "instrumental" than semantic way, while the melodic lines determined by the different levels in the percussion patterns of the *son* and rumba now appear in the trumpets. The vocal lines of the rumbas acquire an essentially instrumental function in the mambo, and all this is enlivened by the sonorities of trumpets, saxophones, expanded Cuban percussion section, and an elaborate stage setup which has provoked arguments as to the mambo's validity and Cuban character.

The *chachachá* represented in its heyday a simplification of elements which were superimposed in levels different from traditional Afro-Cuban music. From the mambo and *chachachá* developed other genres which incorporated styles or elements taken from *comparsa* songs of Santiago de Cuba, restylizing certain customs already using Cuban percussion, or borrowing from other Caribbean musics, or enriching the percussion with doubled instruments, or incorporating new dance steps and figures.   Meanwhile, alongside these developments in urban popular music, the *canción* also took new directions.   After the appearance of *canciones* derivative of the bolero,   the genre gave birth, around mid-century, to the new styles of "feeling" (*filin*) and the modern *canción*, with its weakened chord progressions, ostinatos, and melodies, its rhetorical reiterations, dissonant harmonies, and, eventually, a new character colored by the use of texts concerning social protest.

2

Tambor
(Drum)

One of the most significant developments in modern Cuban culture has been the rescue, promotion, and legitimization of Afro-Cuban culture, especially music and dance. One would be tempted to call this process a "revitalization," but such a term would erroneously imply some prior decline in vigor and creativity within Afro-Cuban culture itself; rather, the process has been one of state and popular recognition of Afro-Cuban culture as an essential element of national identity.

Significant cultivated interest in Afro-Cuban music started in the 1920s and 1930s, with the scholarly work of Fernando Ortiz, the poetry of Nicolás Guillén, and the self-conscious use of neo-Africanisms by composers Amadeo Roldán and Alejandro García Caturla. Yet it was not until the advent of the Revolution that such interest extended beyond the work of a few literati and composers, that intermittent harassment of Afro-Cuban religions was terminated, and that the state itself undertook the promotion of Afro-Cuban culture as a matter of policy. Music and dance have played particularly prominent roles in this process, both as the most celebrated and conspicuous aspects of Afro-Cuban culture, and as the favored objects of scholarly research (to the extent, indeed, that there have been very few studies of Hispanic contributions to Cuban folk culture).

If earlier research of Cuban negritud was conducted by progressive whites like Ortiz, Rogelio Martínez Furé is among the most prominent of a later generation of scholars which includes educated black writers and folklorists who are endowed with a solid academic education as well as a first-hand knowledge of Afro-Cuban culture. Martínez Furé himself is a remarkably versatile individual, distinguished as a poet, essayist, and composer; he is also the co-founder and one of the pre-

sent directors of the Conjunto Folklórico Nacional, which may be said to have done more than any other institution to popularize Afro-Cuban music and dance in Cuba and abroad. Lastly, Martínez Furé is also a prominent ethnologist, as illustrated in this essay, which amply reflects his intimate familiarity with and enthusiasm for his subject, his critical materialist perspective, and his literary talents. "Tambor," indeed, is at once a personal document, a survey of Cuban drums and drumming, and a metaphorical sketch of the historical vicissitudes of black Cubans in general.

2

Tambor
(Drum)

Rogelio Martínez Furé

I

History: Struggle and Ascent

Object of veneration and cult worship for some, cursed and prohibited by others; regarded as a messenger of the gods and an incarnation of the ancestors in the black religions of Cuba; victim of confiscations and slashings by racist and reactionary authorities, the drum has had a fate parallel to that of the black man, its creator *par excellence*. All the political and social vicissitudes experienced by this sector of the Cuban population have been reflected in its most characteristic instrument. No one like the black man has known how to extract its telluric music nor how to carve it with such love and reverence; no one else has endangered his life so many times by protecting it from the persecution of the police, nor has anyone else known how to take it on such triumphant tours throughout the world, conveying the variety and richness of its rhythms to the public.

The history of the drum, whether from the squalid slave barracks or the colonial *cabildo* quarters up until the present, symbolizes the vicissitudes suffered over the centuries by the descendants of the Africans, and their secret struggle to conserve the remains of their cultural patrimony in spite of the measures taken by the colonial authorities and the first

Republican governments to destroy all vestiges of the black heritage in Cuba.

The social ascent of the drum reflects that of blacks and mulattos themselves. Today one cannot conceive of Cuban music without the measured or fiery strokes on a drumhead, marking the rhythm of romantic ballads or making one's blood surge in *sones, congas*, rumbas and *mozambiques*.

The drum is the king of our musical instruments; but its path has been long -- long and difficult.

The Colonies: *Cabildos* and Slave Barracks

In his monumental work *Los instrumentos de la música afrocubana*, Don Fernando Ortiz documented the existence of more than a hundred different types of drums that sounded, or even today sound, in the countryside and cities of our island.

The different African peoples arriving in captivity reconstructed their musical instruments, which were essential for the celebration of their rites. Along with and by means of the Afro-Cuban religions survived many cultural elements (dances, songs, philosophical conceptions, foods, words, oral literature, and even some plastic arts) that went on to blend with the cultural forms brought by the Spaniards, and which, over the course of four centuries, came to constitute one of the fundamental bases of Cuban culture.

Drums from diverse ethnic groups -- Yoruba, Carabalí, Iyesá, Egbado, Mina, Arará, Mandinga, Yolofe, and many more -- resounded in the halls of the *cabildos* (religious mutual-aid societies) where urban slaves gathered, and also in the slave barracks of the sugar mills and coffee plantations, where the drums were often used to send messages of revolt to neighboring plantation slaves, or to accompany dances in fiesta days.

Compared with the aural richness of the African-derived drums, the Spaniard offered an undeniable poverty [of drums] that were all but left out of Cuban music. The Spanish *bombos* and *redoblantes* used in military bands only managed to enter popular music after being Africanized in *congas* and *com- parsas*. As for the *timbales* of the theater orchestras and "salon music," from an early period they, too, incorporated Afro-Cuban influence.

During the entire colonial period the drum remained con- fined to the *cabildos* and slave barracks. It was considered denigrating to dance to its rhythms, "fitting only for slaves," but via the contemporary ensembles, generally comprising blacks and mulattos,[1] its rhythms furtively entered the salons of the dominant class.

Argeliers León argues:

> As musicians, the blacks integrated the orchestras which opera companies used to assemble for tours in the island, or they joined the *piquetes* [small bands] that played in churches or in the elegant soirees of the coffee plantation owners. And thus coalesced a process of mutual relations between that which the blacks brought to such music, and that which the European musicians performed.[2]

Orchestras like that of Tomás Alarcón at the end of the eigh- teenth century, and those of Claudio Brindis de Salas (father), Tomás Buelta y Flores, Raimundo Valenzuela, and Miguel Faílde in different periods of the nineteenth century all enjoyed great popularity.

In periodicals and books of the nineteenth century, com- ments about this process of "mulattoization" of music and dance were common. In 1849 Pichardo[3] wrote that the Cuban *con-*

---

[1] Blacks and mulattos were often euphemistically referred to as *pardos y morenos*.

[2] León, *Música folklórica cubana*. Havana: Departamento de Música de la Biblioteca Nacional José Martí, 1964, p. 117.

[3] Pichardo, Esteban. *Diccionario provincial casi razonado de vozes y frazes cubanos*. Havana: Ed. de Ciencias Sociales, 1976, pp. 223-23.

tradanza[4] was charming the population, and was danced even "in the most solemn function of the capital, just as it might be in the most indecent *changüí* of the far end of the island. . . Already the dancers are gyrating voluptuously in the *Cedazos* with all the aptitude and coquettry of an African."

Years later Antonio de las Barras y Prado affirmed pejoratively, "The *compas* [measure, i.e., of the *contradanza*] is the same which the negroes play with their drums and instruments for the grotesque and sensual dances."[5]   Such harsh denunciations would also come to be written about the *danza* and *danzón*, provoking considerable arguments among "genteel" city-dwellers.

---

[4] The *contradanza* [also known as *habanera*] is a couple dance derived from the French *contredanse*, introduced in Cuba near the end of the eighteenth century by immigrants from Haiti and Louisiana.   The dance rapidly became widely popular among Cubans.   Its steps, simple and inspired by line and circle dances, were, according to Pichardo, "executed only with the hands and arms, because the legs always reiterated the same movements" (*ibid.*, p. 256).   Each step had a specific name, such as *paseo, lazo, ala, cadena, cedazo, latigazo,* etc.

The musical structure of the *contradanza* consisted of two parts, each of eight bars in 2/4.   Each part would repeat, affording thirty-two bars in all. Pichardo notes: "Its music is at times composed of agreeable bits of operas, or of vulgar songs, with a playful bass distinctly its own, regularly in the second part, always varying, tender, happy or sad, sentimental or passionate, whose measured sounds correspond to the meters of the imperturbable *escobilleo* of the sons of this region . . ."(*ibid.* p. 223).   The ensemble used for the *contradanza* was called *orquesta típica*, comprising an ophicleide, a *güiro*, two violins, two clarinets, a trombone, a cornet, a contrabass, and a pair of *timbales*.   Until the second half of the nineteenth century, the *contradanza* remained the favorite dance of the Cuban people, although subsequently replaced by other genres, like the *danza* and the *danzón*, which developed out of it. [Ed.: The *danza* and *danzón* are primarily European and light-classical in derivation and character, although enlivened by a Afro-Cuban-influenced percussive ostinato, the *cinquillo.* The *changüí* is a folk dance and music genre originating, like its close relative, the *son*, among the lower classes of the eastern part of Cuba.]

[5] De las Barras y Prado, Antonio. *La Habana a mediados del siglo XIX.* Madrid: Impr. de la Ciudad Lineal, 1925, p. 89.

The essayist of Matanzas, Osvaldo Castillo Faílde, in his magnificent book *Miguel Faílde, creador musical del danzón*,[6] transcribes some of the vitriolic attacks published in diverse periodicals of 1881. One of these states, "It has been quite some time, esteemed colleague, since we have read your attempted defenses in favor of the *danza* and the *danzón*, dances that you and another call Cuban when they are in fact nothing but degenerations of the African tango."[7] Further on, Faílde quotes:

We energetically reject the sentences that "The Echo of Las Villas" directs at "The Voice of Cuba" and its minions, because we idolize this land, into which, to our disgrace, the negro race has managed to introduce in the family such disturbance, in such a way that we hardly noticed; and that dominion into which we admit the negro race starts with the *danza* -- the *danza* that speaks to the body, never to the soul. Would you care, dear colleague, to prove for us that the *danza* and *danzón* are moral and good? Would you care to prove to us that they are Cuban? Well, do it -- that we may recognize our own injustice -- give us a reason to do so.

Until then, for us the *danza* and *danzón* will remain foreign dances, because for us the dance which originated in this country, and which still thrives in it, is called ZAPATEO.[8]

The Polemic: Spain and Africa

As in other moments in our history, attempts were made in this period to contrast, with racist criteria, Hispanic-derived

---

[6]Castillo Faílde, Osvaldo. *Miguel Faílde, creador musical del danzón*. Havana: Editorial C.N.C., 1964.

[7]*Ibid.*, pp. 145-46.

[8]*Ibid.*, p. 147. [Ed.: *Zapateo* is a Hispanic-derived folk dance of the rural white campesinos, generally accompanied by *tres* and guitar, and lacking the percussive character of Afro-Cuban dances as well as of the *danzón* and *danza*.]

Cuban musical creations with those admitting African influence, alleging that only the former were genuinely Cuban.   In fact, neither was the *zapateo* exclusively Cuban, as it belonged to a large family of *zapateados* which had taken root throughout the Americas, nor did the *danza, rumba,* or a *bembé* ceremony cease to be a genuine expression of our music, conserved, developed, and executed by our own people.

The journalistic polemics cited above regarding these dances are so illustrative of the mentality of the epoch, that we have transcribed here another criticism of the same year, 1881 (also reprinted in Castillo Faílde[9]):

> . . .We believe that even if the *danza* and *danzón* were born in Cuba, they are nevertheless of African origin. The music of these dances embodies the concupiscence and sensuality that characterizes the unruly natives of passionate Africa.   The essence of African character is to be found in them.   The banging of the *timbales* demonstrates this clearly.   Further, the rhythms of the *danza* and *danzón* are very similar to those of the tangos that the sons of uncultured Africa dance in our streets.
>
> How many times, upon hearing a *danzón*, does one recall the mysterious *cocuyé*, reminding one of the disgrace of that portion of the earth called Africa, that is ignorant of the incalculable benefits of civilization?   Further, can we not ask of our colleague, who first conceived of the *danza*?   It was a son of our country, true, but a descendant of Africa.   A son of our country, through whom ran the sensual African blood, the blood of his fathers and ancestors.
>
> Today as before in Cuba, the composers of the *danza* and *danzón* are descendants of Africa.   They, indeed,

---

[9]*Ibid.,* p. 148.

have imprinted on the *danza* this distinctive stamp of African music and dance.[10]

It is interesting to compare such opinions with those proclaimed years later, in the middle of the Republican period itself, by Sánchez de Fuentes[11] and others similarly led astray, who, with attitudes similar to those of the racist collumnists of the nineteenth century, attempted to establish the *danzón* -- rather ironically -- as an example of *white* Cuban music, without any African influence.

In fact, the *danza* and *danzón* were neither white nor black, but Cuban. Neither African, as viewed by the commentators of the nineteenth century, nor European, as in the eyes of those who wished to "whitewash" them. In their general structures both genres remained faithful to their origins, as deriving from the French *contredanse* introduced in our country at the end of the eighteenth century; but in their rhythms, their ambience, and their creole intensity, they demonstrate clearly the mulatto character introduced by the blacks and mulattos of Cuba.

Insofar as every new musical genre -- even if played on European instruments -- seemed to incite new waves of polemics, drums derived from slave society could scarcely be used in the music called "respectable."

It was not possible to exploit an entire race, to alienate an entire society after terminating slavery, and to create separate economic, political, religious, and mental structures while at the same time dancing to the drums of the captives, who were regarded as inferior beings, as simple objects.

---

[10]*Ibid.*, p. 149.

[11]Sánchez de Fuentes, Eduardo, *Folklorismo*. Havana, 1928; *Los orígenes de la música cubana* (Havana: Pro Arte Musical, Nov., 1929; and "La música cubana y sus orígenes," in *Boletín Latinoamericana de Música*. Bogotá, 1938).

The Republic: Prohibited and Profaned

With the arrival of the Republic, the first administrations, full of European vanities and motivated by the same racism inherited from their colonial predecessors, attempted to eliminate all that represented the African presence in Cuba, reaching extremes even beyond those of Spanish rule. A culturally whitewashed black minority supported the official campaign to de-Africanize Cuban customs. These "model men of color" aspired to ascend economically and socially by means of politics and the liberal professions in order to enjoy the benefits and sinecures of the new ruling class.

The black religions were persecuted. The use of "African drums" was prohibited. The repressive forces attacked the cult sanctuaries and burned or slashed the sacred drums. Nevertheless, the persecuted cults continued to gain in popular appeal. Gradually they went on attracting new white and mulatto converts.

In the face of economic, political, and social frustration, large sectors of the population, now united in opposition to the exploitative regime, sought refuge in the cults, and precisely in those which, by being the most persecuted, had not prostituted themselves to the ruling class, and which over the preceding centuries had nourished a rebellious spirit among the enslaved masses. Hidden away were the drums of most pure African descent, the most sacred, those which had been kept in secret, away from the eyes of the uninitiated. And in the recesses of the mountains, on the banks of rivers, and in dwellings in the interior of the island, the faithful continued making offerings to their gods and dancing to the sacred rhythms.

As the law specifically prohibited the use of "African drums," subterfuges were devised to ridicule the sanctions. The construction of some of the drums was modified, attaching metal pegs and making them with barrel slats or with jars of olives. Various possible transformations were effected in order to disguise the African origin and suggest similarities with "white" drums, thereby enhancing the creole character of the drums. The believers went so far as to create some instruments, such as the "viola," adorned with colored belts so as to resemble Spanish tambourines (*panderos*).

An old informant related to us,

> When Menocal came into power [1913] they tried to prohibit us from playing the bongo and the *son*. They even prohibited *comparsas* [Carnival processions]. And if we had to perform a *toque de santo* [a *santería* rite, with music, dance, and possession], we had to transport the drums all wrapped up as if we were carrying something criminal!

Another remarked, "When one least expected, the police would appear and carry off the sacred vessels and ornaments and even slash the drum heads in front of our very eyes."

Nevertheless, just as with the persecutions of the early Christians and Jews, the cults went underground and increased in fervor. The lessons of all the experiences of the previous religious persecutions in history were ignored by the dimwitted administrations, and the undisciplined troops contributed to creating a sentiment of martyrdom among the cult members.

But the drums survived the persecutions under the Republic.

The *Son*, with Bare Hands

The *son* was the first popular Cuban musical genre to use a drum played with the bare hands. It descended from the eastern mountain ranges at the beginning of the twentieth century, and went on to slowly invade the provinces of Western Cuba. In this mulatto, quintessentially national genre were integrated instruments of both African and Spanish origin, *viz*., bongo, *marimbula, claves, maracas, tres,* and guitar.

Very soon the *son* came under attack from the dominant class, which, with a mental attitude similar to that of its slave-trading ancestors, regarded every creation of the people themselves as lascivious, primitive, and contrary to refined manners. From 1910 on, the *son* established itself in the rooming-houses and dance academies of Havana, undergoing a gradual process of evolution. Its musical structure became more complex; new instruments replaced some of the traditional ones; the famous sextets and septets formed.

The *son* came to be prohibited, but the public went on dancing to it. Associated with black society, it was not danced in white social groups, nor in those of "cultured negros," who, alienated to such a degree, allied themselves with racist attitudes. But, little by little, its *sabrosura* ["deliciousness"] continued to break down social barriers, such that it finally penetrated the salons of the whites, and, quite a bit later, those of the "respectable" blacks. The decade of the twenties marked the apogee of this genre.

The Consecration: From the *Son* to the *Mozambique*

The acceptance of the *son* and the bongo rhythms by the Cuban upper class was a reflection of the profound economic, political, social, and cultural changes occurring in the world. The First World War, which had definitively liquidated the last vestiges of the nineteenth century and its conceptions, initiated the decline of European hegemony; beyond this came the triumph of the October Revolution and the spread of its economic and social ideas, which constituted a decisive element in the realm of international politics; the rediscovery of African arts and their subsequent influence in European visual arts; the impact of black musics of America in the primary capitals of the Western world -- all these were elements which contributed to create a new conception of human cultural values.

In Cuba, these changes were reflected in the monumental work of Don Fernando Ortiz, who opened breaches against prejudice and in favor of a more complete acceptance of our cultural reality, in the literary and musical *afrocubanismo*, and in the revolutionary movements against intellectual mediocrity and against the concessions to foreign investors -- movements which culminated in the toppling of the Machado dictatorship.

Starting with the *son*, the drum had definitively entrenched itself in Cuban music. The foreign recording companies discovered a rich mine in Afro-Cuban rhythms, and in order to satisfy the taste for the exotic among the publics of Europe and North America, they undertook to disseminate them, in however deformed a manner, throughout the world.

In 1936 the sacred *batá* drums appeared for the first time outside of the *ilé osha* or *lucumí* temples, in a conference on Yoruba music in Cuba organized by Fernando Ortiz. Performing on that occasion were the famous drummers Aguedo Morales, Jesús Pérez, and Pablo Roche -- known as "Okilapka" or "Strong Arm." The sacred drums timidly began to appear before the uninitiated eyes, offering their musical riches.

Soon after, *batá* drums were incorporated in a symphony orchestra directed by Gilberto Valdés, one of our first composers to explore the sonic world of Afro-Cuban liturgical music.

In 1937 the *comparsas* reappeared, but not without provoking intense polemics between their defenders and those who were horrified by this "return to the colonial period."

The drums, cowbells, maracas, *quijadas* (donkey jaw-bones used as scrapers), and all the rich arsenal of Afro-Cuban instruments invaded popular music ensembles throughout the world. And finally, the rumbas and *congas* were made into extravaganzas that shook the salons of the most elegant clubs.

The last barriers fell after World War II, which marked the death of imperial colonies and the liberation of Afro-Asiatic peoples. The mambo, *chachachá* and other Afro-American rhythms spread throughout the world, transforming international musical and choreographic conceptions. In all these contexts, the drum imposed its lively syncopations and polyrhythms.

Today the *mozambique* [a Carnival rhythm and dance popular in the 1960s] is the definitive consecration of percussion in drum-heads and metal. Our people, free of social vices, with full awareness of their historical and cultural reality, dance the drum rhythms rendered with bare hands -- and thus the drum has been the most persecuted and revered of our instruments, but always, that which energizes and infuses the blood of even the most reserved Cubans.

I I

The Drums: Sacred and Secular

In traditional Africa the drum is the instrument which symbolizes the tribe. It is the medium between man and god, between the living and the spirits of the dead. It calls to war, resounds in weddings and funerals, and transmits messages to neighboring peoples. More than just a musical instrument, it is a living entity, "fed" during propitiatory sacrifices, and surrounded with carefully executed and rhythmically complex ceremonies. The well-being of the group is considered intimately linked to the drum. Its loss or destruction can carry with it disgrace and even death.

The captives taken to Cuba brought with them religious and philosophical ideas which they transmitted to their descendants over the centuries.

Today, different types of drums (Yoruba *ilú*, Carabalí *nkomo*, Congo *ngoma*, etc.) continue to maintain their status in our country. The drum is that which confirms the rebirth of the initiates into the religions. It is believed that the drum conveys this confirmation to the gods, whether they are Yoruba *orishas*, *arará* vodoun spirits, or even the ancestor spirits worshiped in the secret *abakuá* societies. The drum invokes the different deities, and even *obliges* them to manifest themselves

among mortals by "mounting" their devotees. The drum also
resounds lugubriously on the day of death, dispatching the soul
of the deceased from those of the living.

The sacred drum is only used in ceremonial rituals. Its construction, associated apprenticeship, and the ability to play it
are limited to a small group of individuals initiated into priest-
hood. The sacred drum's construction is difficult. It requires
ceremonies, chants, and special offerings. Only special types of
wood, indicated by the oracles of *ifá* divination and of the *dilogunes* [12] -- shells -- can be employed in its carving. After its
construction is complete, its head adjusted, and it has been endowed with the "secret of Añá," other previously consecrated
drums are needed to bestow its special voice upon it, enabling
it to be used in liturgical *toques*. Only after this ceremony, in
which solely selected male drummers participate, is the drum
regarded as no longer *"judío"* ["Jewish" -- i.e., un-baptized].
From then on it is a living entity, charged with all the powers
of the deity Añá.

The sacred drumskins cannot be tightened by means of fire,
so when their players wish to tighten the heads, they strike its
edges, or its tuning pegs, according to the type of drum, or they
place it in the sun.

During important occasions the drums are adorned with silk
scarves, with beaded petticoats, or with beautiful aprons --
banté -- covered with mirrors, shells, and crystal necklaces.

Only the initiated male drummers can care for the sacred
drums, rendering the necessary offerings, cleaning them,
changing broken skins, and playing them. It is considered

---

[12] The oracles of *ifá* and of the *dilogunes* are the two primary systems of
divination used in the Yoruba-derived cults of Cuba. The oracle of *ifá* is
reserved for the priestly class of *babalaos* ("the fathers of the secrets"),
consecrated in the cult of Orula, the god of divination. The *dilogunes* are
used by the *babalosha* and the *iyalosha*, that is, the priests (male and
female) of *santería*.

sacrilegious for a woman to touch or even approach the drums, for a woman would "weaken" them. As in all ancient religions, women are believed to be impure and their contact debilitating to cult objects.

So rigorous and scrupulous is the care of the sacred drums that a drummer, before playing one of them in a ceremony, must undergo certain rites and abstain from sexual relations for at least twenty-four hours before touching the drum heads. The intimate contact with the "messengers of the gods" makes drummers themselves objects of respect and admiration. As priests of Añá, they are expected to be upright men of strong character

The secular drums are used in non-religious music -- *congas*, rumbas, *sones* -- and do not require any ceremonies for their construction or usage. They are generally made from trunks of avocado or almond wood, ribbed like barrels. Their skins are tightened by candles or by a system of metal keys.

Nevertheless, even in secular music, drumming is considered to be for men only. It is regarded as inconceivable that a woman beat the head of an instrument whose creation is attributed to Changó, god of lightning and fire, who changed the divining boards and the sedentary life with his wild drumming, which had imprisoned the rumbling of the turbulent clouds.

III

Some Cuban Drums

The *batá* are drums of ancient Yoruba origin, of sacred character [ed.: text says "secular," but this is presumably an oversight]. They are double-headed, with closed, hourglass-shaped bodies, played with the bare hands, generally on both heads. The system of tension consists of leather straps. They are carved out of cedar or mahogony trunks. A set consists of three drums. The largest, which always occupies the central position, is called *iyá* (mother). Its skins are circled by two belts with bells called *shaworó*. The medium-sized drum is the *itótole*, and the smallest is the *okónkolo*. It is believed that the secret of the deity Añá, the messenger of the gods, resides inside these drums, which are perhaps the most musically versatile and potent of Cuban drums. On the large skins of the *iyá* and *itótole* are circular objects made of a special substance called *faddela* or *idá*, which, apart from its liturgical significance, helps make the timbre deeper.

The *yuka* are secular drums of old Congo origin. Their cylindrical bodies, open on one end, are made from trunks of avocado or almond, hollowed with fire. The leather skins are affixed with pegs. The large drum is called *caja*, the medium *mula*, and the smallest, *cachimbo*. The *caja* is played with the bare hand, and the others, with one bare hand and a stick.

The *abakuá* drums are ritual instruments derived from the Carabalí, used for the Cuban secret societies of the same name. They are made of cedar with goatskin heads. The single head of each drum is affixed with hemp and bone pegs. The *bonkó echemiyá* is the largest; the others are called *obí apá*, *biankomé*, and *kuchi yeremá*.

The bongo (*bongó*) is a small pair of attached drums, originating in eastern Cuba. It consists either of a trunk of one piece or else it is ribbed. This secular drum was popularized by *son* ensembles.

Arará drums derive from Dahomey, and have been preserved in Cuba by the *arará* cult, which is practiced primarily in the provinces of Matanzas and Havana. These drums are what Ortiz has called *abotinada* ["shaped like a legging or spat"], for their system of tension consisting of pegs disappearing into the body of the drum. They are painted with symbolic colors and, in some cases, adorned with ritual scarves. The most important *arará* drums are: *ñoñufó, ñonajo, güegüe, asajún, aplití,* and *achebolisá*. Their skins are played with small sticks of flexible wood.

The conga is a secular drum made of ribbed wood with skins attached with pegs or, traditionally, heated with candles. It is used most characteristically in music of Carnival *comparsas* and in *congas* [i.e., the most typical genre used in the *comparsas*]. At present, due to its extensive usage in theaters and night-clubs, it has acquired metal tuning pegs.

Iyesá drums are sacred instruments of Yoruba derivation. Although double-headed, only one head is played, with small sticks of guava wood, except for the drum called *bajo*, which is played with the bare hands. There are four cylindrical drums, closed on one end and hewn of a single piece of wood. The heads are affixed by rope strung in a zigzag fashion. They, too, "possess Aña."

The *bokú* is a ribbed drum from eastern Cuba with a skin attached by pegs. It is used in the Carnival music of eastern Cuba, and is distinguished by its shape from other secular drums. It is played with the bare hands.

I V

Omí Asaindé: Water Crashing against the Reefs

Seeing him bent over his drum, working on the thick tree-trunks with his gouges, hammers, and straps, watching him tear out the vegetal pith, I am reminded of some verses of a poem Miguel Barnet wrote of him:

> This old man raises his voice
> and moves the tip of his fingers
> as if they were releasing something. . .

My name is José del Carmen de la Trinidad Torregrosa y Hernández, but my name in *santería* is Omí Osaindé, which means "the water that crashes against the reefs," because my mother is Yemayá [Yoruba goddess of the sea].

His hands are deformed by so many years of tanning goatskins and beating the sacred *batá*, messenger drums of the gods.

My mother was a negress named Marcelina Rosalía Hernández, and my father, a mulatto cook and pastry chef named Juan Torregrosa y Séneca. He spoke English, French, and German.

Year after year he guarded the secret of the construction of his drums, which would be relied upon to convey prayers, joys, and hopes to the other world, the distant *ilé* of the *orishas*, where the gods celebrate assemblies, eat, and dance -- as far as there, where the *lucumí* and their Cuban descendants locate their ancient deified kings.

During the War, at the time of the invasion,[13] my father was a cook in central La Julia, in Aguacate, in the province of Havana, and the general Weyler[14] sent him a message: "Tell this mulatto to get ready for me to tear off his head. He looks too much like Maceo . . ."[15] But Weyler let him live.

Trinidad is seventy-two. He is tall, lean, and sinewy, but strong, and of an indefinite complexion which I would call bronze-black.

---

[13] One of the most important episodes in the liberation war against Spanish colonial rule (1895-96). The rebel troops ("mambises"), led by Antonio Maceo and Maximo Gómez, crossed the island from one end to the other, in spite of Spanish military positions, carrying the war to every corner of the country.

[14] Valeriano Weyler, general of the Spanish colonial army, whose methods foreshadowed those of the Nazis.

[15] Antonio Maceo y Grajales (1840-96). Lieutenant General of the *mambí* army and one of the principal heroes of the Cuban independence struggle.

My grandfather was a Andalusian from Jérez de la Frontera who fell in love with a Dominican mulatto, Claudia Séneca. That's why my name is genuinely Spanish. I was born in Zaragoza #27, in el Cerro,[16] in the house of Papa Silvestre, a famous *santero* of back then. Everyone called him Salakó. He was there in 1893. . .

This old man is like a library. He tells us stories of the Yoruba brought to Cuba, and of the songs and *décimas* of *claves*, choral groups of blacks and mulattos which formed in Christmas time in the barrios of Havana. He can also make us a bongo or a *kinfuiti*, a small, loud drum of the *cimarrones* [escaped slaves].

I've done more jobs than a cot-blanket. I've been a flower-vendor, soldier, apprentice coachman, artist . . . and now I find myself here. [His muscles are taught with exertion.] It's not easy to make drums, especially ones like these. It takes a lot of patience to learn to play them, but much more to learn how to make them. Now, of course, after finishing, when you put them on the stand and play them, you feel as if there's nothing grander. It's like with women, or with liquor: once you try it. . .

The air is redolent of ripe fruit. As if he had divined my precise thoughts, he exclaims, "These are canistels[17] for Oshún."

I had the good fortune to learn from the masters: Matías Mesa, Eduardo Salakó, Andrés "the Sublime" -- they called him that because he played the *batá* so well. The old ones were strict; they wouldn't enter in *guachitas* [have sexual relations] with boys; that's how it was back

---

[16] El Cerro is a working-class barrio of Havana.

[17] The canistel is an edible tropical fruit of yellow-orange color. "It is the *Poutería campechiana* (H.B.K.) Bachai (*Lucuma nervosa* A.D.C.), of the family of *Sapotaceas*" (Roig, Dr. Juan Tomas, *Diccionario botánico de nombres vulgares cubanos* (Havana: Editorial de Consejo Nacional de Universidades, 1965), vol. I, p. 233). It is offered to the goddess Oshún.

then. Sometimes they would play in the house where I lived, and I would just sit and watch them. They were real men! They would get such music out of the drums that one felt like crying!

It is midday, and hot. The wind whirls around the wood shavings in the little patio of the rooming-house where Trinidad has improvised his workshop. From a distant radio a man's voice announces the time with annoying repetitiveness.

"Looks like rain. Let me take some precautions."

The old man grabs some ashes and makes the cross on the floor. "San Isidro of Labrador, get rid of the water and bring the sun."

He laughs. "I learned this when I was a kid. Let's see if I can finish my work."

I came to admire these people so much that I wanted to become a drummer myself, and I started my apprenticeship. In those days the apprentices would stand behind the drum, in order to see how the old people played. Since we didn't have any money to pay for classes, we would devote ourselves to the masters. We would do them favors, carrying the drums to *toques*, and sometimes even helping to make them. In exchange they would teach us. We learned the rhythms by ear. It wasn't easy; you had to be alert and have a good memory, and on top of all that, it still took years to learn the *batá* rhythms, or at least, the important ones.

Trinidad waits, and asks me to hold up the gouge with which he is hollowing the cedar trunk. Already the hourglass shape of the *batá* is visible, with its narrow waist, like that of a woman. Trinidad continues, smiling:

I have a helper, but he's at school now. That's why the house is so quiet, and if not, it's only because of me. He

doesn't leave me for an instant when I'm working on the
drums.   I think he'll be a good player -- he's got a good
ear, and that's at only eleven years old.   It's good that
he's starting now.   It took me at least a year to learn to
play the *okónkolo*, the small drum, and about two years
to learn the medium-sized one, and I was in such a trance
that I built a bench and on each edge I attached two bongos made of some little barrels that used to come with
nails.   And I made my music, practicing at night what I
had learned.   Even with all that, it still took me five years
to learn how to play the *iyá*.

"Trinidad, who taught you how to make the *batá* drums,?" I
asked.   He was quiet for a few moments, and then replied:

One time Emilio Estrada, who was another famous drummer, seeing how much I enjoyed the drums, and that I
even knew the rhythmic patterns for each saint,[18] suggested that I help him finish the drums, putting on skins;
and seeing my devotion, he said to me, "I'm going to show
you how to make these."   I was only eighteen then.

I still remember the first time that I played with the
masters, with the "professors" of *batá*.   I recall that it was
in the house of Papa Silvestre, who lived then in 18
Ayuntamiento St., in front of the Loma de la Mulata, in el
Cerro.   When the fiesta was reaching its peak, Andrés
"the Sublime" got up for a moment and went out to the
patio, but as he was all sweaty and not dressed warmly
enough, he felt ill very soon.   There was no one else to
take his place, so they called me to play the *itótole*.   I remember it was a drummer named Luis Prékete, who said
to me, "You dare to play it?"   "Sure, I dare!"   I was nervous and frightened because playing the *iyá* was Eduardo
Salakó, and on the smaller drum was Juan el Sordo, who

---

[18]That is, he was able to perform the special rhythms dedicated to each
individual   deity.

knew drumming better than anyone. I felt my heart in my throat. All the dancers were watching me. But I managed to play for two hours. When Andrés recovered and saw me playing, he was so moved that he kissed me on the forehead and hands and said, "I'm going to teach you how to drum."

A gust of wind blows down one of the goatskins set out to dry on the wall, to be affixed to one of the drums. Sheets of rain start falling. I help Trinidad move the little improvised workshop inside his house. From there I listen to the commotion of neighbors grabbing clothes off the patio, and without knowing why, I think of the cross of ashes that the rain was slowly washing away.

3

The Rumba, the Guaguancó, and Tío Tom

If much of the Cuban scholarly and journalistic attention to Afro-Cuban culture and music since 1959 has been directed toward religious phenomena, secular music genres like the rumba have not been neglected. The rumba, insofar as it has merged with the son to form the backbone of modern Cuban dance music, is certainly Cuba's most renowned and quintessential music style. Nevertheless, the traditional rumba -- an urban folk song and dance form using only drums and voices -- was strictly a product of lower-class black and mulatto society, and tended to be disparaged as such by the predominantly white upper classes.

Leonardo Acosta's article reproduced here provides an overview of the traditional rumba, stressing its vital role in proletarian culture and, by extension, in modern Cuban culture as a whole. Acosta further attempts to refute the facile, depersonalizing notion of the "anonymity" of folk music creation by reminding us that, given sufficient sources, a closer look at any folk genre will reveal live performers and composers with distinct, individual talents and artistic personalities. Gonzalo Asencio, or "Tío Tom," was one such figure, who embodies, in Acosta's portrayal, the dynamic musical vitality of Afro-Cuban culture and, at the same time, the spirit of proletarian anti-imperialist protest which was undiluted by the Cuban bourgeoisie's identification with North American or European culture. (Asencio died in 1991.)

Intended for the general reader, this article well conveys the importance accorded in contemporary Cuban scholarship to Afro-Cuban proletarian culture and what is seen as the revolutionary and nationalistic tendencies within it. Acosta himself is one of Cuba's most distinguished and prolific authors of scholarly and journalistic literature on music. He is the author of nine books, including "La música y descolonización," "Canciones de la nueva trova,""Del tambor al sintetízador"(from which this essay is translated), and other volumes of poetry, criticism, and short stories. At present, Acosta works for the Instituto Cubano de Radio y Televisión.

3

The Rumba, the Guaguancó, and Tío Tom

Leonardo Acosta

What is the boundary between legend and reality, and where does it lie?   Sometimes a genuine person or event becomes a legend, obscuring the reality.   And at other times someone becomes legendary to the detriment of the person himself, who is relegated to obscurity.   Such cases are common in the realm of popular music, where we find such men and women of flesh and bones, who are forgotten or ignored as people, but whose legends continue to enjoy renown.   And such is the case of "Tío Tom" ["Uncle Tom"], of whose hundreds of songs, several are well known to us, yet who remained to us like an entelechy, a legend. . .Until finally he was paid homage in a fete in the Casa de la Cultura of the Plaza de la Revolución district, which was attended by dozens of distinguished *rumberos* of the country -- and there he was, in person, singing and dancing, as real as any of us.

Who is Tío Tom?

We may start by clarifying that our Uncle Tom has nothing to do with the famous character of Harriet Beecher Stowe, who is certainly neither historical nor legendary, but a fictitious person, subsequently attaining the status of an archetype of the "good and submissive" negro of the southern United States, according to the standards of a sector of the North American bourgeoisie. This other Tom, by contrast, is Cuban and rebellious, although, like his namesake, is also black and aged. His real name is Gonzalo Asencio, and he is the best and most prolific author that our country has produced in the field of the type of rumba called *guaguancó*.

Although he cultivated other genres, especially within what our musicologists call the "rumba complex" (*yambú, tahona, columbia, guaguancó, papalote, jiribilla*), the special contribution of Tío affirms, without any exaggeration, that if Pérez Prado can be called the "King of the Mambo," then Gonzalo Asencio, whose crown no one has been able to usurp, should be called the "King of the Guaguancó."

Who among us has neither danced, sung, nor at least listened to some melody of Tío Tom's without knowing it? For outside of his circle of friends and musicians -- especially *rumberos* -- there are very few who have seen him or known him personally, but almost everyone has heard and danced to numbers like "Consuélate como yo," with its much-loved refrain that says: "Por eso ahora ya yo no vuelvo a querer" ["That's why I'll never fall in love again"]. The same has happened with several other pieces of his, like "Los cubanos son rareza," "Bombón,""Color de alelí,""Se ha vuelto mi corazón un violín"["My heart has turned into a violin"],"Al señor marqués,""Changó va vení,""La Reforma va,""Ya me estoy poniendo viejo," and "Siento que me regaña el corazon," with its famous refrain "¿Si tú me lo das, por qué me lo quitas?" ["If you give it to me, then why do you take it away?"]

A Parenthesis about the Rumba

Much has been spoken and written since the last century about the rumba and its origins, which some have tried to trace to the ancient cultures of Egypt and Phoenicia. But in spite of the opinions of some scholars, the rumba is a wholly Cuban product, derived from various, albeit more or less similar forms of African music and dance, which blended here as a result of the mixing of different West African ethnic groups, giving birth to a new culture, a "folklore of the plantation," as Roger Bastide called it, in reference to several different American countries.[1]

In a text of 1967 we find an adequate definition of the rumba, which states:

> It is the mulatto sonorous daughter of the Spanish and the negro. In it one finds diverse elements derived from Congo, Carabalí, or *lucumí* [Yoruba] sources. Textually it follows the Spanish language and meters. It is largely urban, and can be considered a song, a dance, or a general ambience. It is the genre of our music most influenced by direct Spanish elements: the *clave* and street-vendor's *pregón*. It comprises three principal forms: the *columbia* (of rural origin), and the *yambú* and *guaguancó* (of urban origin). The latter is primarily narrative. The dance represents the pursuit [lit., persecution] of the woman by the man.[2]

This explication is somewhat unsatisfactory in its excessive stress on the Spanish elements, which in any case cannot be considered as essential elements of the rumba.[3] We should also point out the frequent presence of African phrases and words in various rumbas. Further, I have always been somewhat skeptical of categorizations of whatever musical features of ours as either strictly rural or urban. Because if indeed in our music there are genres or styles of clearly urban origins --

---

[1]Roger Bastide, *Las Americas negras: las civilizaciones africanas en el Nuevo Mundo* (Madrid: Alianza Editorial, 1969).

[2]Program notes by the Consejo Nacional de Cultura y Sociedad Cubana de Autores Musicales, for "Festival de Música Popular Cubana," held in the Teatro Amadeo Roldán, 8/14/67.

[3]The researcher Rogelio Martínez Furé has referred on various occasions to the inappropriateness of the term "Spanish-African" in relation to the roots of our culture and has proposed instead the term "Euro-African" in order to avoid equating one country with a continent.

as is the case with the *guaguancó* --, these may often derive from an older and relatively unknown rural antecedent. In the case of the *son* of eastern Cuba, for example, we can say that its urban variants were preceded by the rural *son montuno* because we have enough data to that effect; to delve further than that we would have to be able to reach its very origins, which might even be closely tied to the *changüí* [an eastern Cuban variant of the *son*].

As for the rumba, data from the nineteenth century (including the common reference to "rumbas from the Spanish period") and other sources allow us to assert that in the 1880s, considerably before the abolition of slavery in Cuba, rumbas were danced and played in slave barracks and in certain festivals tolerated by the slave-owners.[4] I accept, nevertheless, as undeniable that in the present century the rumba is primarily urban and suburban, concentrated above all in Matanzas and Havana (including nearby townships like Guanabacoa, Regla, Marianao, Güines, Colón, Jovellanos, and Unión de Reyes, as well as parts of Pinar del Río and the central and western provinces).

Among the rumba variants, the *guaguancó* has undoubtedly acquired a predominantly urban character (especially of Matanzas and Havana), and it is in the *"rumbero"* barrios of Havana that Gonzalo Asencio, or Tío Tom, grew up several decades ago as one of the most versatile, sensitive, and original cultivators of the rumba. The *guaguancó*, which is sung as well as danced and played, has served in the cities (as do other genres in the countryside) as *a social chronicle of the dispossessed*, of the humble and marginalized, like a chronicle of home or tenement, of the barrio and the hearth, in which familiar ev-

---

[4]See, e.g., the revealing chronicle in which there is a description of what is undoubtedly a rumba, in the middle of the last century (ca. 1842), of Anselmo Suarez Romero, "Ingenios," in the anthology *Artículos de costumbres cubanas del siglo XIX* (Havana: Editorial Arte y Literatura, 1974, pp. 194-95). And from 1851, a similar description in Fredrika Brenner, *Cartas desde Cuba* (Havana: Editorial Arte y Literatura, 1980).

eryday events are related, but which also comments on con-temporary politics, and sometimes even assumes an anti-im-perialist stance, as in the case of Tío Tom.   Thus we can affirm that the *guaguancó* is the "sung rumba" par excellence.

Of course, the "social chronicle" of the humble folk consisted mostly of "crime pages," which brings us to the proper Marxist appraisal of the bourgeois presswithin which the dominant classes occupy the prime news spaces, while the working classes appear only in the sections on crime.   In neo-colonial Cuba this situation was doubly alienating due to the creole bourgeoisie's dependence on the imperialist metropole and the submission of this class to the metropole's values.   Naturally, the values promoted by the bourgeois press influenced those of the marginal and dispossessed sectors of the populace.   But if the bourgeois media chronicled, for instance, violent crimes in the form of versions *directed at* the poor, the same events narrated in a *guaguancó* reflected the *perception of the dispossessed themselves.*[5]

More Regarding Roots

Further adressing the rumba in general, we may cite a para-graph from Helio Orovio's *Diccionario de la música cubana* :

> RUMBA, LA.   Song and dance genre, of Afro-Hispanic ori-gin, and especially the former.   It originated in urban contexts where poor black people abounded (in homes and tenements) and in semi-rural areas around the sugar

---

[5]A more profound analysis of this matter could be the subject of an article.   We can only note here the difference between the naturalness and authenticity of the sung "popular chronicle" as opposed to the typically hypocritical attitude of the bourgeoisie, which wrote of itself in "society" pages while using sensationalistic reportage of crimes and the like to portray only the dominated classes.   The crimes of the bourgeoisie, meanwhile, were carefully hidden, except for certain particularly notorious exceptions which came to constitute a distinct genre: the chronicle of "scandals" (typified in magazines like "Confidential").

plantations. It is played on drums (*tumba*, *llamador*, and *quinto*) or simply on wood (a codfish box, or a ship's carton), accompanied by *claves* and, occasionally, spoons. It is a collective feast. The African influence is most evident in the rhythm. Lacking any ritual significance, the rumba is completely secular.[6]

Regarding the *guaguancó* specifically, musicologist Argeliers León states:

> The initial part of the song is extensive and assumes the character of a long narrative, generally referring to an event or a person. . .The melodic line is more fluid (than that of the *yambú*), with some sustained, long tones. Sometimes *décimas* are used, or else simple couplets or even prose. In the *guaguancó* the rhythm is more figurative and rapid than in the *yambú*. The steps are more disjointed, and the couple plays a game of attraction and repulsion, of dodging and surrender. . .[7]

León further writes of the *columbia* (a rumba variant in which Tío Tom was also renowned):

> When the rumba "breaks" [starts], a solo male enters the ring, dancing with acrobatic gestures derived to a large extent from the dances of the *íremes* or *abakuá diablitos* [spirits represented in the dances of the *abakuá* cult] . He dances in front of the lead conga player, whom he engages in a kind of animated dialogue.

Similarly, in support of our assertion of the essential Cubanness of the rumba, we may note the view of musicologist Odolio Urfé regarding the *guaguancó*: "The rhythmic language

---

[6]Orovio, *Diccionario de la música cubana* (Havana: Editorial Letras Cubanas, 1981).

[7]A. León, *Del tiempo y el canto* (Havana: Editorial Pueblo y Educación, 1974).

of the drums in the *guaguancó* does not derive directly from African expression, but is the result of the outpouring by the Cubans of surviving African materials."[8]

Don Fernando Ortiz, the great promoter of our national popular culture, situates the *yuka* and the drums of the same name as probable direct antecedents of the rumba, and the *calinda* as a probable earlier predecessor.[9] But one must also mention the influence of the *abakuá* march (of Carabalí origin), and of Congo (Bantu) music, as manifest in the instruments used. Even more, certain influences from Dahomey have been detected; it is known that the Haitian *vodoun* cult (of Dahomeyan origin) left superficial traces in Cuba, but with the massive immigration [of Haitians] in the nineteenth century this cult was further introduced, as was discovered by the traveler H. Piron in Santiago de Cuba, and some of its rhythms persist in the *tumba francesa* societies.[10]

Similarly, it is known that the *loa* [deities, equivalent to the Yoruba *orisha*] in *vodoun* rituals use the serpent as a fertility symbol, whence certainly come the ancestral songs which have reached Brazil, Cuba, and other countries, such as that cited by the Brazilian, Arthur Ramos, and which would appear to be an incipient rumba:

> La culebra se murió, calabasón, son son.
> La culebra se murió, sanga muleque
> Mírale los ojos parecen candela
> mírale los dientes parecen filé;
> La culebra se murió, sanga la mulele[11]

The snake is dead, calabasón, son son

---

[8]O. Urfé, "Factors que integran la música cubana," in *Islas*, 9-12/59.

[9]F. Ortiz, *La antigua fiesta afrocubana del "Día de Reyes"* (Havana: MINREX, Departamento de Asuntos Culturales, 1960.

[10]H. Piron, *L'ile de Cuba* (Paris: 1886).

[11]Arthur Ramos, *Las culturas negras in el Nuevo Mundo* (Mexico: Fondo de Cultura Economica, 1943).

The snake is dead, sanga muleque
Look at its eyes, twinkling like candles,
Look at its teeth, sharp as if they were filed
The snake is dead, sanga la mulele.

These last few words are a *bricamo* (Carabalí) phrase, which is an invitation to dance, wherein we can see the complex syncretism of the real rumba spirit.   Similarly, we find some elements of the rumba in the pantomime of the "Día de Reyes," with its couple of the *diablito* [lit., little demon] and the young negress, which also still survives in the colloquial pair of the *ereno* and the *molañé*.   The following strophes are from the *diablito* and the *negrita*:

> *Negrita* :   Mamita, Mamita, yen, yen, yen
> Que me traiga serpiente [Mama, the serpent is swallowing me],
> yen, yen, yen
> *Diablito* :   Mentira, mi negra, yen, yen, yen
> Son juego'e mi tierra [Lies, my dark one, it's just a game of our land]
> Yen, yen, yen.

Phrases like "yen, yen" appear later in many rumbas of the 1930s-1950s, especially in those of the famous *rumbero* Luciano "Chano" Pozo, who used nonsense syllables like "blen, blen, blen," or those of another popular song of his: "Con tu cara de parampanpín / pin, pon, pan. . ."(another version is "pin, pan, pun. . ."), or in the rumba which announced the end of World War II: "Pin, pin, cayó Berlín / Pon, pon, cayó Japón" ["Berlin fell. . .Japan fell. . ."].   We may also recall that the rumba inherited many refrains from the nineteenth century, which have continued to change, like that which used to go "O-ñaña-ó", and which most of us recall as used later by *rumberos* like Chano, when he called "O-leri-ó, O-tintine-ó, O-chachiri-ó" and other similar expressions.[12]

Conga, Rumba, Guaguancó

We have mentioned the Congo influence on the rumba, which remains evident even in the instruments used (the "conga" drum). The Congo contribution is also evident in other ways. For instance, it is significant that many performers of *comparsas* and *congas* [*conga* being the main dance and song genre used in *comparsa* processions] are also *rumberos*, such as Rigoberto Leyva, author of the famous "Chambelona" and of various *columbias*, or the well-known Eduardo, of the "Las Jardineras" *comparsa*, or even Chano Pozo himself, author of the "Los Dandys de Belén" *comparsa*: "siento un bombo, mamita me están llamando. . ."["I hear a big drum, Mama, they're calling me"]. The examples are infinite, and we can also recall that two great musical artists of ours, Rita Montaner and Bola de Nieve, were both active in Los Dandys.

Nevertheless, in terms of dance the rumba and *conga* are quite different, occupying, indeed, opposite poles. The *conga* needs open space, empty streets in order to proceed, being, as Alejo Carpentier called it, a sort of "walking ballet." In contrast, the rumba site is finite, like a room, in which can be made a circle or *valla* of participants, which, in the street, can take any shape. This traditional setting dates from the first half of the nineteenth century, as described in chroniclers of Havana and Matanzas. The following rhymed description appeared in *El Faro Industrial de La Habana* in 1842: "Un negro alto, corpulento / baila mirando contento / a los que hay en torno dél" ["A

---

[12]Could the locution "O-leri-o" come from songs in North American cowboy films starring people like Roy Rogers and Gene Autrey? In either case there could be a common African origin, since it is well known that country-Western music has incorporated quite a bit of influence from the blues of Southern, rural blacks, which went on to influence genres like rhythm and blues, rock 'n' roll, and contemporary rock music.

tall, fat black man danced, contentedly watching those around him"].[13]

The choreography of the rumba, and especially of the *columbia*, reflects influence of the *diablitos* or *íremes* of Carabalí (*Añaña, Apapá, Bricamo*) origin, although several ethnologists and musicologists have alluded to a similar tradition, of Congo origin, in Cuba and Antioquía, Colombia. We should note that costumes like those of the *diablitos* have appeared in almost all the continents, including in the old pagan festivals of Europe, which Frazer has described.[14] And if the *diablitos* persist in parts of West Africa, they [or similar hooded figures] also accompany Corpus Christi processions in Spain. The Cuban *diablitos* used to come out on the "Dia de Reyes," as described by Landaluce in his chronicles of his epoch. The fiestas of San Juan and "Reyes Magos" are celebrated in a more Christian manner, but as Dr. José R. Rodríguez has noted, "When the black Magi king appears before Christianized blacks, the drums start pounding." According to Hutchinson, our "Día de Reyes," about which Fernando Ortiz has written an important study, seems to reflect strong Calabar origins dating from the massive importation of slaves from that area; these origins are independent from its Christian and Spanish ones.[15]

As for the *guaguancó*, it may have borrowed its name from a pre-existing form, as there was a *danzón* by that name danced in Havana in 1893. But everything seems to indicate that this variant of the rumba already existed by then, with distinct characteristics. Manuel Piedra has documented, for instance, a

---

[13]Vicente, article in *El Faro Industrial de La Habana*, 1/6/1842. The same form was danced in Matanzas, as can be seen in Dolores M. Ximeno's "Memorias de Lola María," in *Revista Cubana*.

[14]Sir James George Frazer, *La rama dorada* (Mexico City: Fondo de Cultura Económica, 1961).

[15]Dr. José R. Rodríguez, "Tío Tom: el de la rumba soy yo" (unpublished); T.J. Hutchinson, *Impressions of Western Africa* (Londres, 1958); and F. Ortiz, *op. cit.*

guaguanco that was very popular in that period, "Tú ve, yo no lloro, tú ve. . ."["You see, I don't cry..."][16]

The typical structure of a *guaguancó* has been described as follows: an introduction (*nana* or *diana*), in which the leader establishes the melodic line; then the *tema*, in which the singer delivers the basic narrative, which can be sung by a few voices; then the *estribillo*, sung by all the participants (and sometimes preceded by a narrative *décima*); the "inspiration," wherein the leader improvises; and ending with the *cierre* ["close"], that is, a concluding phrase reminiscent of Nahuatl people, "Aquí entre las flores cantaremos, hermano" ["We'll sing here among the flowers, brother"].[17]

In the *guaguancó*, aside from the author, there is also the lead singer, the dancer, and the player of the lead drum (the *quinto*). Tío Tom was among those who excelled at everything. Although his voice and physique naturally declined as he grew old, he imprinted his melodies with an unmistakeable stamp, and his prodigious sense of rhythm -- which reminded me of Benny Moré -- allowed him to guide the singers and players through the complex polyrhythmic contortions of this music of ours which is so difficult to execute and at the same time, so contagious.

---

[16]Manuel Piedra Martel, *Memorias de un mambí* (Havana: Ediciones del CNC, 1966).

[17]The use of *décima* and *estribillo* were described by Ontanio Lorcas, in "Los diablitos o el día infernal en La Habana," in *Prensa de La Habana*, 1/6/1856. The leader and *estribillo* appear in the description of Amelio Pérez Zamora, "El día de los reyes en La Habana," in *E l Abolicionista Español*, 1/15/1860. [Ed.: I find this description of the *guaguancó* to be atypical, as does Acosta himself (personal communication). Normally there is a very short (two or three phrases) introductory *diana*, followed by the narrative *canto* sung by the solo vocalist (occasionally with short choral refrains), leading to the call-and-response *montuno*.]

The Adventures and Misadventures of Tío Tom

Gonzalo Asencio Hernández, or Tío Tom, was born on April 5, 1919. An old acquaintance of his tells us, "He was born in El Modelo house, a typical old house, with its fights, its music, and its poetry." It was located at San Rafael y Hospital, in the Cayo Hueso barrio. Tío's father, Nicanor, loaded sacks for a pittance in the dock La Machina. His mother, Carmelina, was a beautiful negro pastry cook, who always had work in the kitchens of the rich. She brought something from there to her children, Gonzalo, Hilda, and, the youngest, Santa. In the 1920s they moved to an apartment in San Nicolás street between Marqués de la Torre and Calzada del Diez de Octubre. At that time Gonzalo was attending Public School #65, where he studied up to the third grade and later on took night classes. Life was hard, as he worked as a bottle cleaner, magazine vendor, a mason's peon, and a day-laborer.

In the thirties the family moved again to Estévez y Nueva del Pilar, where his father died in 1946. They then moved to Consejero Arango y Zequeira, in Carraguao, El Cerro, and thence to Pila street, in Atarés, and later, in the fifties, to Güines, on Reina street, and finally to their present place in Camarera street in Guanabacoa [outside Havana]. Such, in a few words, have been the taxing peregrinations of Tío Tom and his family.

Gonzalo composed his first rumba at the age of fifteen. He already knew some rumbas from the colonial period, like "Tú ves yo no lloro,""Coco mangurria", and the one which went "En la puerto del presidio yo vi cantar un gorrión"["At the prison gate I saw a sparrow singing"]. He knew the leading *rumberos* of his time: Roncona, Mario Alan, Alberto Noa, Carburo, El Güinero, El Checa, and others. And making the rumba his medium, he composed another that became genuinely popular: "Mal de yerba," which narrated a love story using the titles of contemporary popular films:

El cartero llama dos veces,

Mal de yerba, El suplico de una madre,
Tener o no tener, El gran bar,
La luz que agoniza, ya lo ves. . .
Murieron con las botas puestas.
En todas estos parrafitos
que componen mi rumbón
hay mas de un peliculón
que yo llevo en la memoria
para grabarlo en la historia
del libro de mis amores.

The Postman Calls Twice, Herb Sickness,
The Pain of a Mother, To Have and to Have Not,
The Grand Bar, The Dying Light, Now You See,
They Died with their Boots on. . .
In all these little paragraphs
which make up my rumba,
there is more than one film which I carry in my memory
to record it in the storybook of my loves. . .

In those days, when wages were low and work hard to get, Tío lived from rumba to rumba, where aside from partying he could earn some money. His voice, his dancing, his drumming, and his creative talent enlivened the houses called El Palomar (in la Víbora), La Siguanca (El Cerro), El Africa (Cayo Hueso), and others in Belén, Atarés, Jesús María, Los Sitios, Pueblo Nuevo, and other *rumbero* barrios of Havana. Undoubtedly many of these fiestas ended in fistfights, from which Tío did not always emerge unscathed. Nevertheless, the worst problem was that which he faced for political reasons, during the misrule of Carlos Prío Socarrás.

The Anti-Imperialist Guaguanco

We all recall with indignation the abuses, and the criminal, arrogant acts perpetrated by the Yankee marines and Navy children, whose ships often docked in Havana. Their most infamous act of vandalism was the desecration of the statue of our

nation's father, José Martí.   As was customary, the offending
marines -- whose colleagues more than once got their just
desserts in confrontations with Cuban workers -- escaped, due
to the servilitude of the government -- Carlos Prio's at the time.
Among the many protests by real Cubans was that of Tío Tom,
who popularized his *guaguancó* that spread from mouth to
mouth, ending with the cry, "Cubans! Where are the Cubans?"

The punishment was swift, and Tío Tom was sentenced to
six months and a day for his patriotic rumba questioning the
"Honorable señor Presidente."   The incident further shows that
whether in the colonial or neo-colonial periods, Cuba has never
lacked for "protest songs," be they in the form of *son, guaracha,
criolla, punto, habanera, danzón,* or patriotic hymns and
marches.   Many of their authors suffered harsh consequences
for such songs, as did Tío Tom, whose *guaguancó* is worth
quoting further:

> ¿Cubanos, dónde están los cubanos?
> Yo quisiera saber dónde están los cubanos?
> ¿Cómo los americanos han venido desde afuera
> a atropellar la bandera y la estatua de un mártir cubano?
> Cuba no debe favores a ninguna extraña tierra,
> todo el misterio que encierra es de la plata y el oro.
> Oiga señor presidente,
> quiero saber tu opinión sobre la reclamación
> que ha presentado el cubano contra esos americanos
> que han venido desde afuera
> a atropellar la bandera de nuestro suelo cubano.

> Cubans, where are the Cubans?
> I want to know where are the Cubans.
> How is it that these Americans came from abroad
> to trample our flag and the statue of our martyr?
> Cuba owes no favors to any foreign country,
> All the mystery it holds is in silver and gold.
> Listen Mr. President, I want your opinion
> about the punishment which Cuba demands

against these Americans who have come from abroad
to trample the flag of our Cuban soil.

The theme of Cuban identity is common in Tío's rumbas, although occasionally focussing on our merry and festive character, as in the composition "Los cubanos son rareza":

Los cubanos son rareza, con un tambor en la mano
hacen la tierra temblar, y dicen los mexicanos
cuando sienten los tambores, a Cuba voy a gozar
(Refrain:) Si tú quieres divertir, escucha esta rumba
buena

The Cubans are unique, with drums in their hands
they make the earth shake, and the Mexicans say
when they feel the drums, "I'm off to Cuba to have a good
time"
(Refrain:) If you want to have fun, listen to this rumba

After the triumph of the Revolution, Gonzalo Asencio continued to compose anti-imperialist and revolutionary rumbas, and went on constituting, with his group, a kind of popular chronicle, in song and dance, of the achievements of our country during these twenty-some years of struggles and victories.

The *Rumberos* are Many

As can be guessed, Tío Tom didn't spring from barren earth, but from the same fertile soil that produced a legion of distinguished *rumberos*. Although impossible to honor them all in a brief space, we should mention a few of the most distinguished, who would include Calixto Callava, Peñita, Ignacio Quimbundo, Silvestre Méndez, Juancito Núñez, Chano Pozo, Wilfredo Sotolongo, Remberto Bequer, Jorgito Tiant, Evaristo Aparicio ("El Pícaro"), Mario Dreke ("Chavalonga"), Macho el Guanqui, Macho el Guapo, Alambre, Francisco Borroto, Santos Ramírez and others from different provinces, like Juan Bosco, Saldiguera, and Virulilla from Matanzas. Among the distinguished *quinto* play-

ers have been Angel Contreras ("Caballerón"), his brother
Orlando, Julio Basave ("El Barondó"), Pedro Izquierdo ("Pello"),
Félix Xiqués, Eloy Martí, Juan Romay, los Embales, los Papines,
Candito, El Patato, Armando Peraza (Mano de Plomo), Aristides
Soto ("Tata Güines"), and many more.

We might also mention here a few "classic" pieces from this
inexhaustible genre, such as "Xiomara por qué," of Evaristo
Aparicio, "El telefonito," of Silvestre Mendez, "No te detengas,
voy pa Pueblo Nuevo" of Mario Dreke, "Tiene mi barrio de
Atarés" of Angel Contreras, "Nicasia la Escolera" of Alambre,
"Dirán de mí todo lo que quieran" of Juancito Nuñez, "Crucé de
las Antillas el mar," of Guillermo Valdés Quintana, "Baila
Catalina con un solo pie" by Víctor Marín, and "La rumba tiene
valor" by Pablo Cairo.　And we should remember that many
composers renowned for other genres also contributed familiar
rumbas, like Julio Cueva ("Alamán, alamán con chévere"), José
Antonio Méndez ("La última la traigo yo"), or Bienvenido Julian
Gutierrez ("Cuatro platos por un coco").　The latter prolific and
versatile composer, the co-author of "Convergencia," may well
have been inspired by Tío Tom's mother, who, according to
him, lived "easy" through his composition "Carmelina."　One
wonders if his song was the origin of the familiar phrase "to
live like Carmelina," or if he took it from another source.　The
field is open for research.

In this account we have not yet mentioned composers like
Ernesto Lecuona, Eliseo Grenet, and Armando Oréfiche, who
popularized the rumba internationally, although in a more
"sophisticated" salon style.　Similar contributions were made, in
their own way, by singers like Desi Arnaz and, above all,
Miguelito Valdés, who popularized Chano Pozo's classic rumba
[about the death of the famous *rumbero* Malanga] "Malanga
murió": "Siento una voz que me dice, Oguaniyé-ó" (or sometimes "Aleriyé-ó").　This latter phrase, which we find in several
variants, brings us again to the question of African words
which are found in rumbas from the nineteenth century to the
present (including in Pérez Prado's mambos).　Some refrains of

the last century, like "Senseribó, senseribó, epe manco-ó" and the aforementioned "Oñañá-ó" have reached the present in many variants. To mention just one example, we recall the tense and troubled Daniel Santos shouting "Anacobero, mi rumba, o-yamba-ó. . ."

From Lecuona to Tío Tom

The influence of the rumba in our music is scarcely limited to the above names. Mentioning Ernesto Lecuona, it is interesting to note that a composer who achieved great renown in the forties and fifties, Juan Arrondo, used to say, "My music goes from Lecuona to Tío Tom." And, indeed, Tío's impact on our music has been considerable, although seldom acknowledged so explicitly as did Arrondo. The point is that the rumba has exercised great influence on other Cuban music genres and on their various interpreters. For just as the *son*, as we have noted elsewhere, has permeated and revitalized, at different times, the most varied styles of our music (from the *danzón* to *nueva trova*), so must we realize that the rumba gave new life to the *son* when the latter reached Havana and Matanzas. It is not coincidental that the leading *sonero* of Havana, Ignacio Piñeiro (who was born in Jesús María and raised in Pueblo Nuevo), was an inspired *rumbero*, who in 1906 formed part of the *clave* and *guaguancó* group "Timbre de Oro," and later directed the *guaguancó* group "Los Roncos."

Benny Moré himself, although generally associated with the *son, trova, bolero*, and mambo, was an ardent *rumbero*, as is reflected in his style, his improvisations, his refrains, and his own big-band *guajeos* [instrumental ostinati]. He himself proudly proclaimed to be a *rumbero* and *guaguancosero* in "Elige tú, que canto yo"["You choose it, and I'll sing it"], whose refrain has an ineffable *guaguancó* flavor, and is essentially identical to that of Chano Pozo's "Cubano be, Cubano bop," performed with Dizzy Gillespie's jazz band. In rumba parties I've also heard very similar refrains, like "Con un solo pie, con un solo pie." The rumba remains present in the most dissimilar groups, from Rumbavana to Irakere, and in authors of *boleros* and *canciones* like Guillermo Díaz. Similarly, one of the most popular *nueva trova* songs, Pablo Milanés's "Los caminos," is a typical *guaguancó*, which starts with a short, traditional *nana*.

We should also recall the presence of the rumba in Cuban poetry, and especially in Nicolás Guillén's internationally famous poems "Sesemayá," "La canción del bongó," "Canto negro," "Rumba," "Chévere," "Velorio [wake] de Papá Montero," "Mulata," and "Sóngoro Cosongo." A recent and less-known poem of his, "Yo nunca digo," could be called a "protest *guaguancó*," like those of Tío Tom:

> Yo nunca digo
> que mi canción es de protesta;
> yo siempre dejo
> que lo diga ella. . .
> Si mi guaguancó protesta,
> ay, también protesto yo.
> Mi cuchillo tiene filo,
> no le sujetes, no, no.
> Guaguancó, que guaguancó,
> que guaguancó, guaguancó. . .
>
> I never say that my song is protest
> I just let it speak for itself;
> If my guaguanco protests,
> then so do I.
> My knife has a blade, don't grab it,
> Guaguancó, what a guaguancó. . .

We can affirm, then, that our national poet is not only a poet of the *son*, but also of the rumba. And Guillén is not alone in this respect, but shares this feature with poets like Emilio Ballagas, Ramón Guirao, Marcelino Arozarena, and José Z. Tallet, whose poem "La rumba" was used as a text in the magnificent symphonic work of Alejandro García Caturla.

Tío and the Rumba: Prejudices and Plagiarisms

If I have insisted on the importance of the rumba in our culture, it is because the rumba has been so disparaged, and at the
same time so adulterated in deformed versions, especially,
though not only, in commercial Yankee music. Denunciations of
the rumba date from the nineteenth century, when diverse
chroniclers --noted by Fernando Ortiz -- castigated it as im-
moral, licentious, savage, and primitive, etc., leading to the
classic definition of the rumba as "a popular Cuban dance cultivated in a certain licentious ambience by happy people."[18]
Even during the neo-colonial republic period, despite the great
work undertaken by Fernando Ortiz, Amadeo Roldán, Alejo
Carpentier, Alejandro García Caturla, Nicolás Guillén and others
who militated against elitist and racist traditional prejudices,
the rumba coninued being the object of derision and persecution by the upright and proper bourgeoisie. Something similar
had happened with the *danzón* and *son*, but undoubtedly it was
the rumba which had to wait the longest for its total vindica-
tion.

As for plagiarism, the rumba proved to be quite favorable as
a victim, since the *rumberos* traditionally had little to do with
the mass media and commercial mechanisms in general; their
compositions spread spontaneously from house to house, street
to street, and barrio to barrio, sometimes falling into the hands
of "professional" musicians who registered the "anonymous"
compositions as their own. Such practices were exacerbated by
the musicologists who promoted the myth of "anonymous
folkore." In innumerable cases, it was eventually discovered
that some or other "anonymous" composition had an author,
with a name, address, and identity card.

Many *rumberos* were deprived of the fruits of their work
by such practices, as was Peñita, the author of "Sepárate mujer,
suelta ese reja"["Out of the way, woman, let go of those bars"].

---

[18]Ricardo Orta Nadal, cited by José R. Rodríguez and by Fernando Ortiz,
who mention many similar opinions.

But the most deprived, plagiarized, and imitated author was Tío Tom. For example, there is an old rumba of his which describes a cockfight in the old stockade at the corner of Tejas, with the refrain "Veinte le voy a mi gallo pinto"["I'll put twenty on my spotted cock"]. While Tío's authorship remained largely unknown, the piece became famous, with a few changes, and with "gallo" replaced by "pelón"["bald"]. Another celebrated *guaguancó* of his, which has also traveled "anonymously" abroad, is called "Siento que me regaña el corazon"["I feel my heart scolding me"], whose refrain is well known: "Si tú me lo das, por qué me lo quitas..."

More recently, a Venezuelan group performed that song. How did it reach there? Not even the musicians themselves knew of the author. Even his masterpiece "Consuélate como yo" had various supposed authors or claimants until the Revolution, which cleared everything up and did justice to Gonzalo Asencio, who today is the registered author of his songs and goes on giving the people more songs, one after another.

Gonzalo Asencio's production is so copious -- reaching the hundreds -- that not even he remembers it all, in its variety of themes and ambiences. For example, Tío has ventured into the forgotten genre of the *pregón* [based on the street-vendor's call]: "Estiro bastidores, cunitas de niño y camas de mayores" ("I stretch bed-springs, of cradles and adult sizes"). He also turned to traditional themes dealing with neo-African beliefs, like "Changó va vení":

> Ya empezó el tambó, oye la tambo tá soná
> y todos los santeritos cantan así:
> Changó va veni (3x) con el machete en la mano
> Tierra tiembla y sarabanda manomo, mundo acaba
>
> The drumming has already started, listen to it,
> and all the little devotees are singing:
> Changó is coming, with a machete in his hand,

The earth trembles and, sarabanda manomo, the world ends.

Among Tío's themes are comic situations, domestic tragedies, social problems and more.   One feature that is particularly notable in his compositions is his treatment of barrio machismo and bravado, a favorite subject of our authors, especially in the context of women and infidelity in romance.   Thus, in "Ya ves que me la jugué"["See, I took a chance"] and "De qué me sirve una mujer?"["What good would a woman be to me?"], Tío Tom sagely combines love, nostalgia, violence, irony, tenderness, Cubanness, and so on.   Never does he lapse into the tastelessness characteristic of so many *boleros, tangos, rancheras, canciones*, and even rumbas throughout Latin America.   For example, Tío knows how to present the infidelity of a woman in a remarkably graceful and picaresque manner, as in his *guaguancó*   "Tun tun, quién es."   Thus there are several compositions of his which our singers, after fifteen and more years, have never tired of singing, such as: "Tú era una coqueta, que a nadie respeta. . ."[You were a flirt whom nobody respects. . ."].

But he also has pieces like "Con ese caminaíto que tienes tú,""Caballeros qué mujer,""Corazón que naciste conmigo,""Cuando yo la vi por primera vez,""Escondido en las aguas,""Pensé darte mi nombre,""Yo no tuve la culpa," and many more, in which the woman appears like a true companion rather than an untrustworthy seductress.   And, of course, as mentioned above, revolutionary and anti-imperialist themes have always occupied an important place in his works, as in: "Este es mi país"["This is my country"],"Tierra brava,""La Reforma va"["The reform proceeds"], "Camilo Cienfuegos,""Ché Guevara,""Viva Fidel,""Ahora tenemos armas y aviones" ["Now we have arms and planes"], "Señor Marqués, váyase pa España" ["Señor Marqués, go to Spain"], "Que canten los bandoneones, que ha nacido el Ché Guevara"["Let the accordions sing, Ché has been born"], "Vamos pa el cañaveral,""Y siempre es 26," and "Quita la mano, americano" ["Get your hands off us, Americans"].

Nor does Tío Tom's work lack for satire of bourgeois society, as in "A la fiesta de los caramelos no pueden ir los bombones"["At the fiesta of the candies, chocolates aren't allowed"], or the catchy refrains still popularly sung, "Tan chiquitica y ni ná ni ná, salsa," "Oye como suena la chancleta," and "Mambo Guana-hacabibes, si tú me quieres, tú no me olvides." The thematic variety of his rumbas is evident in titles like "Bemba colorá"["Red lips"],"A Juan Arrondo le gusta el pollo"[Juan Arrondo likes chicken"], "Sangre africana"["African blood"], "Viento en popa a toda vela"["Full sails ahead"],"Coco pelao baila pacá"["Dance over there, bald-head!"], and other more tender and sentimental ones like "Madre no llore" ["Mother don't cry"], and the marvellous synthesis of comedy and affection of "Qué quiere la niña?"

> ¿Qué quiere la niña que le compren
> en la bodega del primo?
> Una chambelona.
> No te puedo complacer, nené
> El primo nada más que vende ron;
> ahora, yo de corazón, nené,
> te compraré una chambelona

> What does the little girl want from her cousin's store?
> Only a lollipop.
> I can't satisfy you, nené,
> Cousin's store has only rum;
> But now, nené, I'll get you a lollipop.

Clearly, we can't conclude without quoting part of his most famous *guaguancó*:[19]

> Consuélate como yo,
> que yo también tuve un amor, y lo perdí;

---

[19][Ed.:] This familiar rumba is recorded in traditional style by Carlos Embale on Areito LD-3428, and in modernized, salsa-style by Eddie Palmieri on "Cheo y Quintana" (Coco CLP-109XX).

Y por eso digo ahora
ya yo no vuelvo a querer;
¿De qué te sirvio el querer
si a ti también te traicionó, como a mi?

Console yourself like me,
that I also had a love, and lost it;
And that's why I say now
that I won't return to love again;
What good will love do you
if you've been betrayed, like I was?

Recently Tío Tom composed another quite popular *guaguancó* in which he confronts old age and death with his perpetual grace: "Ya me estoy poniendo viejo, ¿qué es eso? La muerte me llama, ¿que es eso?" ["I've gotten old, what's going on? Death is calling me, what is it?"]. But Tío Tom will never get old, nor will his work, which is so representative of our music. As José Rodríguez has well said:

> The *guaguancó* and the *columbia*, musical expressions of the rumba, have never had a more explosive, spontaneous, and fecund creator than Tío Tom. . .Tio never limited himself to the trite and insipid theme of the rhythmic mocking and gossip, but he sang of the Revolution, of the homeland, of love and life.

4

The Tumba Francesa Societies and their Music

At the turn of the nineteenth century, in the wake of the Haitian Revolution some 30,000 Franco-Haitian refugees immigrated to eastern Cuba. Many of these were Frenchmen and their families, who brought to provincial and undeveloped Oriente an unprecedented level of European culture, from opera to Moliere. Most of the refugees, however, were patois-speaking blacks, who, for their part, introduced their own distinctive culture, much of which centered around the tumba francesa societies and which continues to color eastern Cuban culture. After nearly two centuries of acculturation to greater Cuban culture, these societies and their characteristic music and dance have naturally declined, and, as the following article points out, they have lost their mutual aid function since the advent of the Revolution in 1959. Nevertheless, the societies, their art forms, and creole dialect do persist, and have been amply documented by Cuban ethnographers, particularly Olavo Alen, in his recent book "La Música de las sociedades de la Tumba Francesa en Cuba." The recreational and artistic activities of the tumba francesa groups have also been encouraged such that they now form a familiar sight at the frequent folkloric festivals in eastern Cuba.

Olavo Alen, since obtaining his doctorate in musicology at Humboldt University in Berlin (formerly GDR), is director of the Centro de Investigación y Desarrollo de la Música Cubana (CIDMUC) in Havana.

4

The Tumba Francesa Societies and their Music

Olavo Alen Rodríguez

The slave trade in the Americas lasted nearly four centuries, bringing several million Africans of diverse ethnic origins to the New World. The commencement of the trade coincided with the decline of European feudalism and the origins of capitalism. From this period on, slave labor in the Americas changed the extent and nature of European primary capital accumulation. The slave trade itself became one of the most profitable businesses of the time.

The shipment of Africans to the Americas occurred in a series of waves involving various African ethnic groups and cultures. The slaves found themselves placed into a very different socio-economic world with highly unfamiliar modes of production. In the course of the four centuries of the slave trade, Africa also underwent significant transformations. The dispersal of slaves of distinct ethnicities into diverse socio-economic conditions in the New World contributed to an intricate and complex process of transculturation among the slaves introduced to the greater American ethnic complex. Of course, the process of merging and transculturation involved not only the mutual influence between the different African ethnic groups, but also that with Europeans of diverse origins, aboriginal Americans, and with some Asians subsequently imported as manual laborers. On the cultural level, mixture was thus a product of the interaction of diverse African and non-African cultures within a new socio-economic and geographic environment. Many African cultural traditions were lost, some managed to endure relatively unchanged, and others -- perhaps the majority -- became the authentic traits of a new, distinctively American cultural complex.

The nature of New World slavery also played an important role in shaping neo-African culture in the new environment. In many cases, Spanish landowners kept slaves of diverse ethnic groups in separate compounds in order to facilitate supervision, lessen the risk of collective revolt, and enhance labor productivity among the slaves.

The slave trade eventually led to the emergence of another new social group in the Americas -- that of the freed black. Indeed, freed blacks played an essential role in the intensive rural and urban transculturation which was crucial to the development of neo-African culture in the New World. Freed Africans and their descendants were allowed to gather in associations called *cabildos*, as long as current legislation regulating them was observed. Cofraternities of Africans from their native lands were thus reproduced or imitated in the Americas. The *cabildos* also served to preserve ancestral rituals and song and dance practices associated with religious beliefs. Thus, the greatest social significance of the *cabildo* was its preservation of African cultural traditions and many of the elements that would later integrate in the new cultures of the American environment.

The custom of forming fraternal associations according to ethnic groups was already common among blacks in Seville, and from there it spread to most of Hispanic Latin America. Initially, the New World *cabildos* were patterned after the practices and mores left behind in Africa. Later, with the ever-increasing inclusion of acculturated creole blacks, the *cabildos* changed in function to become associations of mutual assistance, instruction, and recreation, generally named after a

Catholic saint and regulated by the colonial Spanish Act of Associations.

The societies of *tumba francesa* in Cuba are a special case among neo-African mutual aid and recreational groups in the Americas. They merit attention for the manner in which they continue to preserve African-derived art forms.

A considerable Haitian population -- comprising blacks and mulattos, slaves and freedmen -- arrived in Cuba at the turn of the nineteenth century as a result of the revolution in Haiti. These immigrants were referred to by Cubans as "French" (*francés, francesa*, etc.), along with their descendants and other slaves subsequently imported by French slaveowners who had fled Haiti. These groups, whose culture had been shaped by an earlier process of transculturation in Haiti, knew French as a language of domination and had assimilated elements of French culture. Their primary language, however, was not pure French but a creole or patois derived from French and the variety of African languages spoken in Saint Domingue [subsequently Haiti]. In Cuba they continued their distinctive "French" culture and retained patois as their primary idiom, while being subject to a second process of transculturation in their new socio-economic situation.

In Cuba, the *"francés"* denomination was applied not only to the Haitian immigrants but also to their dances, music, instruments, and cultural societies in general. The immigrants preferred to be regarded as French rather than as Haitians, especially since the latter were regarded as troublesome by Spanish colonial authorities after the Haitian Revolution challenged European colonialism in the last decade of the eighteenth century.

The *tumba francesa* associations were founded by the first generation of descendants of the immigrants, and were subsequently joined by increasing numbers of Cuban creoles. They grew quickly, reaching their peak by the turn of the twentieth century. The associations thus incorporated the contributions of black slaves and freedmen, both Cuban and African, and the descendants of Haitian immigrants, who retained the family name of the French master of their ancestors in Haiti. Festivities held on specific occasions were the main vehicles for the preservation of folkloric traditions in the process of transculturation that took place in Cuba, in which the distinctive Franco-Haitian character persisted. The societies have declined in importance since their peak; at present there are only two.

The music and dances of the *tumba francesa* societies have become one of the most distinctive features of Cuban cultural heritage, and they have exerted influence, whether directly or indirectly, on other urban artistic expressions, such as the *congas* and *comparsas* of Cuba's easternmost provinces.

Life in the *tumba francesa* societies centers around festivities in which songs are created and performed by a soloist, or *composé* (the cantor), with the accompaniment of a chorus or *tumberas*. The festivities also feature a dance led by a *mayor* or *mayora de plaza*, a few drummers (*tamboreros*), and other followers led by "queens" and "kings" (referred to in modern times as "presidents").

The most important figure is the *composé*, the solo singer, who improvises song texts and leads the chorus in alternating call-and-response passages. The chorus comprises women (*tumberas*) who attend the festivities wearing pale, beltless, stiff, well-ironed dresses with broad collars, sleeves, and ruffles, trimmed with lace and ribbons. The *tumbera*'s broad skirt hangs to her feet, with a short train behind; lace-trimmed petticoats can be seen beneath the skirt. Colored, artfully-knotted bandanas are worn on the head and large kerchiefs on the hand. The women also wear necklaces with the low-necked gowns, along with earrings, bracelets, and huge finger rings with fancy jewels; they also carry fans with chains for hanging them. The men wear predominantly white shirts and trousers. Traditionally they attended festivities wearing a suit, formal shirt, and necktie, with large kerchiefs around their necks when dancing.   Both men and women wear comfortable, low shoes.

The instruments used in the festivities include three large single-headed drums called *tumbas*, a *catá* (a cylindrical wooden idiophone), and a *tambora* (a two-headed drum played during the dance called *masón*).   Drumming is always accompanied by metal rattles called *chachás*, played by the *mayora de plaza* and the *tumberas*.   The three *tumbas* are individually called *premier, bulá,* and *segón*; they each function differently in the ensemble.   The *premier* is the biggest of the three, has the largest head, and is lowest in pitch.   It is the last to perform and functions to introduce virtuoso improvisations which become the focal point of the music.   The *bulá* is somewhat smaller than the *premier* and has an accordingly smaller head and higher pitch.   Its function is to maintain a fixed pattern of discrete tones within a polyrhythmic structure.   The *premier*'s rhythms are richer and more varied than those of the third drum, the *bulá-segón,* or *segón* or simply *bulá*, which also plays fixed patterns.   The *toques*, or basic rhythmic cells, played on the *segón* are the same as those of the *bulá*, although it remains silent at certain points in the dance.

It appears that previously several dances were performed, but many have disappeared.   In the opinion of this writer, the *yubá*, which still exists, represents a synthesis of some of these older, extinct dances.   Only memories remain of the *toques grave* (or *gravima*) and *mangasila* in the *yubá*; even the oldest informants were unable to illustrate the individual *toques* and archaic steps which were eventually synthesized in the *yubá*.

At present there are only two dances, the *yubá* and the *masón*, which appears to be of more recent origin.   In the beginning of the twentieth century the *masón*, a couple dance, was used to attract the attention of young people and stimulate them to dance at festivities. According to Fernando Ortiz, the word *masón* derives from the French *maison* (house), and the dance represented an imitation of the dances seen by slaves at the mansion of their French masters.   All festivities of the *tumba francesa* traditionally begin with a *masón*.

The *yubá*, as noted above, is the oldest remaining dance.   It consists of a series of *toques*, dance steps, and other choreographic elements, which likely derive from different older dances.   The *yubá* today can be danced to rhythms called *toque macota* and *cobrero*.   The finale of the *yubá* is called the *frente*, a section in which the rhythm and dance are markedly different.   In the *frente* the *premier* and *bulá* drums are played laying horizontally on the floor.   The dance consists of a duel between the rhythmic improvisation of the *premier* and the intricate steps of the solo dancer, who stands alone in the middle of the room in front of the drums, dancing with colored kerchiefs around his body until he "defeats" the drummer or is defeated.

The fest extends throughout the night, with several dance sessions from fifteen to thirty-five minutes, between which cool beverages and sweets are enjoyed, and a new *composé* takes over.

Like other phonetically similar words, *tumba* is a generic term of the word *tambor* in Bantu and semi-Bantu cultures.   In Cuba this word designated a meeting of negro slaves dancing around their instruments.   Many members of the *tumba francesa* refer to the accompaniment of the *bulá* as *bular*.   In some Bantu idioms the words *bulá* and *babulá* mean "to beat" or "to strike."

The Arará drums from West Africa serve as models for the parchment-tightening method of the *tumbas*.   Several hook-shaped stakes pierce the drum body; to these are attached looped strings themselves affixed to the head.

The use of the *catá* and the cylindrical shape of the drums are of Bantu ancestry, along with most of the African terminology.   Paintings on the drums often take the form of ellipses, five-pointed stars, and lines and triangles.   These are presumably New World innovations, along with the use of mechanical nut-and-bolt tightening mechanisms and metal rings around the body of the drum to reinforce its structure when cracks appear.

The practice of hanging the *tambora* from the neck of the performer and playing it with a stick rather than the palm of the hand illustrates its affinities to the French *tambourin*. The French contribution to the process of acculturation is also obvious in the many words applied to instruments and dances, such as *masón, premier*, and *segón* (second).

A guitar string is stretched across the head and attached to the rings which bind it to the pegs. Originally, a strip of twisted leather with a feather of a chicken or buzzard in the middle was used in place of the guitar string. This strip was called the *ficelle*; as explained to this writer by the president of one *tumba francesa* society, it serves to alter the timbre of the drum, partially by making the head vibrations more complex. In the evident absence of African precedents, this element appears to be of European origin.

The arrangement of the rhythmic functions of each drum according to register is clearly African in character. In Cuba, as a result of the process of transculturation, improvisation is generally performed on the higher-pitched drums, while the lower-pitched ones provide rhythmic accompaniment. This practice (as described here from a European perspective) is not, however, found in the music of the *tumba francesa*. Here, the improvisational function is rendered by the lowest-pitched drum, the *premier*, while the higher-pitched drums provide recurring accompaniment patterns. In recent field work carried out in Santiago de Cuba in 1978, however, we did hear at one festivity a *premier* tuned to a higher pitch than the *bulá*. In response to our questions, the drummer, a 25-year-old man who had played in the society for ten years, said, "I tuned the drum this way because I wanted it to be heard better and to sound higher than the *bulá*." The man had not been playing the *premier* for long, having taken up that drum, rather than the *bulá* to which he was accustomed, only recently when the

former *premier* player fell ill. The young drummer's preference for the higher pitch illustrates the continuation of the process of transculturation and the way in which progressively
fewer elements of the original culture persist in Cuban culture.
In the case of the *tumba francesa*, such changes, although
spontaneous and natural, may not be able to rescue the societies from the decline they have experienced in recent years.
This change also illustrates the adoption of the practice referred to above, wherein improvisations are rendered on the
higher-pitched drum.

The *tumba francesa* societies have evolved under different
successive socio-economic systems. Initially, the French aris-
tocracy and pre-Revolutionary courts served as important
aesthetic models. Later, they became societies of mutual aid
due to socio-economic transformations in the Republican period
in Cuba. With the victory of the Cuban Revolution, their economic function of mutual assistance became obsolete, although
it was deemed desirable to preserve their aesthetic value as
part of the social patrimony of the country. The Ministry of
Culture (the former Consejo Nacional de Cultura, or National
Council for Culture) undertook the necessary steps to revive
the two societies which in 1959 were still capable of functioning. Both are located on the easternmost coast of the island.
One of them, Santa Catalina de Riccis -- better known as La
Pompadu -- is in the city of Guantanamo, and the other, La
Caridad, is in Santiago de Cuba. The most important steps necessary for the preservation of their folkloric values are the
following:

--the performance of *tumba francesa* festivities by the
Folklore Ensemble of Oriente;

--the edition of an LP record to preserve separately
and in unison the drum *toques* as well as the songs of
composés and complete sections of a fest [ed.: This record
has since been issued as volume VII (Areito-Egrem LD
3606) of the series *Antología de la música afrocubana*];

--photographs and videotapes to be kept in the archives of communities where these societies exist;

--the restoration of the place of the *tumba francesa* in Guantánamo and the preservation of its distinctive elements;

--the performance of typical dances and music by the members of these societies in local and national festivals and in main theaters in Havana;

--the edition of newspaper articles and books about these societies;

--the transcription of rhythms and songs;

--the promotion of the interest of local researchers in the history and cultural contributions of these groups;

--the production of a documentary film about the origin and history of the *tumba francesa* societies.

The essential aim of all these efforts is to research and spread the musical and cultural patrimony of the *tumba francesa* societies, preserving them from oblivion and the present-day decline.

5

The Décima and Punto in Cuban Folklore

The term punto is applied to the wide variety of Cuban song-types which employ the ten-line décima as their text. In their vocal style, chordal vocabulary, predominantly triple meter, and usage of stringed lutes and the décima form, they clearly reflect their origins in the folk musics of Spain and the Canary Islands. The décima itself, a product of sixteenth-century Spain, reached Cuba in the early eighteenth century. By the early nineteenth century, through the works of poets like Francisco Pobeda and El Cucalambé, the punto had become the foremost poetic and musical genre of the white campesinos, with whom it remains closely associated. While retaining the Hispanic features noted above, the punto cubano evolved in a rich variety of regional substyles, becoming distinctly Cuban in the process.

Like many other Spanish-derived folk styles in the New World, the punto is a text-dominated genre, in which the melodic setting consists primarily of a finite number of stock tunes. This feature, while making the punto an effective vehicle for traditional poetic expression, has tended to limit its popularity in the modern period, as literacy, the mass media, and other forms of communication eclipse folk versification. Since 1959 the Cuban government has sought to arrest the perhaps inevitable decline of the genre by sponsoring folkloric programs, recordings, daily radio broadcasts, and, last but not least, scholarly documentation of the punto in its numerous variants. Nevertheless, while Cuban folklorists have written extensively on the décima as poetry, the punto as a musical style has received less scholarly attention from Cuban musicologists than have Afro-Cuban musics, and, moreover, it has never been researched by non-Cuban writers. The introductory article included here is one of the relatively few studies of the punto as a musical genre.

María Teresa Linares is a senior Cuban musicologist, who has authored several articles and edited a number of records of Cuban traditional music.   She currently directs the Music Museum in Havana.

5

The Décima and Punto in Cuban Folklore

María   Teresa   Linares

The *punto* is the most widespread music genre of rural Cuba. It constitutes a broad song repertory represented in character- istic styles of different regions. *"Punto"* -- whether *libre, cam- agüeyano, sanjuanero, spirituano, pinareño*, etc. -- is a generic term, denoting the melodic setting (*tonada*) whose text always consists of a *décima*,[1] whether pre-composed or improvised. The tradition of improvising *décimas* has allowed the campesino to use the genre as a chronicle, as an epic song, or for a lyrical message, or to express his ideological struggles.

The *punto* has occasionally been disparaged as being simple, primitive, archaic, and monotonous as a song form; but in spite of such criticism and the present fondness of Cuban youth for other musical genres, the *punto* has been adopted by many ur- ban dwellers and maintained by rural migrants to the cities.

Although it is certainly true that the poet-singers of the *punto* pay more attention to the improvisation of the text than

---

[1] [Ed.:] The *décima* is distinguished by the use of verses of ten lines, with a specific number of syllables in each line, usually employing the rhyme scheme *abbaaccddc*.   In Cuba the *décima*, when sung, is generally referred to as *punto guajiro* or *punto cubano*.   The term *guajiro* denotes a Cuban peasant, implicitly of Hispanic rather than African descendency.

to the music, and that they study the precepts of the *décima* without becoming interested in the technical aspects of the music, still, there are many campesinos who *create* their own melodic settings, and it is possible to collect hundreds of totally different melodies in different regions.

We have suggested above that the campesino song repertoire constitutes a grouping of songs perfectly identified with the people that sing them, and with special characteristics which give it the right, if not to be called autochthonous, to possess the most legitimate trademark of Cuban identity. This presence and vitality of campesino songs suggests characteristics so well defined and differentiated through the different songs of the Cuban people that they constitute distinct entities. The *punto's* innumerable melodies, its instruments and tunings, and its rhythms, styles, and texts are the patrimony of a great nucleus of our people, whether located in the countryside or in the cities. Its characteristics are so well defined that they absorb foreign elements only with difficulty, and they manifest themselves in all the occasions of campesino life, from *guateques* or fiestas, to the chores of the home or field, whether in love or in battle.

The *décima* is the text form most widely used in the *punto guajiro*, and it constitutes a common denominator in all the Spanish-speaking peoples in the Americas. Its provenance is invariably rural. Well-known, for example, are the *payadas* or *trovadas* of the Argentine *gauchos* [cowboys], who also use the *décima* as a text form for genres like *cifras, media cifras, trovadas, estilos, tonos,* and *milongas*; in such genres the *décima* is used in the form of *décima glosada, décima con estrambote o estribillo* [with refrain], *décimas improvisadas a lo humano y a lo divino* [improvised, secular or devotional], and *el encadenado* [lit., "chained"], wherein two rival singers alternate, each taking the last line of the other as their first line. The verbal duel we call *controversia* is called *contrapunto* there, and is used in diverse forms; it is especially known for its difficult references to astronomy, geography, and mythology, which are used for the wakes of the *Altares de Cruz.*

We can take the verses below as an example of *décimas a lo divino* [devotional *décima*], which appears in a booklet of Oreste Plath, *Santuro y tradición de Andacollo,* sung by Nicasio García to the miracles of the Virgin of Andacollo, of which we take the first and last *décimas.*

A ver la Reina del Cielo
Ocurre bastante gente
Llega el humilde devoto
Hincado se hace presente

De diferentes lugares
Vienen a rendirle culto,
El pobre, el jurisconsulto
Lloran junto a sus altares;
Algunos cruzan los mares
Deseosos del tal consuelo
Andacollo, feliz suelo,
Que el mes de diciembre atiende,
Todo el orbe se desprende
A ver la Reino del Cielo

Ciegos han tenido vista,
Los tullidos han andado,
El enfermo ha mejorado,
Refiere una larga lista;
Dicha princesa conquista
Que ocurra inmediatamente
Todo estado de viviente
Si quiere ser perdonado,
Confesado y comulgado,
Hincado se hace presente.

So many people have gathered
To see the queen of the sky
Humble devoted people arrive
Kneeling, they let their presence be known;

Coming from different places,
They come to offer their worship,
The pauper along with the jurist
Cry together before her altar;
Some must journey across the seas
Desirous of the consolation
Andacollo, a happy earth,
Which the month of December attends to,
The whole world then releases itself
To see the queen of the sky.

Blind ones have regained their sight,
The crippled have walked again,
The sickly have become well again
This is referred to on a long list;
Happiness that princess conquers
That this may occur immediately
Every state where the living are found
If they want to be forgiven,
Be confessed and given communion,
Kneeling, they let their presence be known.

Eminent American folklorists like Carlos Vega, Isabel Aretz,
Angela de Cufré of Argentina, Luis Felipe Ramón y Rivera and
Juan Liscano of Venezuela, Oneida Alvarenga of Brazil, Lauro
Ayestarán of Uruguay, Oreste Plath of Chile, Vicente Mendoza
of Mexico, and others agree in recognizing the use of the
décima in their countries; these scholars affirm the existence of
vocal genres which incorporate improvisation within this
framework, along with others that do not, in which the *décimas*
would have to be learned and known by both singers.
Examples of the latter include the songs called *apareados* or

cruzados, in which one vocalist commences by singing two or three verses, the other sings a few more, and both conclude the *décima* together.   Isabel Aretz observes:

> In the *cruzado* song, the singers alternate rendering a fixed number of verses of a poetic composition known by both, or else each singer selects one text whose verses are rendered in an interweaving manner by the two vocalists.   These verses can be precomposed, or improvised, whether on the same or different themes.   The strophes can be elongated by the repetition of certain verses, by the insertion of refrains, or by the addition of new verses which complete the sense of the composition.

This *cante cruzado* is occasionally performed by Cuban singers, when there is a *candente* (lit., burning) *controversia* in which a singer "snatches away" the song of the other before the *décima* is finished, such that the *décima* continues with such "thefts," with both singers improvising two lines apiece, or one line apiece, alternating retorts, insults, and so on, until the affair concludes with broken guitars and broken heads!

The adoption and spread of the *décima* among the American peoples took place during the seventeenth and eighteenth centuries, from which period we have several examples surviving in Lauro Ayestarán's compilation, "Un antecedente colonial de la poesía tradicional uruguaya," which cites a *trovo* written in Montevideo in 1798.[2]

The Hispanic origin of the *décima* is clear, as even Cervantes gives several examples of contemporary *décimas* in his *Don Quixote*.   The form may well have been brought to the Americas along with the very first Spanish colonists, although Antonio Iraizoz situates its appearance in Cuban literature in the seventeenth and eighteenth centuries, as in the works of

---

[2]"A Colonial Antecedent of Traditional Uruguayan Poetry," in *Revista Histórica*, XLII:17 (2nd ed.).

Padre Capacho.[3] Joaquín Llaverías has also discovered in the
National Archive some *décimas* sent by the Marqués of
Someruelos to the Governor of the island in 1808, which circulated in the form of loose papers, like proclamations; Llaverías
has also unearthed a number of political *décimas* dating from
1838.[4]

Of the popular Latin American poets who most used the
décima, aside from the thousands of unknown singers who
have well employed the genre without becoming widely recognized, we may mention Hilario Ascasubi (1807-1875), known
for his poem "Aniceto el Gallo"; José Hernández (1834-1886),
author of "Martín Fierro"; Estanislao del Campo (1834-1880),
author of "Fausto"; "guachesco" poets (although they did not
use the *décima* in these poems mentioned); and our own Juan
Cristóbal Napoles Fajardo, "El Cucalambé," born in 1829 and
disappearing in 1862. Cucalambé, who lived in the same period as the others, albeit with less longevity, wrote neither long
epic poems like "Martín Fierro," nor complete works like
"Fausto"; memorable, nevertheless, are his love songs devoted
to Rufina, the patriotic fervor of his songs dedicated to Hatuey
and Guarina,[5] and to Cuba's natural beauty, and his verses regarding springtime, Cuban customs (as in his *décimas* "La lidia
de Gallos"), and perfidious love (as in the *décimas* "El amante
despreciado"). In all these *décimas*, Cucalambé used indigenous
terms, to the extent that at times the reader must consult
Zayas' *Lexicografía antillana* in order to understand his meaning. According to the biographer who edited the last editions of
Rumores de hormigo, Cucalambé adopted the meter then popular in Cuba, namely, the *décima* of eight-syllable lines, rejecting
the use of ten-syllable and eleven-syllable lines used in *silvas*,

[3] Iraizoz, in "La décima cubana en la poesía popular," in *Archivo del Folklore Cubano*, vol 4, no 2.

[4] Llaverías, "Unas décimas políticas," in *Archivo del Folklore Cubano* (date not given).

[5] [Ed.:] Hatuey was a Taino prince of Cuba who fought valiantly against the Spanish conquerors; Guarina was his princess.

liras, and *quartetas*; thus, we can infer that the eight-syllable meter was already in vogue in Cuba by Cucalambé's time.

The *décima* reflected more than bucolic ambience. Because of the Cubans' marvellous love of lampoon, we have been able to recover a large collection of political *décimas* from the *Revista Archivos del Folklore Cubano*. Further, in old song anthologies appear genuine romances and stories of famous victories, murders, ill-fated loves, and the like, which were printed and sold in loose-leaf form. The commercial *décima* in which form street-vendors sang the praises of their products, also came to be used by the magnates of sophisticated new advertising agencies, in which *décimas* were skillfully elaborated to announce products on radio and television.

In terms of music, there is no marked similarity between our *punto guajiro* and the other genres which employ the *décima* text form in Argentina, Brazil, Colombia, Mexico, and Chile. However, a Venezuelan folklorist, upon hearing some Camagüey-style *puntos* which we had recorded, remarked that they were almost exactly the same as the *galerón* of his country. Luis Felipe Ramón y Rivera has also commented on this similarity, adding that the *décimas* sung to the Altar of the Cross in the island of Margarita are still called *punto*, as in Cuba; Ramón y Rivera has hypothesized that these songs were brought by sailors who travelled throughout the Caribbean in galleons.

The following example of *trova margariteña* [i.e., from Margarita], using *décimas a lo humano* [secular *décimas*] is taken from an anthology entitled *Poesía popular venezolana*, and is sung in the *galerón* style.

> El ave busca la cima
> Busca la abeja la miel
> Busca el hombre a la mujer
> Busca el poeta la rima.
>
> Busca el prado el colibrí

la niña busca el jazmín,
el edén el serafín
busca el alma el frenesí
busca el color carmesí
el pintor y lo sublima
busca el escultor la lima
busca la pupila el llanto
y para arrullar su canto
busca el ave la cima.

Busca el cantor la velada,
busca el celo la malicia,
busca el amante caricia
con que halagar a su amada,
busca el adalid la espada
busca la mirla el vergel
busca el insecto el clavel
busca el vuelo el pensamiento
y para su mas sustento
busca la abeja su miel.

Busca el imán al acero,
busca el tigre la llanura,
el salvage la espesura,
busca el viento el marinero,
busca el avaro el dinero,
busca al malo el padecer,
busca el alegre el placer,
el corazón la ambrosía,
y para su compañía
busca el hombre a la mujer.

Busca la ola a la playa,
las nereidas a la mar
y busca el cielo el palmar,
busca el cura el atalaya,
el ariete la muralla,
el espadachín la esgrima,

busca todo el que se estima
la paz en el universo
y para escribir un verso
busca el poeta la rima.

The bird searches for the summit
The bee searches for the honey
Man seeks a woman
The poet searches for the rhyme.

The meadow looks for the hummingbird
The little girl looks for jasmine
Eden looks for great beauty
The soul is in search of its frenzy
The painter looks for the color crimson
And then he harnesses it;
The sculptor searches for his file
The eye's pupil looks for a tear drop
And a way to woo the song that breaks
The bird searches for the summit.

The singer looks for the night's soiree
And jealousy searches for malice,
The lover searches for affection
With which he may then flatter his lover,
The gallant leader searches for his sword
The blackbird seeks the fruit garden
The insect looks for the carnation
Thoughts that bloom seek a way to fly
And for his greatest sustenance
The bee searches for the honey.

The magnet looks for the attracting steel
The tiger searches for rolling fields,
The savage in the wild searches for the thicket,
The wind that blows looks for the seafarer
The miser looks for money and gold,
The villain seeks his victim

The happy person looks for his pleasure
The heart for the sweetness of ragweed
And to have as a companion,
Man searches for a woman.

The rolling wave looks for the beach
The Nereids seek the ocean
And the heaven looks for the palm grove
The priest searches for an onlooker
The battering ram for the wall,
The swordsman looks for his foiling tool,
All those who appreciate what they have
Look for peace in the universe
And in order to write these verses
The poet searches for the rhyme.

Our *punto*'s ancestry can be traced to Andalusian genres like the *peteneras, bulerías*, and *seguidillas*.[6] But it must be remembered that the Spanish galleons mentioned by Ramón y Rivera stopped off at the Canary Islands after embarking from Cádiz or Sanlúcar, and that many peasants from the Canaries immigrated to the Spanish colonies. Thus it is that our *punto* has many features of Canary Island music, such as the narrow and constricted vocal timbre, and the use of ornaments and inflections which resist transcription insofar as they deviate from conventional tempered tuning, and which lend a certain flexibility to the overall sound. The principal characteristic of the western Cuban *punto*, which is also called *punto libre, punto pinareño* or *punto a gusto*, is its use of an elastic pulse which gives greater freedom for expression, following the prosodic inflections of the text in free-rhythmic style; this may also derive from Canary Island songs or from related genres; indeed,

---

[6] [Ed.:] The *seguidilla* is a serious, Castilian-derived verse form, generally consisting, since the seventeenth century, of four-line stanzas, with lines of seven, five, seven, and five syllables, respectively. *Peteneras* is an old Andalusian folk song-type; *bulerías* is a gypsy flamenco *cante* (song-type) in fast 12/8 meter.

the provinces of Pinar del Río, Havana, and Matanzas, where these stylistic features abound, were populated by large contingents of Canary islanders and their descendents. We have found peasant singers who use the *pinareño* style in the San Luis Valley of Oriente, where more than fifty Canary Island families settled in the early twentieth century.

From Canarian immigrants' singing -- which many regard as out-of-tune -- were popularized, around the end of the nineteenth century, satirical *seguidillas* which were sung, or even recited, in a shrill, out-of-tune manner:

> -Seguidillas me pides,
> ¿De cuales quieres?
> -De las amarillitas
> Que son alegres.

> -- You ask me for *seguidillas* --
> Which would you like?
> --The little yellow ones,
> which are so joyous.

We have collected several melodies in the *pinareño* and *camagüeyano* style which are referred to as *seguidillas*.

The presence of two distinct tendencies can be detected in campesino melodies, namely, the western or *vueltabajero* style of the aforementioned *punto libre*, and the *punto en clave* or *punto cruzado*, also referred to as *punto camagüeyano* or *punto fijo* ("fixed,", i.e., in steady meter), which was first used in melodies of Sancti Spíritus province, where, according to some, the *punto* proceeds "entering the meter." Here is where can be found *punto* settings with the *estrambotes* (triplets) noted by Isabel Aretz, in the form of our *puntos coreados con estribillos* (*puntos* with refrains). The *punto en clave* takes the name *cruzado* ("crossed," or cross-rhythmed) when the song incorporates syncopated cross-rhythms with a rigid rhythmic accompaniment, rapid and rich in figuration, measured throughout by the *clave* and *güiro*. These syncopations provoke breaks or caesuras which divide the text phrases and alter their prosodic accents, producing a melodic line structured in relatively short phrases or segments of phrases, quite distinct from the melodies of the *punto pinareño*, which is rendered in a more continuous and sometimes almost melismatic style.

Another distinctive feature that the *punto guajiro* shares with the Venezuelan *galerón* is its use of modality. In all the *puntos* we have collected and analyzed, both in *pinareño* as well as *camagüeyano* styles, we have encountered a major modality without any clear resemblance to either the medieval Mixolydian mode, or to the minor "Spanish" modality which corresponds to the Phrygian mode.

Ramón y Rivera says of the *galerón*:

> At first it was a long song, a sweet recitative (also expressed over a Hypophrygian scale, descending from sol to sol), which was accompanied with guitar and *laúd* (formerly with *bandurria*). But it is very probable that in some enthusiastic moment, and for lack of other music, people who wanted to dance to this music did so, and from this practice derived the custom of dancing the *galerón* in Venezuela, while in other countries like Cuba (where it is called *punto guajiro*), the genre remains a mere song [i.e., not for dance].

In mentioning the Hypophrygian scale, Ramón y Rivera is evidently referring to the ancient Greek mode which corresponds to the medieval Mixolydian scale which we have noted.

The danceable genre of *guajiro* music was the *zapateo*, the "*tonada de punto*" played in *tempo giusto* on string and percussion instruments (guitar, *laúd, güiro*, machete, and *clave*). The genre is almost extinct today, and is performed only by a few old instrumentalists.

The rhythmic structure of the *punto* is quite simple, regular, and constant, marking a 3/4 meter. Folklorists have often transcribed the melody in 6/8 and the accompaniment in 3/4. Having observed a large number of songs, we have come to the conclusion that both should be transcribed in 3/4, not only in the vocal *punto* but in the *zapateo* as well.

The melodies without refrains are most common in the *pinareño* style, which is preferred by improvising singers because its free meter gives them time to spontaneously compose without being distracted by the music. The use of refrains is more common in the Camagüey style, where the refrains may consist either of verses extraneous to the *décima* text (called *coros* in the *spirituana* style), or of onomatopaeic phrases imitating the accompanying instruments.

On some occasions these refrains divide the *décima* into two parts, of four and six lines, or they may occur at the beginning or end of the *décima*.

> Ave María, Ave María
> ¡Qué muchacho!   (twice)

> Le encargué una chiva hembra
> y me trajo un chivo macho   (twice)

> O Mary, what a boy!

> I gave you a female goat
> and you've brought me a billy goat.

One famous *tonada* was that invented in the early twentieth century by the old and equally famous poet and singer Juan Pagés, "El Cojo" ("The Lame"), which, according to tradition, he sang upon the occasion of the inauguration of Tomás Estrada Palma as first president of Cuba. The refrains imitate the strumming of the guitar, and were performed for us with a *décima* typical in style of the mid-nineteenth century.

> Apreciable señorita guambán
> desde que te conocí guambán

siento una rebambarama guambán
de amor que no se me quita guambán
Y al mirarte tan bonita guambán
yo quisiera ser tu novio guambán
y aunque parezca un oprobio guambán
hermosísimo alelí guambán y guambán y guambán y
guambán
desde que te conocí guambán
brinco, relincho y "corcobio" guambán

Desirable young woman (guambán)
ever since I met you (guambán)
I feel a rebambaramba guambán
of love that will not leave me alone (guambán)
and as I look at you so lovely (guambán)
I would like to be your boyfriend (guambán)
and although it seems like an opprobrium (guambán)
the most beautiful gilly-flower (guambán)
ever since I met you (guambán)
I jump, whinny, and buck [like a young stallion]
(guambán)

Another onomatopaeic verse, which was sung for us by an old
woman from Cienfuegos, imitates the plucking of the *laúd* in
passages inserted between the phrases of the *tonada*:

Con el dinero que junto
de mis pollos y gallinas
compro buena muselina
y un pañuelito de punto
gua tiqui miniqui
y quiti jay

With the money that I collect
With my chickens and with my hens
I buy myself good muslin
and a little knitted handkerchief

gua tiqui miniqui
y quiti jay

Refrains of laughter are found in the so called *tonadas de la risa*, such as we encountered magisterially rendered by "Hilguero (goldfinch) of Cienfuegos." Other variants include the *tonada del burro*, with a refrain imitating the braying of a donkey, the *tonada* of the cat, of the "nervous one," and that of "two voices," wherein the vocalist sings one part in his natural voice, and the other in a shrill falsetto.

As for the form of using the *décima*, aside from the styles common throughout much of the Americas -- improvising on a *pie forzado* (a given line), *controversia*, and so on, whether devotional or secular -- also in frequent use are nonsense stories, such as the following:

Ayer pasé por tu casa
yo para adentro miré
en la sala había una rana
abrochándose el corsé
más palante había un ciempies
abrochándose zapatos
echábase polvo un gato
una pulga vaselina
y una vaca en la cocina
salcochaba unos boniatos

Estaba un cangrejo pando
un zorro tocando un pito
muerto de risa un mosquito
al ver un burro estudiando
un buey viejo regañando
muy sentado en su butaca
a una ternerita flaca
que de risa estaba muerta
al ver una chiva tuerta
remendándose una hamaca

Yesterday I walked by your house
I decided to look inside
In the living room I saw there was a toad
Putting on a corset
Farther in there was a centipede
Tying his shoes
A cat was throwing dust on himself
And a flea putting on vaseline
There was even a cow in the kitchen
Boiling some potatoes with salt.

There, too, was a crab inching along
And a fox playing on a whistle
Dying of laughter, a mosquito
Watching a donkey immersed in study
And an old ox scolding everyone
Seated comfortably in his armchair
And there was a skinny little calf
That had laughed itself to death
At the sight of a one-eyed goat
Trying to mend a hammock for itself.

Décimas have expressed and preserved popular sentiment in every historical moment. The following examples are taken from different works published in the *Archivo del Folklore Cubano*.

Entre los sesenta modos
que se han hallado de hurtar
uno es decir que Alvemar
pide donativo a todos.
Peñalver hasta los codos
a sacarlo se ha empeñado
y yo tengo averiguado
que no hace por el Conde
sino ver lo que es-conde

y quedar aprovechado.
Arrójese al fementido,
mas protéxase al honrado,
extermínese al malvado,
y sea el bueno querido:
El laborioso cumplido,
merezca la estimación,
mírese con atención,
aquel que adicto a Fernando
no se matricule al bando
perverso de Napoleón.

En la tienda del Vaivén
vi llegar a yo no sé
a comprar yo no sé que
para darle a no sé quién.
Amo de tal almacén,
puritos los dos hermanos,
a donde existe fulano,
preguntó por yo lo vi
y entonces le respondí:
ayer he visto a ciclano.

Among the sixty ways people have found
In which to cheat
One is to say that Alvemar
Asks donations from everyone.
Peñalver is up to his elbows
In enriching himself this way,
And I have been able to figure out
That he isn't doing it for the Count,
But rather to put it into his own ac-Count [untranslatable pun]
While continuing to enjoy respect.
Let this treachery be exposed,
and protect the honorable!
Let the evil be exterminated,

And the good be beloved;
Careful perfection
Merits our approval;
So watch with great care,
That he who is a follower of Fernando
Should not register
With the perverted faction of Napoleon.

In the store of the seesaw
I saw arrive who knows who
To but I don't know what
To then give it to I don't know who.
I love of that warehouse
The two brothers,
Wherever so-and-so may exist,
I asked, for I have seen him
And then I responded   to him
Yesterday I have seen "ciclano."

Still very popular among campesino singers is this old *décima* which dates from the anti-colonial Independence War.

Maceo llegó a un potrero
de una viuda con amor
pidiéndole de favor
unos caballos ligeros
ella dijo "¿Caballero
ese objeto nada más?

"Tengo un potrero que está
lleno de ganado en brete
y ademas tengo un machete
que pide la libertad"

Maceo arrived at the cattle ranch
Of a widow and her lover,
Asking her to donate

A few fleet-footed horses,
And she said to him, "Sir,
that lone favor and nothing more?"

"I have a ranch which is full
Of livestock still in their shackles
And I have a machete as well
which asks for its liberty."

From the renowned campesino poet José Marichal, "La
Estrella de Govea," are the following *décimas*, which he improvised in 1950 at the University of Havana, using as a base the
opening quartet:

La familia campesina
base de nuestra riqueza
vive en la mayor pobreza
en un estado de ruina.

Cuba, tu dicha soñada,
tu sueño de amor y paz
está en tu tierra feraz
tan rica como olvidada.
En el llano y la cascada
de agua pura y cristalina
la abundancia se advina
por lo que no se concibe
la miseria conque vive
la familia campesina.

Allí bien cerca del monte
se alza un gracioso bohío
que tiene rumor de río
y gorjeo de sinsonte
soñando un bello horizonte
toda una familia reza
con la infinita tristeza

de saberse abandonada
aunque es su labor honrada
base de nuestra riqueza.

Y así el pobre campesino
cultiva su rico suelo
seimpre esperando del cielo
lo que pocas veces vino.
En lucha con el destino
pide a la naturaleza
que le ayude en la pobreza
de darle a su prole el pan
la que a pesar de su afán
vive en la mayor pobreza.

Pues no teniendo manera
da canalizar el río
muere de sed su plantío
casi en la misma ribera.
La sequía horrible y fiera
que su colonia calcina
duro golpe le propina
a su hermoso porvenir
y tiene que proseguir
en un estado de ruina.

The campesino family
the base of our richness and wealth
lives in the direst poverty
in a condition of ruin.

Cuba, your dreamed-of happiness,
your dream of love and of peace
lies in your fertile soils
so rich that they are forgotten.
In the plains and waterfalls
made of pure and crystalline water,

the abundancy can be imagined,
but that which cannot be conceived of
is the misery in which lives
the campesino family.

There close to the mountain
an odd-looking shack is erected
that murmurs like a river
and gurgles like a mockingbird
dreaming of a beautiful horizon
a whole family plays together
with an unending melancholy
at having found themselves abandoned
even though it is their honored work,
the base of our richness and wealth.

And in this way the poor peasant
cultivates his rich soil
always expecting from the heavens
what seldom comes,
in struggle with his destiny
he requests the aid of nature's hand
that she may help him through his poverty
to provide bread for his children,
the children that despite his hard work
live in the direst poverty.

Because of lacking the means
to make canals from the river
his garden patch must die of thirst
almost on the river-bank itself.
The horrible and fiendish drought that comes
and that tramples on his farmlands
delivers such a hard blow
to his cherished occupation,
and yet he must carry on
in a condition of ruin.

The *tonadas* always have an instrumental accompaniment which commences with a brief introduction, featuring flashy ornamental phrases on the *laúd*, giving the singer time to improvise the first four lines of the *décima*; after these are delivered, another interlude follows, and then the last six lines. Aside from the *laúd*, a guitar or *tres* is often used to provide the bass, and in the *puntos fijos*, rhythmic accompaniment is provided on the obligatory *clave*, and a *güiro* or *guayo*, or, in the absence of these, a machete and a fork which, when rubbed together, produce a sound like that of the *guayo*.

In some parts of the provinces of Las Villas and Camagüey, these ensembles are supplemented with a *quijada* (scraped jawbone of an ass), a *botija* (a jug, overblown as a bass instrument), and an accordion with two ribbed grills. Occasionally a small bongo is also used, reflecting some influence of the *son*. The oldest ensembles we have seen use accordion, guitar, *bandurria* (which today is called *laúd*), and earthen *botija* (which used to have a hole in its belly through which it would be blown, while the player would insert his fingers in the mouth of the jug in order to vary the intonation). Sometimes the *tiple* (another guitar-like lute) and mouth-bow would also be used, but these, along with the *botija* and accordion, have fallen into desuetude.

The campesino singer pays little heed to "correct" vocal production. His timbre is nasal and shrill, although his intonation is generally sure. Some singers have poor voices, while others may be well-endowed, but it invariably seems to be the case that the best poets lack fine voices, but express their verse and melodies so well that the listener soon forgets their vocal deficiencies.

In this sense, it is as a poet, and especially as a improviser, rather than as a singer, that the campesino is revered. It is in this role that the folkloric tradition of the *punto* continues, inseparable from the guitars and *laudes*, and the singer-poet sings verses about his daily life, brings people together with his songs, performs at their festivities, competes at festivals and contests, and performs on the radio and television. Through the singer-poet the *punto* makes history out of a rich Cuban tradition.

II

Cuban Music in New York

6

The Charanga in New York
and the Persistence of the Típico Style

Charanga ensembles, with their distinctive flute and violins, have played an important role in the development of Cuban dance music since the late nineteenth century. For fifty years it was charanga groups that performed the danzón, the syncretic, salon-derived dance enlivened with enough Afro-Cuban flavor to charm all Cubans except the most negrophobic purists. Later, charangas adopted the son, guaracha, and other uptempo popular dances, maintaining their traditional instrumentation, and their popularity, alongside the horn-based conjuntos who became identifed with "salsa" in the late 1960s.

Both in Cuba and New York City, many of the couples -- young, old, black, and white -- who flock to clubs to dance to charanga groups may regard them as essentially interchangeable substitutes for horn-based conjuntos. Yet it is clear that a large part of the dance music audience associates charanga with a certain classicism, both for its use of flute and violins -- to play fiery Afro-Cuban music, of course --, and its redolence of Cuba in bygone days. This "típico" -- loosely, "traditional" -- aspect of charanga's image accounts, on the one hand, for its shrinking audience, and, on the other, for its continuing and persistent appeal to a certain dedicated minority of dancers and listeners. The enthusiasm of these audiences, the versatility of the musicians, and the inherent vitality of the repertoire prevent the charangas from ossifying, as can be seen from the controlled pandemonium of the dance floor at virtually any charanga performance.

In the following article, John Murphy, a saxophonist and ethnomusicologist currently completing his Ph.D. at Columbia University, outlines the features which define charanga music as típico and explores the significance of this aesthetic for charanga music in contemporary New York City.

6

The Charanga in New York
and the Persistence of the Típico Style

John P. Murphy

The típico style is the traditional way of playing Cuban-derived dance music in the charanga ensemble, which features flute and violins. New York charanga musicians have maintained the típico style through several cycles of high and low popularity over the past several decades. The use of the term "persistence" is meant to suggest two senses of the expression "persistence of vision," which refers to visual images that remain on the retina after the stimulus -- a glimpse of the sun, a distinctive shape -- has been removed. In a passive sense, the típico style of charanga performance is a strong image that has remained with Cuban charanga musicians in New York long after their separation from the initial stimulus -- music in Cuba in the 1950s. In the second, active sense, the típico style is an artistic vision that New York charanga musicians have fought to keep alive and develop. Both senses of "persistence" are applicable to the charanga in New York. This article describes the típico style of the charanga, discusses the charanga in the context of New York Latin music in general, and interprets the típico style as a residual element of Latino musical culture.[1]

---

[1] This article is based on fieldwork carried out in New York between 1987 and 1990. See my M.A. thesis, "The Charanga in New York, 1987-

The Típico Style

The típico style has identifiable historical antecedents. Since the background of the charanga ensemble has been described elsewhere, I will provide only a summary here.[2] The roots of the charanga ensemble date from the late-19th century, when the Cuban *danzón*, a stylized, light-classical derivative of the Franco-Haitian *contredanse* and the Cuban *contradanza habanera*, evolved in connection with *orquestas típicas*, which featured clarinet, cornet, trombone, *timbales*, and *güiro*. The *danzón* later came to be associated with a new ensemble, the *charanga francesa*, made up of five-key flute, strings, piano, contrabass, *timbales*, and *güiro*. With the exception of the vocalists, conga, and *cencerro* (cowbell), which were added in the first half of the 20th century, this instrumentation is preserved in the present-day charanga.

As the *son* became part of the musical environment in Havana during the 1920s, eclipsing the *danzón*'s popularity, its anticipated bass and *tres* (guitar) patterns, the latter imitated by wind instruments, began to be incorporated into the *danzón's* coda. Members of the Antonio Arcaño orchestra carried this fusion further in the livelier, more Afro-Cuban

1988: Musical Style, Performance Context, and Tradition" (Columbia University, 1988). I thank the members of Orquesta Broadway (especially Eddy Zervigón, Mike Amitin, Ruben Rivera, Ronnie Baró, Ricardo Whittington, Danny González, Felo Barrio, and Mike Collazo), George Maysonet, Karen Joseph, and Enrique Orengo of Charanga América, Willie Ellis of Orquesta Típica Novel, José Fajardo, John Rodríguez, Rene Lopez, Max Salazar, Larry Florencio, Awilda Rodríguez, Ana Araya, and Landy Soba for their assistance. Both article and thesis benefited from the guidance of Peter Manuel; Roberta Singer and Gage Averill made helpful comments on earlier drafts of this article. The responsibility for any errors is of course my own.

[2]For example, see Cristobal Díaz Ayala, *Música Cubana Del Areyto a la Nueva Trova* (San Juan: Editorial Cubanacan, 1981), Argeliers León, *Del Canto y El Tiempo* (Havana: Editorial Letras Cubanas, 1984), Peter Manuel, *Popular Musics of the Non-Western World* (New York: Oxford University Press, 1988), and John Storm Roberts, *The Latin Tinge* (New York: Oxford University Press, 1979).

danzón-mambo, which helped the *danzón*, and with it the charanga ensemble, to become widely popular again. The *mambo*
was further popularized by *conjunto* ensembles (i.e., featuring
brass instruments), especially that of Arsenio Rodríguez, and
by Pérez Prado in a big band format. The leading Cuban charanga since the mid-1950s has been Orquesta Aragón, which
was founded in 1939.[3] The popularity of the charanga sound
spread throughout much of the world in the 1950s with
Enrique Jorrín's innovation, the *chachachá*.

Since the Cuban Revolution of 1959, the charanga ensemble
and its music have followed separate but related paths in Cuba
and the U.S. In Cuba, the group Los Van Van has integrated
string and brass instrumentation and, along with Orquesta
Aragón, Ritmo Oriental, and other charangas, helped popularize
new genres such as the *songo* and the *mozambique*. In the U.S.,
the Cuban style of Orquesta Aragón has been perpetuated by
Orquesta Broadway, José Fajardo, and others. Since the late
1960s charangas have shared the Latin dance music field with
salsa, the modernized variant of Cuban dance music that became a vehicle for socio-musical expression for the growing
population of New York Latinos (especially, but not exclusively,
those of Puerto Rican descent). Charanga music can be regarded
as a sub-category of salsa, but it is distinguished by its instrumentation (see below) and its more conservative style.

Orquesta Broadway and the Típico Style

The word "típico" came up in virtually every discussion of charanga music I had with musicians during 1987-88. Típico can
be translated as "typical," but the word clearly has broader
connotations, more akin to "traditional" or "old-fashioned," especially in a way that suggests cultural (in this case, Cuban)

---

[3] See Roberto Nodal, "La Orquesta Aragón: Cuarenta Años de Éxitos,"
Areito 8/32(1983):33-34. According to Díaz Ayala, Aragón in the mid-
1950s was, "musician by musician and as a group, better than any other
charanga of the period" (*Musica Cubana*, p. 223).

roots. The word is often applied to music. In this regard, Roberta Singer has written:

> Típico is perhaps the most semantically laden of all music-related concepts and terms in use by contemporary Latin musicians. Most often it refers to a range of Island-rooted styles of performance, each country having its own típico styles. The precise referent can only be known in the context of conversation. Puerto Rican típico can be the jíbaro [Puerto Rican peasant] cuarteto styles as well as the Afro-Puerto Rican styles either as performed in traditional ways or in the more urban conjunto format. Cuban típico includes the later charanga groups and the son septeto and sexteto styles. All típico styles, on some more or less removed levels, contributed to the development of contemporary salsa styles.
>
> Some contemporary performers in New York City define típico as "source" music: the non-commercial styles from which contemporary commercial styles are derived and reinterpreted. A performer in commercial Latin music may be complimented by other performers if the latter feel he is a "real típico player."[4]

The charanga is distinctively típico in instrumentation, repertoire, and playing style. The típico aspects of charanga music are well illustrated by the foremost and longest-lived charanga ensemble in New York, Orquesta Broadway.[5] This group was founded in New York in 1962 by the Zervigón brothers (Eddy, Rudy, and Kelvin, from Güines, Cuba) and

---

[4]Roberta Singer, "My Music is Who I Am and What I Do: Latin Popular Music and Identity in New York City" (Ph.D. dissertation, Indiana University, 1982), p. 226.

[5]Orquesta Típica Novel began earlier than Orquesta Broadway but has had periods of inactivity. Orquesta Broadway has been performing consistently in New York since 1962, with a brief relocation to Florida in 1974 (interview with Felo Barrio, 5/27/90). See Max Salazar's history of the group, "Eddy Zervigón & Orquesta Broadway," *Mambo Express Latin Magazine* (Los Angeles, CA) no. 2, issue 13 (June 1989).

singer Roberto Torres. The band has a high reputation in New York, and has toured throughout the U.S., the Caribbean, South America, and Africa. The members of Orquesta Broadway have direct personal links with previous generations of Cuban musicians. They are proud of the flute and violin sound, and regard themselves as actively maintaining continuity with the charanga's historical antecedents. The connections with the Cuban charanga tradition are direct. After beginning musical studies on trumpet and piccolo, Eddy Zervigón was encouraged by Richard Egües, flutist with Orquesta Aragón, to change to the five-key flute; Zervigón later studied with Egües. Band members say the group consciously patterns itself after Orquesta Aragón. Several motifs from Aragón's arrangements appear in those of Orquesta Broadway. Broadway has also recorded several Aragón songs, such as "Pregúntame Cómo Estoy" and "Sin Clave y Bongo."

Orquesta Broadway's instrumentation includes five-key wooden flute, two amplified violins, upright electric bass, electric piano, *güiro, timbales, cencerro*, conga, and lead and supporting vocalists. Both the modern C flute and the wooden five-key flute are used in New York charangas; musicians regard the latter as more traditional.

While instrumentation is the most overtly típico aspect of the charanga, its musical style is also regarded as distinctively típico, compared to the related but more modern styles of salsa and Latin jazz. First of all, típico flute improvisations use a vocabulary of stock melodic phrases and rhythmic motives in order to maintain continuity with the charanga tradition. Two examples of such stock phrases are given in ex. 1.

Ex. 1a Melodic figure, "Tres Lindas Cubanas" (Orquesta   Aragón)

Ex. 1b Melodic figure, "Pare Cochero" (Orquesta Aragón)

The style can also be understood as the avoidance of certain elements, such as swing phrasing of eighth notes and excessive chromaticism, which are associated with jazz. Rene Lopez pointed out one obvious explanation for this: while the charanga's flute and violin are more commonly used in Western art music than in jazz, brass players are more likely to be able to play both típico and jazz styles.[6] On the other hand, charanga music has much more improvisation than *conjunto*-style salsa. The flute often solos throughout an entire song, and piano and violin solos are plentiful.

Violins are amplified and play four types of passages: On the instrumental introduction, the violins play a melodic line as a section, with vibrato and coordinated bowing. During the vocal section, violins play short background figures, often along with the flute, or in counterpoint with the flute, depending on the arrangement. Once the *montuno* section begins, the violins play a *guajeo* (or *tumbao*), a melodic-rhythmic ostinato. Three examples are given in ex. 2.

[6]Interview with Rene Lopez, 5/25/90.

Ex. 2 Violin guajeos: (a) "¡Ahora Es Cuando Eh!"; (b) Isla del
Encanto"; (c) "Barrio del Pilar"

When the flute improvises, the violins often play a tremolo
which lasts up to 16 bars as the solo builds to a climax.   It is
this type of passage that clearly shows the different range of
choices an arranger has when writing for the charanga.   It
would be difficult for brass to play a constant background figure like the violin *guajeo* without overpowering the soloist.
Violin improvisations follow conventions similar to those described for the flute.   Melodic motion is usually diatonic, with
the exception of chromatic slides. Common violin techniques
include grace notes, glissandi, rapid cross-string bowing, and
double stops.

Típico piano *montunos* are harmonically simple.[7]
Although more harmonically adventurous *montuno* patterns
can be heard in New York salsa, and especially in Latin jazz,
solos by pianists such as Ruben Rivera and Sonny Bravo, who
perform with both charangas and *conjuntos*, are often quite sophisticated in terms of harmony. Típico bass lines usually are
confined to roots and fifths of chords and remain rhythmically
simple.   They form the foundation for the upper parts, and are
an especially important focus for the dancers.   Bass players
provide a consistent, rhythmically precise pattern which lends
itself to clocklike coordination with the rest of the rhythm section.

Both charangas and salsa *conjuntos* use the standard 2-3
and 3-2 clave time-lines (played on the *clave* sticks) almost
exclusively (exx. 3a and 3b).

Ex. 3 Clave patterns: (a) 3-2; (b) 2-3; (c) rumba

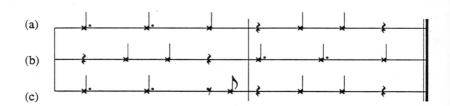

The choice between the *claves* is made by the arranger, depending on which one fits best with the melody.[8] New   York

[7] See, for example, those shown in Charley Gerard and Marty Sheller,
Salsa!: The Rhythm of Latin Music (Crown Point, IN: White Cliffs Media
Company, 1989), pp. 33-41.
[8] Interview with Rubén Rivera, 5/27/90.

charangas avoid the use of the *rumba clave* (see ex. 3c), because, some musicians say, it would confuse their dancing public. However, Mike Collazo, percussionist with Orquesta Broadway, says that the *rumba clave* is used occasionally without any noticeable effect on the dancers.[9] Charanga percussion, according to Collazo, is lighter and more consistent than that of the conjunto, which often plays rhythmic kicks with the brass. This consistency may explain the preference some accomplished dancers express for charanga music.[10]

Cuban charangas employ the *rumba clave* frequently in the *songo* genre without losing a dancing public. The use of the *rumba clave* in recent Cuban music is just as típico as using the 2-3 and 3-2 *claves*, since it comes from the *rumba guaguancó*. However, New York charanga musicians say they associate the *rumba clave* with Afro-Cuban jazz, and avoid it because they want to avoid turning their music into a listeners-only music.

Orquesta Broadway plays all of the basic genres of Cuban dance music: *danzón, chachachá, son montuno, guaracha, mambo, bolero, guajira,* and *rumba*, as well as the Dominican *merengue*. Many of the pieces thus classified -- especially the *sones, montunos, guarachas, mambos,* and *rumbas* -- might be labelled simply as *son* by Cuban musicians, especially if they have the *son*'s rhythmic style and formal structure, consisting of a *canto* (featuring verses in a "song"-like form) followed by a longer *montuno*, with call-and-response vocals and/or instrumental solos over a harmonic ostinato. "Montuno" may also denote the piano ostinato played during the *montuno* section. The charanga and the *danzón* are closely associated with each other for historical reasons. Although the *danzón* is seen as somewhat archaic and is not played at all by *conjuntos*, charangas

---

[9] Interview with Mike Collazo, 5/27/90. Brittmarie Janson Pérez also mentions the need to keep the clave to avoid losing a dancing public (in "Political facets of *salsa*," *Popular Music* 6/2(1987), p. 157).

[10] Interview with dancers Larry Florencio and Awilda Rodríguez, 3/5/89, and L. Florencio and Ana Araya, 5/24/90.

still play *danzones* occasionally.[11] Orquesta Broadway's repertoire includes new songs as well as Cuban classics like "Pare
Cochero," "Tres Lindas Cubanas," and "Fefita." Others were hits
for Orquesta Broadway in the past: "Como Camina María," "Isla
del Encanto," "Yo Bailo Con Ella," and "Mi Sosio."

Musicians and knowledgeable listeners still make distinctions among these genres. But for younger audiences and musicians, their differences are becoming ambiguous. The dance
music repertoire that one hears in nightclubs, especially as
performed by *conjuntos*, is relatively uniform in terms of
tempo, form, and arrangement. Some musicians claim that
younger musicians group all of these genres under the term
"salsa," and predict that over time the differences between
genres might disappear altogether.[12]

---

[11] Some bands preface their performances of the *danzón* with an
introduction, reflecting their awareness of its archaic nature for some
listeners. See Robert Baron, "Syncretism and Ideology: Latin New York
Salsa Musicians" (*Western Folklore* 36/3(1977):209-225, p. 219).
However, I witnessed Orquesta Broadway playing a *danzón* without an
introduction at the Sidestreet club in the Bronx in May 1990 for an
audience of mostly young Latinos. A few older couples danced during
the first part and many younger couples danced during the *mambo*
section.

[12] When asked whether the genres that predate salsa are starting to
sound the same, John Rodríguez, percussionist and former co-leader of
Típica '73, replied: "They sound the same to people who don't know the
difference. Because the people you talk to who are on the scene playing
nowadays with [one of the younger Puerto Rican salsa bands], they don't
know what a *danzón* is, they don't know what a *son montuno* is. They
know salsa.' They have this one thing, this one concept of this music"
(interview, 9/12/88). Rodríguez went on to explain that many younger
Latin musicians and audiences are uninformed about the variety of
song genres because of the power of promoters and radio stations to
limit airplay to current salsa rather than a wide variety of styles.   Tito
Puente made comments on the same topic from the stage of the Village
Gate on May 21, 1990: "What is 'salsa'? It's tomato sauce. It's spaghetti
sauce. In the old days we had the *son montuno*, the *guaguancó*, the
guaracha. . ." See my thesis (1988) for description of the genres
performed by the charanga.

Arrangements have a standardized form, with variations possible within it. There is usually an instrumental introduction lasting eight or sixteen bars. Several verses follow, with short instrumental interludes between. A final instrumental interlude with a particularly definite rhythmic break leads to the *montuno* section. Here call-and-response singing alternates with solos for flute or piano, and less often for violin, *timbales*, conga, or (rarely) bass. Often a song ends by repeating the instrumental introduction, stopping where the voice would have entered.

The use of the term típico in reference to repertoire was not explicitly articulated by musicians, but the choice of songs for a given nightclub performance does relate to what can be termed "the típico aesthetic." Songs composed in the 1920s, such as "Tres Lindas Cubanas," are still played and danced to, especially when charangas play for older audiences. New songs in the charanga repertoire generally imitate these models -- to the frustration of some younger charanga musicians. The lyrics of songs performed by charangas concern the traditional topics for much 20th century Cuban and Puerto Rican dance music: sentimental love, Cuba and Puerto Rico in times past, and the act of playing and dancing to Cuban dance music itself.[13]

The Charanga in the Context of Contemporary New York Latin Music

Charanga ensembles perform at nightclubs, private functions, social clubs, concerts, and at outdoor concerts. The principal performance site is the nightclub. While at earlier periods in its history the ensemble may have catered to a predominantly

---

[13]The trivial nature of salsa texts in general was confirmed by Rene Lopez, who believes that the lyrics' "message is, for most Latinos, a faded message," with the exception of songs by Rubén Blades, Willie Colón, and others who address current issues and problems facing Latinos (interview, 5/25/90); see also Jorge Duany, "Popular Music in Puerto Rico: Towards an Anthropology of *Salsa* ," *Latin American Music Review* 5/2(1984):186-216.

Cuban and upper-class audience, this is no longer the case in New York. Charangas perform in the same nightclubs as do salsa bands, and to an extent they share the same pan-Latin audience. There is, however, a part of the audience which prefers charangas to salsa groups, and these audience members tend to be old enough to have been charanga fans during the 1960s and '70s. Virtually all of the musicians I interviewed agreed that the market for charangas, and for salsa in general, was worse during the late 1980s than at any point in the past. The most recent period of high demand for charangas in New York was between 1974 and 1984. During this period, there were between 25 and 30 Latin music nightclubs in the city, and in a routine week Orquesta Broadway, for example, played fifteen dances. On a busy Saturday they played five, each lasting around two hours. During 1987-88, Orquesta Broadway averaged between five and ten jobs per month, and there were less than ten nightclubs in the city that featured charangas regularly.

The decline in number of performance sites is a serious problem for the charanga ensembles. Touring opportunities and special concerts still exist, but the nightclubs are the main source of regular musical employment for musicians who reside in the New York area; according to producer and musician Rene Lopez, however, as many as 90% of Latin musicians have to support themselves with nonmusical employment.[14] Nightclub rents have risen sharply, along with insurance and salaries. The fact that Latin dance music audiences in general go out only on the weekends reduces the clubs' potential business even further. Short of closing, nightclubs cope with increased costs by employing fewer bands, paying musicians poorly, and using recorded music. Continuous music still is preferred; in the past, this was supplied by alternating bands, but in 1987-88, Club Broadway was one of the only nightclubs to feature two or three bands per weekend night. Some nightclubs, such as Ipanema, Juan Pachanga, and El Abuelo, had

---

[14]Interview with Rene Lopez, 5/25/90.

eliminated live music from one weekend night altogether during the same period (and Ipanema switched to country-western music in 1989).

Management issues are another factor contributing to the low demand for charangas in 1987-88. Charanga musicians stress the power exercised by booking agents, and feel that the agents have lost interest in charanga. This impression was corroborated by one of the two main salsa booking agents, Landy Soba, who seemed convinced that charangas were passé, appropriate for their specialized audience at a limited number of "charanga rooms," but no longer of interest to the larger audience for Latin dance music.[15]

The "war" between salsa and *merengue* has also been much commented upon, both by musicians and journalists. Charanga musicians have described the competition caused by the recent influx of Dominicans to New York and their subsequent takeover of formerly Puerto Rican nightclubs as a struggle over territory. According to one charanga musician, many of the Upper Manhattan *merengue* clubs were formerly Puerto Rican clubs featuring salsa *conjuntos* and charangas. Due to the Dominican Republic's depressed economy, promoters have been able to bring in *merengue* bands to undercut New York-based bands (both *merengue* and salsa) by working for less pay. In addition, there is a large, young Dominican audience.[16] The popularity of *cumbia* and other musics associated with recent immigrants from Central and South America and the Caribbean has also reduced the potential audience for salsa and charanga.

It would be wrong, however, to portray the charanga as a musical entity in irreversible decline. There are hopeful signs. New charangas are occasionally formed, such as Son Primero, a

---

[15]Interview with Landy Soba, 3/1/88.

[16]Dominicans are by far the largest group of recent immigrants to New York City, constituting, for example, 18% of all immigrants in fiscal 1986. See Samuel G. Freedman, "A Profile of the Newest New Yorkers," *New York Times* (9 August 1987).

group led by Charlie Santiago that includes contemporary
Cuban compositions in its repertoire. Típica '73, an important
and innovative band during the 1970s, combined elements of
the *conjunto* and the charanga into a viable and appealing
sound. The album they recorded in Cuba in 1978 is seen as a
landmark in Latin music. From all accounts the charanga tradition is very much alive in Cuba; further Cuban influence on
North American charangas and innovations by the latter are
possible.[17]

The Típico Charanga Style as Residual Culture

The preceding sections have shown the music of the charanga
in the late 1980s to follow closely Cuban musical traditions of
the 1950s. In doing so, the charanga ensembles have declined
in popularity, while at the same retaining a small, dedicated
audience of mostly older Latinos. The adherence to the típico
style has led to both the decline and the persistence of the charanga in New York; that is, while many consider it too traditional, others prefer it precisely because of its típico qualities.

In view of the decline in popularity of the típico charanga
style, one might consider it a traditional survival that eventually will disappear as its adherents assimilate. From this point
of view, those musics that are open to diverse musical borrowings (like salsa and Latin jazz) survive and perhaps thrive,
while those that attempt to preserve the relative purity of
source musics (like charanga) face either irreversible decline or
a subsidized future. Although the latter possibilities may become apparent only over a longer span of time, it appears that
charangas in New York have avoided them. Instead, they have
remained much the same, performing for a smaller audience
and incorporating an element of nostalgia in their appeal.

---

[17]For example, see the recent LP by the group Bongo-Logic, *Cha-Cha-
Charanga* (Rocky Peak Records RP 52752, 1988), which is a fusion of
charanga and jazz.

In order to understand the paradox of the charanga's simultaneous decline and persistence, it is important to keep in mind both the diversity of Latino culture in the U.S. and the historical conditions that have enabled this diversity to be constantly replenished. New York Latino musical culture can be seen as a mixture of elements that are residual, emergent, or assimilating with the dominant Anglo-American culture.[18] The sentimental ballad, with its pan-ethnic appeal and homogenizing tendencies (see Manuel, "Salsa and the Mass Media" in this volume), could be seen as an assimilating genre. Some scholars of Latino culture in New York describe salsa as emergent, since it can be a source of new meanings that "cross over" to a larger audience. Thus, Flores and Yudice state:

> Crossover does not mean that Latinos seek willy nilly to "make it" in the political and commercial spheres of the general culture. They are vehicles which Latinos use to create new cultural forms that cross over in both directions. The music of Willie Colón, Rubén Blades, and other U.S. based Latino and Latin American musicians is a new pan-Latino fusion of Latin American forms. . .and U.S. pop, rock, even do-wop, around a salsa base of Caribbean rhythms, particularly Cuban *son*. Salsa cuts across all social classes and Latino groups who reside in New York, home ground of this fusion music. [...] Salsa, perhaps better than any other cultural form, expresses the Latino ethos of multiculturalism and crossing borders. [...] Finding one's "roots" in salsa means more creating them from the heterogeneous sounds that traverse the barrio than going back to some place that guarantees authenticity.[19]

Charanga music, by contrast, can be described as a residual element of Latino musical culture. Charanga "roots" have more

---

[18] See Raymond Williams, *Marxism and Literature* (Oxford: Oxford University Press, 1977), pp. 121-27.

[19] Flores and Yudice, "Living Borders," pp. 71-2.

to do with "going back to some place that guarantees authenticity" than with "creating them from the heterogeneous sounds that traverse the barrio," with a few exceptions.[20] Cuban musical models of the 1950s are the stimulus that persists in the vision of many New York charanga musicians. This does not limit the charanga's role, however, to that of a nostalgic survival. It remains a viable form of musical expression, and fits well with Raymond Williams's concept of residual culture:

> The residual, by definition, has been effectively formed in the past, but it is still active in the cultural process, not only and often not at all as an element of the past, but as an effective element of the present. Thus certain experiences, meanings, and values which cannot be expressed or substantially verified in terms of the dominant culture, are nevertheless lived and practised on the basis of the residue -- cultural as well as social -- of some previous social and cultural institution or formation.[21]

Williams is referring to abstract cultural institutions, such as the idea of rural community, but a musical institution like the típico charanga style can function in analogous ways: it was formed in the past, and expresses a musical worldview that cannot be expressed in terms of hegemonic musical styles like rock or rap, but is effective for its audience in the present, especially the energized, transformed present of live musical performance. Conceiving of the charanga as residual culture, then, accounts for both the passive and active aspects of its stylistic "persistence of vision."

An important function of the típico charanga style, like other típico styles, is the reaffirmation of ethnic identity. Though only a minority of the New York charanga audience is Cuban,

---

[20] For example, see Orquesta Broadway's "Barrio del Pilar" (which includes street sounds and a típica *rumba guaguancó*), "Angela Give Me Your Love" (sung in English), and charanga-conjunto fusions by Típica '73 and the Fania All Stars.

[21] Williams, *op. cit.*, p. 122.

the majority being Newyorican, Cuban music has been heard for so long in Puerto Rico, and Puerto Rican and Newyorican musicians have been such an important part of the development of Latin music in New York, that the Cuban-derived musical styles on which it is based have come to be regarded as a common musical heritage. While Cuban and non-Cuban musicians alike regard the charanga ensemble as distinctly Cuban, its musical style is part of this shared heritage, and its songs refer to life in Puerto Rico as well as in Cuba.[22]

Conclusion

The charanga in New York is a musical entity that has lost much of its former popularity, but still retains its musical vitality and its core audience. Both aspects of the present state of the charanga can be explained by interpreting the persistence of the típico charanga style, whose features have been described in detail above, as residual culture. The maintenance of the típico style assures the charanga of the core audience that has followed it for decades, while at the same time making it difficult to attract new audiences. The presence of this important traditional style in the field of Latin dance music, however, demonstrates that New York Latino musical culture is neither trend-driven nor rigidly traditional, but possesses a rich and healthy diversity.

Discography

Arcaño y sus Maravillas
   n.d.   Arcaño y sus Maravillas. Havana: Egrem Areito LD-
         3917.

---

[22]For example, when Orquesta Broadway performed the song "Isla del Encanto" at the Sidestreet club in the Bronx on 5/27/90, the following coro was sung: "De cuál parte de la Isla tú eres?" (What part of Puerto Rico are you from?). Audience members shouted out Puerto Rican place names that were repeated by the vocalists. A second coro proclaimed, "Soy puertorriqueño" (I am Puerto Rican).

Charanga América
   1985   The Very Best. New York: Combo Records RCSLP 2042.

Fajardo, José
   1977   Selecciones Clásicas. New York: Coco Records CLP 141X.

Fania All Stars
   1986   Viva La Charanga. New York: Fania JM 640.

López, Belisario
   n.d.   Y Su Orquesta. Ansonia SALP 1410.

Los Van Van
   n.d.   Los Van Van. Havana: Egrem Areito: LD- 4045.
   n.d.   Los Van Van. Havana: Egrem Areito LD- 4118.
   n.d.   Anda Ven y Muévete. Havana: Egrem Areito LD- 4164.
   n.d.   La Habana Sí. Havana: Egrem Areito LD- 4282.

Orquesta Aragón
   1983   Los Grandes Éxitos de Orquesta Aragón. Mexico: RCA International IL5-7234.
   1984   Orquesta Aragón Recorded "Live" in New York City, July 15, 1983. New York: Monitor Records MFS 820.

Orquesta Broadway
   n.d.   Dengue. Santurce, Puerto Rico: Gema Records LPG-1191. [1962]
   n.d.   Broadway Orchestra. Santurce, Puerto Rico: Gema Records LPG 3003 (reissued 1982).
   n.d.   Arrímate Pa' Acá. Venezuela: Gramsa LPS 88943. [1965]
   1975   Salvaje (Savage). New York: Coco Records CLP 119.
   1976   Pasaporte. New York: Coco Records 126CS.
   1981   Paraíso. New York: Coco Records CLP 159X.
   1987   ¡Ahora Es Cuando Eh! New York: Mambo Records MLP 1987.

Orquesta Maravillas de Florida
   n.d.   Orquesta Maravillas de Florida. Havana: Egrem Areito LD-3856.

Orquesta Típica Novel

1980   Que Viva El Son Montuno. New York: Fania JM 585
        Series 0798.
Orquesta Riverside
1983   The Contemporary Charanga Sounds of Orquesta
        Riverside. Sonido Latino Records SLP 5022.
Pacheco, Johnny
n.d.   Pacheco y su Charanga Vol. II. New York: Alegre
            SLPA 8050.
Rodríguez, Tito
n.d.   Charanga Pachanga. New York: West Side Latino
            Records WSCA 4164. Reissued 1986.
Santamaría, Mongo
n.d.   ¡Arriba! La Pachanga. Fantasy 3324.
n.d.   ¡Sabroso!. Berkeley, California: Fantasy OJC 281 (F
            8058). Remastered and reissued 1987.
n.d.   Mongo's Greatest Hits. Berkeley, California: Fantasy
            MPF 4529. Reissued 1987.
Son Primero
1987   Tradición Cubana en Nueva York. New York:
        Montuno Records MLP 524.
Típica '73
1979   Intercambio Cultural. Fania JM 00542.
Various Artists
n.d.   Mosaíco Cubano. Havana: Egrem Areito PRD   073.
n.d.   Qué Linda Es Cuba. Havana: Egrem Areito PRD
            080.
Various Artists
1977   Caliente = Hot: Puerto Rican and Cuban Musical
        Expression in New York. New York: New
        World Records NW 244.
Various Artists
1982   The Cuban Danzón: Its Ancestors and Descendants.
        New York: Folkways FE 4066.

7

Drumming for the Orishas:
The Reconstruction of Tradition in New York City

If salsa is the most conspicuous Cuban-derived musical genre flourishing in New York City, it is certainly not the only one. Since the mid-twentieth century, the major Afro-Cuban religions -- especially the Yoruba-derived santería -- have established substantial followings in the metropolitan area, not only among Cubans, but also among Puerto Ricans, other Latinos, North American blacks, and even some whites. Accordingly, the rich tradition of ceremonial musics intrinsic to these sects has also taken root in the area, although not without considerable difficulties deriving from the original paucity of knowledgeable performers.

Many fundamentally oral cultural traditions have sustained prolonged and complex relationships with ancillary written versions of their own discourses, whether these fixed descriptions be the products of local elites, colonial scholars, or other observers. Such relationships may be competitive, symbiotic, or both. A particularly interesting case of such an interaction is the manner in which enthusiastic, primarily non-Cuban drummers in New York City reconstructed the intricate and dynamic santería music largely by relying on "frozen" documents like published transcriptions and recordings. Once established as authorities among the local santería communities, such performers and their students then had to confront bearers of the living Cuban tradition arriving in the Mariel boatlift of 1980.

Steven Cornelius, currently music professor at Bowling Green State University, is one of the very few Anglo scholars to have penetrated the rather secretive Afro-Cuban religions and written extensively on their music. While achieving acceptance in the New York santería community was not without its difficulties and pitfalls, Cornelius managed to immerse himself sufficiently in the sect in order to document, among other things, the vicissitudes involved in the reconstruction of santería drumming traditions in New York.

7

Drumming for the Orishas:
The Reconstruction of Tradition in New York City

Steve   Cornelius

This article considers the emergence and developments within the New York metropolitan area of the liturgical *batá* drumming traditions from the religion *santería*.[1] It presents a general historical synopsis of musical evolution from the late 1950s to 1990 and highlights the processes by which the reconstruction of performance practice and the transmission of knowledge have taken place. Of special interest in this history is the essential role that both written sources and sound recordings have played in re-establishing an oral tradition, for in the New York musical community, the technical aspects of performance practice were made available and grasped before the religious and social mores that the music supports. The eventual integration of these values with technical understanding has created a unique history for New York ritual drumming.[2]

---

[1] There are two major genres of religious drumming performed at this time for New York *santeros*: *batá* drumming and a style called "drum and *güiro*." This chapter focusses on the *batá* performance tradition because it is considerably more complex, its internal musical structure is more highly regulated, and it is better documented than "drum and *güiro*." All these factors have also strongly influenced the reconstruction that has taken place in New York.

[2] The material for this chapter was gathered between 1986 and 1990. While the majority of informants were New York Hispanics of either Puerto Rican or Cuban heritage, a number of non-Hispanic whites and

Santería (also known as *regla de ocha*) is an Afro-Cuban religion which syncretizes New World Yoruba beliefs with those of Catholicism. It centers around acknowledgement, supplication, worship, and manipulation of the forces of nature, which are personified in various deities called *orishas*. Ritual music expression, found in song, drumming, and dancing, is central to *santería*'s religious conception. Musical sound acts as a doorway, mediating as celebration, communication, and invocation between the *santero* (religious practicioner) and the *orishas*.

Santeros believe that through the proper handling of organized sound (formulated recitation, chant, song, or drumming), they may effectively bridge the gap between the physical and spiritual worlds. By correctly manipulating ritualized musical activity, contact with the *orishas* may be achieved through spirit possession trance, a central aspect of religious experience in *santería*. These ideas are actualized through public music celebrations (known as *bembés, tambores,* or *toques*) which are held in honor of the various *orishas*.

Historical Background

The practice of *santería* is relatively recent in New York City. The first Cuban *babalawo* (var., *babalao*, a priest of the *orisha* Orunmila, specializing in divination) did not arrive in New York until the late 1940s and did not become active until a few years later.[3] It was not until 1959 that the first New York residents were initiated in the religion, visiting Cuba for the ceremony. The first initiation in New York probably took place in the mid-1960s. Since then the *santería* community in New York has grown dramatically.[4]

---

blacks were also interviewed. All of them have been performing since at the late 1970s, and a few since the mid-1960s.

[3]Robert Friedman, "Making an Abstract World Complete: Knowledge, Competence, and Structural Dimensions of Performance among Batá Drummers in Santería." Ph.D. dissertation, Indiana University, 1982, p. 54.

[4]*Ibid.*, pp. 54-55.

There are numerous temples in the metropolitan area today. Some are legally licensed and recognized houses of worship, while others are informally run under the direction of a single leader. While Cuban culture remains the dominant force throughout the religious community in New York, it rules by force of tradition rather than numbers of practicioners. There is no precise documentation of the ethnicity of *santeros* or of the musicians that play for ceremonies, but it seems clear that most are New York Latinos of Puerto Rican heritage, followed by Cubans and other Hispanics. There are also growing communities of non-Hispanic blacks and whites. Within these various groups one finds various factions with different beliefs, goals, and loyalties.[5]

Many of the people involved with *santería* maintain that belief system as their primary religion. However, some practicioners (known as *espiritistas*) are also involved with various aspects of Kardecian spititualism,[6] and a substantial percentage also consider themselves to be Catholic. These and other beliefs come together at public ceremonies where it is not uncommon to see people actively involved in singing, dancing, and occasionally even possession trance who are not *santeros*, but perhaps spiritualists, practicioners of other Afro-Cuban

---

[5]It is virtually impossible to ascertain how many practicing *santeros* there are in the metropolitan area today. Informant estimates have been as high as 100,000, although that figure seems overstated. I am indebted to David Brown for pointing out an article by Gary Langer, "Animal Sacrifice Cult Attracts U.S. Following," *Miami Sunday News* (5/6/84) which cites a 1982 survey by the Roman Catholic Archdiocese of New York estimating that three percent of New York's Hispanic population, or some 30,000 people, practiced animal sacrifice, while 70,000 frequented *botánicas* (stores which sell Afro-Cuban religious goods). However, a large percentage of those frequenting *botánicas* are not initiated *santeros*, while, on the other hand, many New York *santeros* are not Hispanic. Considering continued growth, it seems that an estimate of 50,000 initiates would not be exaggerated.

[6]Allen Kardec was a French spiritualist. His techniques of mediumship are commonly employed within the *santería* community.

cults such as *abakuá* or *palo*,[7] or those who are participating for
purely social reasons.   Should these individuals achieve possession trance, it is often with spirits who are not recognized as
orishas.

There are also numerous temples in the metropolitan area
which are run by North American blacks.   While not denigrating the Cuban religion as it stands, individuals in some of these
temples are investigating beneath the layers of Spanish and
Christian influence, looking to the *orisha* traditions as practiced
in Yoruba Africa for their inspiration and guidance.[8]   John
Mason, an influential leader in these circles, states that the goal
of these believers is "purifying the religious concepts, while
weeding out the influences of European and other religions."[9]

Finally, individuals with neither ethnic nor cultural roots in
either Africa or the Caribbean are becoming associated with
santería.   Many are drawn to the religion for practical reasons,
such as the *santeros'* purported powers to divine the future,
heal, or work magic.   Simple curiosity is also a major allure-
ment.   New World African religions have received prodigous
exposure through the arts establishment, the press and entertainment industry in the past few years.[10]   People may initially

---

[7]*Abakuá* is a Cuban secret society associated with the Carabalí people
from the Bight of Biafra region.   *Palo* (lit., "stick") has its roots in
Congolese religious sects.

[8] One of the larger tasks of this movement is to return the ritual
language from *lucumí* to intelligible modern Yoruba.   At present, the
term *lucumí* refers to Afro-Cubans of Yoruba descent and their
language, which was once spoken on a daily basis but has now
disintegrated considerably and is mostly reserved for religious
incantations.   In New York, as in Cuba, *santería* itself is often referred
to as *lucumí*.

[9] Gary Edwards and John Mason, *Black Gods--Orisa Studies in the New
World* (Yoruba Theological Archministry, 1985, p. v).   Mason and I also
discussed these ideas on various occasions.

[10] I first became aware of this music tradition through a concert
given by Milton Cardona in August of 1984 at New York's Museum of
Modern Art.   Aside from such functions, another important sponsor of
Afro-Cuban religious music has been the Caribbean Cultural Center on

attend ceremonies out of curiosity, but often go on to become more deeply involved.

Musical Tradition

From a historical perspective, ritual drumming in New York can be seen in three major phases. First was the introduction of the music to the New York musical community by Cuban drummers in the late 1950s. The second phase began when a number of New York drummers, who were not Cuban and had little or no direct training in or exposure to *santería* drumming, took interest in the repertoire for the standard trio of double-headed *batá* drums. These musicians, most of whom were already versed in Cuban secular hand-drumming traditions such as rumba, and ranged from highly successful professionals to students, mustered whatever materials they could find and set out to reconstruct the *batá* traditions for themselves.[11] The third phase was marked by the arrival of knowledgeable Cuban musicians via the Mariel boat lift of 1980. With this influx, a new level of authority presented itself which resulted in a major restructuring of the performance hierarchy.

Despite the early presence in the commercial music business of eminent Afro-Cuban drummers such as Chano Pozo, Mongo Santamaría, and Patato Valdéz, who had at least some knowledge of *santería* performance practice, it is Cuban drummer Julio Collazo who must be seen as the catalyst for the first stage of the development of ceremonial drumming in New York.

W. 58th St. in Manhattan, which presents an annual performance series called "Carnival in New York: A Celebration of the African Deities of the Americas." A number of *santeros* are also reaching an expanding audience on the "New Age" lecture circuit.

[11] It is worth noting that while there are numerous opportunities for drummers to perform in ritual settings, the financial incentives for doing so are meagre for all but the most prominent musicians. Most musicians play more from an interest in preserving folk traditions than for money. I commonly found that the *batá* drummers knew not only rumba and *santería* drumming but also substantial parts of other traditions, including those associated with *abakuá*, *palo*, *vodoun*, merengue, samba, and even some West African styles.

Collazo and another distinguished Cuban drummer, Francisco Aguabella, originally came to the USA as musicians for the Katherine Dunham Dance Company. After leaving the company's employment, both musicians stayed in this country. Collazo set up residence in New York City, while Aguabella moved to the West Coast. Various informants have stated that Collazo and Aguabella were probably the only people in the USA during the late 1950s who understood the deeper intricacies of *batá* drumming.

Collazo's roots in the music traditions of the religion are significant. Before coming to the United States, he was a member of a *batá* ensemble headed by the legendary *batalero*, Pablo Roche. Roche was not only acknowledged as being one of the finest ritual drummers in Cuba, but was also a major informant for the landmark publications of the Cuban scholar Fernando Ortiz. These relationships are central to understanding what has occured in the New York performance practice. There are two different major *batá* styles in Cuba, one centered in Havana and another in Matanzas. Both Collazo's style and Ortiz's research came primarily from the same source, that is, Pablo Roche and the Havana style. Therefore, the two sources were mutually supportive when introduced into New York.

Besides working in commercial settings, from the late 1950s through the 1960s, Collazo performed occasionally at religious ceremonies within the New York area. However, rather than using *batá* drums, he generally performed in the less complex *bembé* style.[12] Collazo's playing attracted the interest of sev-

---

[12]In Cuba, *bembé* is the name for a specific type of drum, a rhythm genre, and any public music ceremony that uses this instrumental combination. The lead *bembé* drum is larger than a conga drum, and the support drums are slightly smaller, although they are roughly similar in construction. The *bembé* style is performed with one open hand and a stick held in the other, and only *bembé* rhythms are performed. There is also a style in Cuba called *iyesá* (*yesá*), which also has its own drums and rhythm genre. In New York, both of the standard *bembé* and *iyesá* rhythms are played within the broader *bembé* ceremony on the "drum and *güiro*" ensemble, which also includes bell, from one to three

eral New York musicians, which coincided with the increasing demand for drummers to accompany religious ceremonies throughout the New York community. However, Collazo took few students and proved to be generally unwilling to reveal the intricacies of *batá* performance.[13]

Collazo's reluctance to share the knowledge of *batá* drumming initiated the second historical phase we have referred to. Because of Collazo's secrecy, interested New York drummers were obliged to turn to non-conventional sources for information in order to learn performance practice. Traditionally, the technical and social requirements of ritual drumming for *santería* had been passed down directly from teacher to student. Apprentices learned the different parts in order, beginning with the least complicated drum, the *okónkolo*.[14] By performing in groups, the apprentice gradually learned the other parts from that perspective, next mastering and performing on the *itótole*, and finally carrying the responsibility not only for the entire ensemble, but also for much of the success of the religious ceremony as a whole, from the position of the lead drum, the *iyá*.

With the exception of a very select group of musicians that were able to apprentice with Collazo, the first New York drummers could not follow this method. Therefore, they used a combination of sources, mainly, published transcriptions, commercial recordings, and watching and listening to the few *batá* performances that Collazo was giving.

---

conga drums, and three *shekeres* (gourd shakers strung with beads on the outside). In New York, a ceremony that uses *batá* drums may be called a *bembé, tambor*, or *toque*.

[13]Many New York drummers consider expertise on *batá* to represent the pinnacle of advancement for hand drumming. While *batá* music is clearly the most complex of the Cuban drumming traditions transplanted in New York, one wonders if perhaps Collazo's reluctance to make the music readily available contributed to the genre's mystique.

[14]For further discussion of these drums, see Rogelio Martínez Furé's article "Tambor" in this same volume.

The works of Fernando Ortiz were (and remain) of paramount importance.[15] Ortiz had published a number of volumes in the 1950s which provided a large amount of general information about the music of *santería*, including transcriptions of a major portion of the *batá* repertory. These works became the primary source for most New York musicians, both in terms of understanding the technical aural aspects of musical performance, as well as the proper manipulation of ritual actions that musical performance supports.

In terms of performance specifics, what the Ortiz transcriptions provided was a scheme for understanding how the drum parts interlocked. Examples made explicit the stylistic roles of lead, response, and support that the different drums maintained and the metric spaces that each drum could be expected to fill. Also of major importance, the transcriptions showed the sectional characteristics inherent in the specific salute rhythms to the various *orishas*. This allowed the drummers to distinguish the differences between structurally meaningful musical progressions and mere embellishment.

Nevertheless, there were a number of problems to overcome in working with these transcriptions. First, at least when compared with *batá* performance today, many of the rhythms are transcribed inaccurately. Ortiz placed into duple structure many of the rhythms which are actually played in a triple meter. The overall result is that when performed as written,

---

[15] Because most of Ortiz' works are either out of print or else published only in Cuba, the few privately owned copies of these books are highly prized and guarded by the New York musicians who own them. In fact, many of the Ortiz works dealing with *santería* have been stolen from public libraries in the New York area. I came across some of these during fieldwork. One informant had even gone to the effort of having the entire five-volume set, *Los instrumentos de la musica afrocubana* (Havana: Ministerio de Educación, 1952-55) photocopied and hardbound. The other most relevant works of Ortiz are *La africana de la música folklórica de Cuba* (Santa Clara: Universidad de Las Villas, 1965 [reprint of 1950 ed.]), and *Los bailes y el teatro de los negros en el folklore de Cuba* (Havana: Editorial Letras Cubanas, 1981 [reprint of 151 ed.]).

these transcriptions are too angular in feeling, and hence obscure the underlying (although implicit) bell patterns that form
the musical groundwork.[16]   Finally, the transcriptions are intended to be only concise idealized representations of the various sacred rhythms. They do not account for the fluid level of
variation and controlled "conversation" that is a part of every
batá performance.

In short, the transcriptions represent a single performance
possibility, frozen in time, but which were raised to the level of
a singular authenticity by the New York drummers.   Therefore,
while the musicians involved in reconstructing the rhythms
realized that the transcriptions were problematic, they nevertheless had a tendency, in trying to maintain accuracy to both
folkloric ideals and spiritual efficacy, to stay overly close to the
written examples.

Using the general map that Ortiz had provided, drummers
also turned to various recorded sources and transcribed the
rhythms therein for themselves. Working from these purely
aural sources without visual cues would have made transcrib-
ing the sounds of six interlocking drum heads nearly impossible if the Ortiz works had not existed. But using the recorded
examples (which, like the transcriptions, were static representations) together with the information provided by Ortiz and
further subtleties gleaned from watching Collazo, the musicians
were able to reconstruct most of the performance rhythms.[17]

---

[16]The problem is further complicated by the fact that accurate
Western-oriented transcription for many *batá* rhythms is inherently
unsatisfactory because the rhythms often fall somewhere between
duple and triple meter.

[17]The two most influential recordings were "Afro Tambores Batá"
(Orfeon LP-LAB-0) and "Ecoes Afro-Cubanos" (Orfeon LP-12-138).   The
batá ensemble on these recordings was headed by Geraldo Rodríguez.
Jesús Pérez, a student and former member of Pablo Roche's ensemble,
also performed with this group and was probably playing *iyá* on at least
some of the tracks.

One of the elements lacking in this pieced-together *batá* drumming was the characteristic musician hierarchy found in Cuba. Instead of following the apprentice route that traditional learning would have dictated, New York drummers began as relative equals. They were involved in learning together, with each member trying to contribute to the overall reconstruction process. One consequence of this situation was that (except for Collazo) there were no leaders distinguished by virtue of deep understanding and years of performance. In direct contrast to drumming in Cuba, the New York groups forming in the late 1960s and early 1970s were characterized by equality and a general lack of understanding. Very few of the New York drummers were fully initiated *santeros*.[18] Therefore, even when they had learned the notes and begun to perform at ceremonies, musicians often had only an outsider's understanding of the proper ritual and social functions thay would be expected to maintain, and most of this knowledge came from the Ortiz works. An insider's perspective was only slowly achieved through a gradual socialization into the ideals of the religious community.

As the New York musicians became more qualified, many of the original groups broke up. Some of the performers gradually withdrew from lack of interest, others moved away from New York, and still others formed their own *batá* or "drum and *güiro*" groups. The net result of these various changes was the gradual development of a system of training more similar to Cuban practice. New York musicians naturally developed their own hierarchy in which there were clear leaders ("elder" is perhaps a better term from a religious standpoint) who took the responsibility of training new people.

In the late 1970s, Collazo remained an important figure within the religious music community. However, other groups headed by New York natives John Amira, Louis Bauzo, and others had established themselves as well. The situation changed

---

[18]This generally remains the case today.

markedly, however, with the arrival of Cuban "boat people" in 1980, which inaugurated the third major period in the development of ritual drumming in New York. Musically, a number of interesting things happened. Many of the arriving immigrants initially claimed (falsely) to have been important ritual drummers in Cuba. However, rather than dominating the New York scene, most were surprised to find that the locals had accumulated a considerable amount of knowledge on their own, including enough to discern between truth and fiction and dismiss the false prophets. Therefore, of these new arrivals, only the most knowledgeable were able to establish themselves within the musical community.

Clearly, the most influential of these has been Orlando "Puntilla" Ríos, who was a recognized master drummer in Cuba. Suddenly a virtuoso Cuban musician was on the scene, who unlike Collazo, was more than willing to teach New Yorkers to play. Soon after his arrival, he had established himelf as the primary source for information. Puntilla taught not only novices, but also to many of the more advanced New York drummers who went to him for confirmation and needed adjustments on the material that they had already been playing for years.

Interestingly, these changes have caused yet another schism, this time within the community of elder local drummers. Ironically, it is the New Yorker natives, the newest bearers of the tradition, who may be the most conservative. Because the newly imported styles show many differences when compared to the older sources, the more conventional New York drummers have rejected certain aspects of Puntilla's performance style as being too liberal. Some have even suggested that it may lack in authenticity because it is so far removed from the style documented by Ortiz. Meanwhile, most New York musicians have accepted the innovations brought by Puntilla as proper and have adopted his style. Some musicians have responded to the dilemma by visiting Cuba themselves in order both to verify Puntilla's musical credentials (which turn out to be formidable) and perhaps find an even higher source of information.[19]

At present, Puntilla is clearly the most important ceremonial drummer in the New York area and is in considerable demand for playing "folkloric" performances as well as ceremonies. He not only fronts his own group, but contracts other ensembles to play under his banner, using drummers loyal to him exclusively. During any given Saturday or Sunday he may make brief appearances at several of the temples where these various groups are performing.

As this scenario suggests, Puntilla's relationship with the New York drummers is in many ways symbiotic. While he can be seen as revitalizing the musical community, Puntilla is also indebted to the local musicians who worked to establish *batá* drumming before his arrival. It is they who were responsible for generating the interest and preliminary understanding upon which Puntilla was able to assert his musical knowledge and authority.

The Social Framework

The process of gradual acculturation for New York drummers into the ideology of *santería* is worth noting. Local drummers came to ritual performance for a variety of reasons, including economic incentive, chance, or folkloric interest in learning new rhythmic traditions. However, after getting exposure to the religion, every person that I worked with both stated and displayed a strong respect for *santería*'s religious beliefs and

---

[19] It is of interest that New York drummers also tend to take a conservative approach in their realization of the secular Cuban rumba styles. Perhaps this conservatism in both sacred and secular drumming is in part a consequence of the fact that they have generally found it difficult to achieve musical acceptance from the native Cubans. Consequently, in striving for a stronger sense of legitimacy, they look to higher and older authorities than their contemporary Cuban peers. Interestingly, some of the New York *batá* drummers trace the lineage of their performance style directly to the Cuban masters Pablo Roche or Jesús Pérez, rather than to either contemporary sources or Ortiz.

ritual procedures. In fact, while there are few musicians who are actual practicioners, there are even fewer who deny *santería*'s efficacy or reality.

Perhaps the key to understanding these developments is through realizing the change in perspective of the drummers' values orientation from practical/aural to socio-religious. Native New York ritual musicians have come to express in both their performance and daily life many of the values embedded within the religion. While the musicians' early considerations dealt primarily with issues relating to performance practice, these have been largely replaced with social ideology. One example of this change concerns the rules defining who may or may not play the drums. When the local musicians began learning and performing amongst themselves in the 1960s and '70s, anyone who was interested could come to learn and play. The only real requirements were tenacity and musicianship. Drumming was approached primarily for the sake of musical knowledge, rather than in terms of its ceremonial role or spiritual efficacy. This situation began to change as the New Yorkers became more involved in liturgical performance. By engaging in actual ritual practice the drummers discovered how to use the music to call the *orishas*. They learned how to regulate the process of spirit possession by correctly manipulating the musical and ritual factors under their control. This direct confrontation and integration of the music with the sacred broadened the musicians' overall perspective from a strictly musical focus to a view more in line with general religious values.

The movement toward a philosophical basis for music-making had an insular effect on the performance scene. The doors of knowledge, briefly open to all, quickly closed. For example, because of issues dealing with blood and sexuality, belief structures render it taboo for the *batá* drums to be played by either women or homosexual men. Initially, because their interest was focussed on aural rather than religious practice, New York musicians ignored these restrictions. Today, however, most of the drummers that regularly perform in ritual settings accept these values and carry them to the rest of their *batá* performance relationships. Consequently, because instruction is denied to specific social groups, teaching that briefly took place in institutionalized settings is no longer possible.

The acculturative process works in the other direction as well. Many New York drummers come to this music as mature performers in other styles. In trying to master the subtle differences in feel and timing that ritual drumming for *santería* requires, they take previously understood musical structures and genres as their initial framework for comprehension, and use this basis to build an appropriate style. In a sense, the New York performance style seems to be an organic incorporation of numerous contemporary musical and social backgrounds into an older vessel. The musical ideal maintains the same ultimate purpose -- it calls the *orishas*. But the ingredients that go into the mix are of a different musical palette in New York than in Cuba, and the aural result reflects the New York experience.

While the aural differences may be too elusive to analyze systematically, musicians have cited a number of sources for their inspiration. Some have said that when the music is really flowing, it is the *orishas* themselves that take over and control the per-formance. Other musicians have cited soul music, salsa, rumba, or Puerto Rican folk musics as their personal points of departure. The flow of musical ideas also works outward into secular styles as musicians take rhythmic motives from *santería* and use them in other performance contexts.[20] When musically appropriate, many drummers use motivic ideas from ritual drumming in commercial situations or even in other rit-

---

[20] Such borrowings also occur in Cuba, as in Irakere's "Misa Negra" and other songs.

ual settings, such as ceremonies for Cuban *palo* or Haitian vodoun.[21]

As New York drummers continue to develop their own style of performance, broader changes may be in the making. Drummers have stated that there has been a general increase in musical tempi, variation, and density as a response to the vitality of the city around them. They suggest that the music and the African *orishas* themselves are adapting and coming into harmony with the New York environment.[22] Music will continue to change with the interests and needs of this developing community.

As the musicians become more secure in knowledge and strength of conviction, additional sources for understanding may become accepted within the general community. Although learning the drumming was once confined to books, records, and interpersonal sources, this situation is clearly changing. One musician told of a dream in which he was in Nigeria looking over the backs of drummers who were performing within a ritual context. Upon awakening, he remembered the dream and the rhythms. He considers this experience to be a revalation and the knowledge gained from it to be both authentic and usable within local ritual settings. In another instance, a drummer used a psychic to contact *orishas* who had not made the journey from Africa to the New World. The psychic sang

---

[21]Because of the severe restrictions in acceptable levels of variation in *batá* drumming, this occurence is considerably more common in the "drum and *güiro*" style. It is also not uncommon to hear *batá* rhythms imitated on conga drum or even by an ensemble of *shekeres*.

[22]This process is also happening within other aspects of *santería* practice. For example, in New York the *orishas* (when possessing a devotee) will often speak English, as well as *lucumí* or Spanish. Sandra Barnes, in *Ogún: An Old God for a New Age* (Philadelphia: Institute for the Study of Human Issues, 1980), discusses the transformation of the *orisha* Ogun in modern Yoruba Nigerian society, where he has gone from a warrior deity associated with the forge and the sword to being connected today with car engines and the taxi-driver profession. Similar analogies concerning Ogún have been related to me in New York.

back the deity's spiritual signature, and the musician trans-
ferred the feeling to the drums. Again, the information was
considered to be authentic. As a final example, there have
been instances in New York City in which an *orisha* possesses
an individual and then demonstrates a specific rhythm that he
wants played. That rhythm, coming straight from the sacred, is
considered to be authentic, whether traditional or not.

Conclusion

What course performance practice will take in the future is impossible to predict, but a number of factors will have a clear
impact. *Santería* is continuing to grow within the metropolitan
area. Should it continue to do so, more musicians will be
needed to fulfill ceremonial requirements.[23] Further, the religious community itself is also becoming more ethnically diverse and more integrated into the general metropolitan community. Some temples are looking for musicians to perform
who share their values. An example is the previously mentioned "Yoruba Reversionism" movement, which is attempting
to eliminate the New World influences from the religion. Such
trends may serve to increase innovation, diversification, and
fragmentation among local musicians.

Clearly, United States foreign policy has had a powerful effect on this New York drumming. There is little free exchange
of information between Cuba and the USA. Should the relationship with Cuba remain antagonistic, it may be a long time be-

---

[23]During the time-frame considered in this paper the number of
actively performing New York *batá* drummers has grown from none in
the late 1950s, to probably around ten in the following decade, to
perhaps as many as fifty today. The number of New York drummers
who at present know at least a portion of the *batá* repertoire from the
standpoint of one or more drums may easily exceed one hundred;
nevertheless, there are certainly fewer than twenty who could function
competently as ensemble leaders, in having a firm understanding of the
entire song concerned and the complete drum repertoire, and in being
able fluently to manipulate this knowledge within the ritual context.
Several highly accomplished drummers told me that they consider
Puntilla to be the only master drummer in New York.

fore an artistic blossoming such as that which followed Mariel can be repeated. The lines for artistic communication getween the two nations will continue to depend on individuals or groups obtaining short-term visas to travel between the two countries.[24] Musical practice in both countries will develop and change separately, according to the specific needs of each communities.

As we document performance practice throughout the modern world, it may be relevant to take note of what has happened in New York and accept, for better or worse, the researcher's potential for influencing cultural practice. The impact of both Ortiz's work and commercial or ethnographic recordings strongly demonstrates that documentation can profoundly affect, and thus even become a part of tradition itself.

---

[24] Video tapes made in Cuba of actual ceremonies or of folkloric rehearsals and performances are treasured and well-studied commodities in New York.

8

Salsa and The Music Industry:
Corporate Control or Grassroots Expression?

While it may be commonly believed that the commercial mass media constitute neutral and essentially "natural" vehicles for the dissemination of music, entertainment, and news, contemporary media studies have highlighted the ways in which the mass media, by their very nature, tend to actively shape the content and even meaning of the material they transmit. This process is particularly evident in the history of the music industry's treatment of salsa, a genre which has generally been able to affirm its original intended sense of grassroots community only in live performance or in the hands of non-corporate, independent record companies and radio stations. Similarly, the tendency of the large corporate sectors of the music industry to decontextualize and trivialize salsa suggests that the media are not as neutral as they are popularly held to be.

This brief study of salsa's media dissemination in New York may naturally invite comparison with the media treatment of dance music in modern Cuba itself, and the reader may well wish to regard Leonardo Acosta's article following this one as a comparative companion study.

8

Salsa and the Music Industry: Corporate Control or Grassroots Expression?

Peter Manuel

Salsa, or Cuban-style dance music as produced by Latinos in New York City and elsewhere, has emerged as one of the most significant and dynamic components of the American popular music scene in the last twenty years. Salsa's evolution can be seen to exemplify some of the ways in which the capitalist mass media and corporate music industry actively shape dissemination and consumption patterns, rather than serving as neutral transmitters of music. In general, the relationship between salsa and the music industry can be seen as the conflict and mediation of a set of interrelated dialectic oppositions, *viz.*, corporate/grassroots, upper-class/working-class, Anglo/-Hispanic, white/ black, Euro-American/Afro-Latin, and pan-regional/local. Salsa embodies these and other dialectic oppositions in a process of negotiation and mediation that is, as with any popular music, fundamentally contradictory. This article, while too brief to attempt a detailed treatment of such processes, explores some of the ways in which the mass media have influenced salsa's development and dissemination. In particular, it suggests how the corporate broadcast and recording industries (as opposed to public or independent sectors of the mass media) have tended to neglect salsa in favor of Spanish-language "easy listening" styles in the endeavor to appeal to and create a broader, ethnically more homogeneous audience; further, insofar as the corporate music industry has in fact promoted salsa, it has attempted to shape it into a bland, apolitical dance music rather than a vehicle of working class, barrio identity.

Some of the ideological and socio-musical contradictions embodied in salsa as a genre are implicit in the history of the term itself, which, while originating as an artificial commercial label, subsequently became the standard term for a grassroots musical phenomenon.   In the late 1960s, Jerry Masucci of Fania Records coined the term "salsa" as a rubric for the Cuban-style dance music which his company was then successfully marketing.   Although these music styles were by no means new, the term caught on, largely because of the new significance the music was acquiring as an expression of social identity for New York Latinos.   However, as we shall attempt to illustrate, the widespread adoption of the label did not resolve the fundamentally dualistic nature of the genre as corporate commodity on the one hand, and, on the other, as a grassroots social phenomenon.

The Mass Media and the Emergence of Salsa

The music which came to be called salsa developed out of Cuban dance genres -- especially, the *son, guaracha,* and *rumba* --which had evolved into a cohesive set of commercial popular styles by the 1920s.   By the 1940s, these genres, as promoted primarily by RCA Victor (which monopolized the record industry in Cuba) enjoyed considerable international appeal, and Latino communities in New York had come to play an important role in the evolution of Cuban music.   Puerto Ricans had so eagerly adopted Cuban music for decades (especially since the introduction of radio in 1922) that they had come to regard such genres as the *son* and *guaracha* more or less as their own (generally at the expense of indigenous genres like *plena* and *bomba*).   Meanwhile, since the 1920s, New York City had become the scene of a lively dialectic blending and competition of diverse grassroots Latin American musics and commercialized versions thereof (an ongoing pro-

cess amply documented in John Roberts' *The Latin Tinge*).[1]
Many Cuban musicians had come to base themselves in New
York City, where, together with Puerto Rican bandleaders like
Tito Puente and Tito Rodríguez, they established New York as a
center for the music that would eventually come to be labelled
"salsa" by the record industry.

The Latin music record scene in New York had been monopolized, or more properly, oligopolized, by RCA Victor,
Columbia, and Decca until the early 1940s.   As was the case
with "race records" of black American music, the domination of
these three Anglo corporations had tended to limit the diversity and quantity of Latin records.   However, during World War
II a variety of factors led to a decline of the near-total hegemony enjoyed by these so-called "majors" in the field of ethnic
and minority musics, such that smaller independent record
companies ("indies") were able to enter the market and service
the demand for specialized markets in a more creative, responsive, and energetic way.   These factors included: the majors' abandonment of minority musics as a response to wartime
shellac shortages; the advent of magnetic tape and 45 RPM
records, which lowered record production costs sufficiently for
smaller firms to enter the market; the increasing purchasing
power of minorities, including working-class Puerto Ricans; the
AFM (American Federation of Musicians) boycott of the majors
in 1942 and 1947; and the rise of BMI (Broadcast Music Inc.)
which relied considerably on non-traditional (especially black
and Latin) popular musics in the wake of the ASCAP ban on
radio broadcasts of their own mainstream popular music in the
early 1940s.   Within the realm of black American music, these
factors led to the emergence of indie labels like Sun, Phillips,
Chess, and Atlantic, whose growth contributed significantly to

[1] Roberts, *The Latin Tinge: The Impact of Latin American Music on the United States* (New York: Oxford 1979).   I am particularly grateful to Max Salazar, Carlos Agudelo, Enrique Fernandez, and WADO's Danny Ortiz for sharing their insights with me in interviews between January 1989 and June 1990.   Chris Washburne and John Murphy also provided much useful feedback.

the rise of R&B and, later, rock 'n' roll. In the Latin music scene, such record industry developments, together with the dramatic increase in migration from Puerto Rico during the 1940s and the big-band "mambo craze" of the 1950s, facilitated the emergence of independents like SMC (1945), Tico (1948), Alegre (1960), and others; these labels specialized in Cuban-style dance music and the syncretic mambo which Pérez Prado, Tito Puente, Machito and others had fashioned, primarily in New York City.[2] The competition between the majors and the indies formalized the dialectic opposition between corporate hegemony and grassroots "authenticity" within the record industry -- a dialectic which we shall discuss in greater detail below.

In the latter 1960s, Cuban dance music in New York City underwent a transitional period of reorientation and redefinition. The Cuban Revolution of 1959 had ruptured commercial and touristic ties with the USA and to some extent spoilt the glamorous and idyllic image of Cuban music that the major record companies and the tourist industry had sought to promote. After such a harsh reminder of socio-political realities in the Caribbean, the multinationals that had been involved in Cuban-style music largely withdrew.[3] More significantly, a distinct social identity began to coalesce in New York's Hispanic barrios, as Puerto Ricans and other Latinos came to perceive themselves as confronting a shared urban experience of social, political, and economic alienation and marginalization. Cuban dance music, both as performed live and on record, began to play an increasingly important role in expressing, mediating, and shaping this emergent barrio identity; thus, as we have suggested above, the advent of the new label "salsa," however commercial in inspiration, can be seen to some extent as legitimate insofar as the music it denoted acquired a new social significance and operated in a milieu substantially distinct from

[2]See *ibid.*, pp. 111, 121; also Steve Chapple and Reebee Garofalo, *Rock 'n' Roll is Here to Pay* (Chicago: Nelson-Hall, 1973), pp.9-29, and Max Salazar, "The Pioneers of Salsa," in *Mambo Express* 2/15, 8/89.

[3]Rondón, Cesar Miguel, *El libro de la salsa: Crónica de la música del Caribe urbano* (Caracas: Editorial Arte, 1980), p. 20.

that of its Caribbean parent. To the extent that its texts mirrored their social context, salsa could be seen as continuing the tradition of its predecessors, the Cuban *son* and rumba, whose lyrics frequently dealt with local neighborhood events[4]; what distinguished salsa was that the neighborhood was now East Harlem rather than, for example, Havana's Guanabacoa suburb.

The growth of salsa as a vehicle of social identity was inseparable from its development as a commercial entity. Indeed, the more salsa flourished, the more it was subject to the pressures of the corporate music industry. Some of these pressures -- toward standardization, stylistic conservatism, and absence of socio-political content[5] -- operated in direct opposition to the grassroots attempt to use the genre as an expression of barrio identity. Thus, the development of salsa can be seen as an ongoing dialectic between, on the one hand, the Latino community's attempt to shape salsa as its own subcultural expression, and, on the other hand, the tendency of the commercial music industry to glamorize, decontextualize, and depoliticize the music as a bland and innocuous dance music -- as ketchup rather than salsa.

As we have suggested above, the latter tendency, in salsa as well as other musics, is particularly marked in the case of large, corporate record companies, as opposed to smaller, independent firms, which are generally more reflective of grassroots aesthetics. It may be appropriate at this point to clarify further the distinction between the so-called majors, who control their own distribution and marketing as well as production, and the independents, who produce records but generally market them via separate distribution companies or, very often,

---

[4] The lyrics of the pre-salsa Cuban *son* remained rooted in local experience even in the genre's commercial, mass mediated stage. Most of Arsenio Rodríguez's *sones*, for example, refer to specific individuals or local events familiar to the composer and his contemporary local peers.

[5] See Simon Frith, *Youth, Leisure, and the Politics of Rock 'n' Roll* (New York: Pantheon, 1981), p. 153, for a discussion of these tendencies of the major recording companies, with regard to rock music.

arrangements with the majors. The indies suffer several disadvantages in their competition with the majors. Distribution is by far the biggest problem, but in addition to this, indies have such limited capital resources that they are easily ruined by a few failed records. Paradoxically, due to cash flow problems, a blockbuster hit can also bankrupt an indie if it is unable to meet sudden demand for a particular record. Disc jockeys are often reluctant to play indie records, especially since the independents cannot afford the same sorts of promotion, miscellaneous perks, and, in many cases, payola offered by the majors. Artists themselves often prefer to sign contracts with the more reliable, if exploitative majors. Hence the indies tend to be small companies which cater to specialized markets, with whom they are more in touch on a grassroots level than are the majors. The majors can afford to take risks, but they generally avoid doing so; rather they prefer to wait until a group or artist has made a name on an independent label, and then they buy that act from the indie, thus letting the indie bear the cost of research and development. (While the complexity of industry accounting renders calculations of profit margins difficult, if not meaningless, it may be roughly estimated that a typical record produced by a major currently costs about half a million dollars, including promotion, and has to sell around 70,000 copies to break even, while an indie can produce a record for $10,000 and make a profit by selling only 2,000 copies.) The indies tend to be owned not by large corporations, but by middle-class or in some cases even lower-middle-class entrepreneurs. The indies, accordingly, are intimately rooted in their local, ethnic markets and can be responsive and faithful to those markets in a way which the majors are either unwilling or unable to be.[6]

We have mentioned that in the 1960s, recording of Latin dance music in New York was largely in the hands of a few in-

---

[6] See Frith, *op. cit.*, pp. 138-50 for further discussion of the differences between indies and majors. Fredrick Dannens, in his "Hit Men" (New York: Times Books, 1990), discusses payola in the contemporary recording industry.

dies, especially Tico-Alegre and Coda Records.[7] In 1964, Jerry Masucci and Johnny Pacheco, the gifted leader of a thoroughly traditional Cuban-style ensemble, formed another independent label, Fania Records. By 1970, through a combination of creative marketing (including popularizing the term "salsa"), aggressive signing of local bands, and responsiveness to the growing significance of Latin music, Fania had surpassed its established competitors and had come to dominate Latin music recording in the city. In this initial period, Fania, as an energetic, dynamic indie, remained vitally in touch with "Newyorican" barrio life and did not hesitate to promote "salsa" as a dynamic expression of that subculture. Song texts by Willie Colón, Felipe Luciano and others dramatized barrio alienation and aspirations. Album covers expressed similar themes, as with Ray Barretto's "Que Viva la Música", showing Barretto emerging in chains out of a conga, looming over the Manhattan skyline, and reaching for the sun. Most explicitly, perhaps, Fania produced a 90-minute promotional film, "Nuestra Cosa" ("Our Thing"), contextualizing salsa and its exponents in their Newyorican milieu of barrio squalor, transplanted traditions, and cultural revival.[8]

The period 1971-75 was the creative and financial zenith for salsa and for Fania Records. Despite the appearance of a few more innovative salsa indies (TR, Montuno, Coco, and Caytronics' Salsoul and Mericana), Fania, with 80 percent of the market, dominated the field, and enjoyed such growth and virtual monopoly that it came to operate more like a major record company than an indie.[9] Accordingly, as Cesar Rondón has documented, Fania's management chose increasingly to divest salsa of its barrio ethos and to market it as a typical American pop music industry product, i.e., glamorous, decontextualized, depoliticized, standardized, and aimed at a homogeneous mass audience rather than a local, marginalized one.

---

[7]Pablo Guzman, "Siempre Salsa!," in *The Village Voice*, 6/25/79, p. 92.
[8]See Rondón, *op. cit.*, pp. 19-64 for further discussion of the early Fania years.
[9]Guzmán, *op. cit.*, p. 92. Alegre was by this point leased to Fania.

Hence, Fania promoted several (largely unsuccessful) "crossover" LPs aimed at reaching Anglo audiences. Much of the remaining Fania output -- especially the records of Johnny Pacheco and Celia Cruz -- was devoted to reiteration, however tasteful, of the traditional-style Cuban *son*, in the vein of the Sonora Matancera (a Cuban group) of the 1950s. Aside from crossover ventures, Fania seemed to have forsaken innovation for standardized, reliable formulae, and chose to celebrate a mythically idyllic Cuban past rather than to continue confronting barrio reality in all its complexity.[10]   The contrast became most explicit in another Fania promotional film, "Salsa" (1973), aimed at Anglo audiences and ignoring problematic barrio culture and Cuban roots by implying that salsa came directly from Africa to New York City recording studios. Through such propaganda, salsa and Cuban dance music in general were decontextualized and dehistoricized to the extent that many listeners thought them to be modern New York creations.[11] Meanwhile, innovative, jazz-oriented salsa (like Eddie Palmieri's) and provocative songs which embraced and confronted barrio culture (like those of Rubén Blades and Willie Colón) were largely confined to the margins of the record industry, and came to be avoided by commercial radio stations.[12]

Despite such policies, Latin radio had been actively contributing to the popularization of Latin music in New York since the early 1930s. Cuban dance music -- including live broadcasts from clubs -- had been broadcast on stations like WJZ and WMCA since as early as 1932-34, and continued in subsequent decades to be played in short programs on PIX, WOVZ, WOR,

---

[10]See *ibid.*, and Rondón, *op. cit.*, p. 137.

[11]Rondón observes, for example, that Pacheco's liner notes (e.g., "Pacheco y su nuevo tumbao") led many listeners to believe that he was the inventor of the *charanga* ensemble (which had been in vogue in Cuba for fifty years). See *ibid.*, p. 138.

[12]Thus did Blades' remarkable "Juan Pachanga," with its innovative instrumentation and sensitive text portraying the desperate emptiness of *machismo*, appear originally only on the failed fusion LP "Rhythm Machine." Palmieri won Grammy Awards five times in spite of his low profile on commercial radio.

and other stations. In the late 1940s the owners of Tico Records and SMC, in accordance with the customary promotional practices of the times, started buying air time on radio stations to promote their recordings. From 1947, the "Tico-Tico Show" hosted by Art "Pancho" Raymond and, later, Dick "Ricardo" Sugar, on the English-language station WEVD, attracted wide audiences from both Latino and Anglo communities, as did shows by other English-speaking disc jockeys (e.g., Bob "Pedro" Harris on WJZ and "Symphony Sid" on WEVD).[13] It was not until 1961, however, that WADO was established as the city's first fully Spanish-language radio station (or "SLR"). While WADO, from its inception, made some efforts to orient music programming toward the city's various ethnic groups, Cuban-style dance music, and what came to be called "salsa," never received much airplay on WADO, due primarily to the personal antipathy for the genre on the part of the station's owner, Nelson LaVerne.[14] By the late sixties, however, Jerry Masucci was buying air time on stations like WBNX in an energetic and remarkably successful promotion campaign to make stars out of Fania's upcoming performers.[15] Purchase of radio air time has since become too expensive for most indies, however, and the majors prefer to promote musics other than salsa, as we shall discuss below.

The Contemporary Scene: 1980 to the Present

In the late 1970s, the commercial success of Fania, and of salsa in general, began to decline. While artist-management conflicts beset Fania itself, more significant reasons for salsa's problems relate to broad socio-economic and demographic changes which, although affecting the music industry, did not originate

---

[13]Interview with Max Salazar, 6/90. Also see Roberts, *op. cit.*, pp. 91, 221, and Oscar Hijuelos's *The Mambo Kings Play Songs of Love* (New York: Farrar, Strout, and Giroux), p. 154.

[14]Inteview with WADO's station manager, Danny Ortiz, in 5/90. Also see Max Salazar, "Salsa Losing Popularity to Ballads on City Airwaves," in *Billboard* 1/26/85.

[15]Interview with Max Salazar, 6/90.

in it. Salsa has lost much of its audience to rock, as second- and
third-generation Latino immigrants to New York become increasingly Anglicized, and as middle-class, English-speaking
youths in Puerto Rico and elsewhere come to associate salsa
with backward, lower-class values.[16] Salsa has also been reel-
ing under the extraordinary vogue of *merengue*, fueled by the
dramatically increased Dominican immigration to New York,
and the faddish, inherent appeal of the simpler rhythms and
flashy stage presence of the *merengue* bands.[17]   Meanwhile,
under policies of the Reagan-Bush administrations, the
American lower classes, including the vast majority of
Hispanics, have suffered a dramatic decline in their standard of
living; the markedly increased Latino poverty has hurt record
sales considerably.[18]   Due to the high dollar and currency de-
valuations in Latin America, the Latin record industry in the US
has also been seriously damaged by the phenomenon of parallel importing.   In this practice, copies of records inexpensively
pressed outside the US (e.g., in Venezuela, or Mexico), under
separate licensing agreements for marketing abroad, are ille-
gally imported to the US, where they are sold for less than half
the price of the American-pressed LPs.   More than one Latin
music label has gone bankrupt or abandoned the market due to
the import problem.[19]

A particularly serious problem facing salsa in the 1980s has
been the tendency of commercial radio stations and large, corporate record companies to promote "easy listening" pop ballads at the expense of salsa.   This policy, which has been repeatedly denounced by journalists and spokesmen for inde-

---

[16] See, e.g., Ian Simpson, "Guerra Musical en Puerto Rico: Rock vs.
Salsa," in *Noticias del Mundo* 12/2/88.

[17] See Peter Manuel, *Popular Musics of the Non-Western World: An
Introductory Survey* (New York: Oxford, 1988), pp. 45-46, 49-50.   Note
that *merengue* is often categorized together with salsa as "*música
tropical*."

[18] See, e.g., Max Salazar, "Salsa Losing Popularity...," p. VL-48.

[19] See, e.g., *ibid.*, p. VL-48, regarding Fania's losses due to parallel
imports.

pendent salsa labels,[20] is one of the clearest illustrations of the potential for the music industry to manipulate rather than respond to public taste, and it thus merits some further analysis in the context of this article.

The Latin music scene in the US could be said to comprise four or five broad musical and socio-ethnic categories, which, although overlapping, remain somewhat distinct. Working-class Puerto Ricans, Cubans, and Dominicans, concentrated especially in the northeastern US, and above all New York, constitute one large group, whose traditional music of preference is what the music industry refers to as "tropical music," i.e., salsa and *merengue*. Miami-based Cuban-Americans, while also enjoying salsa, have tended to favor Americanized salsa-pop fusions. A quite separate group would be people of Mexican and Chicano descent, comprising some two-thirds of Hispanics in the US, who tend to prefer other genres, most notably Tex-Mex *rancheras*, or *música norteña*. The growing numbers of Colombians and Central American immigrants, while not averse to these musics, retain a special fondness for Colombian *cumbia* and *vallenato* music -- genres which are not very popular among Cubans and Puerto Ricans. Finally, there are newer genres -- particularly Latin jazz and Latin hip hop -- which have substantial followings in New York and elsewhere.

The demography of New York City's Hispanic population started changing in the mid-1970s, when the numerical dominance of the Puerto Ricans (formerly a majority of the area's Hispanics) was challenged by the increased influx of Dominicans, Central Americans, Colombians, Mexicans, and others, who by 1985 appear to have outnumbered the Puerto Ricans (many of whom were themselves assimilating to Anglo

---

[20]E.g., Enrique Fernandez, "Latin Notas," in *Billboard* 9/6/86, and Carlos Agudelo, same column, 4/25/87. *Billboard*'s "Latin Notas" series, as the numerous citations below suggest, is an invaluable source for data about the Latin record industry.

culture).[21]   The city's four Spanish-language radio stations (all
of which are owned by Anglo corporations) were thus faced
with   the diverse musical tastes of an increasingly mixed listening public.   One strategy would have been for the stations
to divide their programming and audiences along ethnic musical lines, i.e., by having one or two salsa stations, a Chicano-ori-
ented station, a Dominican station, and so on.   Instead, however, each station chose \to follow the monopoly capitalism
model by seeking the largest possible audience -- and, by extension, the greatest advertising revenue -- rather than target-
ing a particular ethnic audience.   In effect, each of the stations
decided to devote over half its music programming to the
common denominator music styles which are enjoyed by *some*
members of *all* the Hispanic groups -- in particular, the sentimental pop ballad (*balada romántica*, or *canción romántica*), as
sung by Julio Iglesias, José José, Emmanuel, and other practicioners of this thoroughly international genre.   Thus, for example, WKDM (formerly WBNX) and WJIT changed their
"tropical music" formats to an "easy listening" policy consisting
of   60% sentimental ballads, and 40% salsa and merengue.
Nearly identical formats were adopted by the other New York
stations (WKAQ and WADO).[22]

    Latin music DJ and journalist Max Salazar asserts that the
switch to ballad programming was largely a result of pressure
exerted by corporate conglomerates, which threatened to with-
draw advertising sponsorship unless their artists, especially
balladeers like Julio Iglesias and José Feliciano, were given

---

[21]Precise figures on the area's Latino demography are unavailable,
due to the high numbers of illegal immigrants, the incomplete census
returns, and the unavailability of 1990 census data at the time of writing
this article.   Estimates here are drawn from discrete sources, including a
conversation with Zeneida Mendes of the city's Latino Affairs office.
[22]Thus, commercial sponsors, who indirectly remain the main
determinant of programming policies, need not duplicate their
advertisements on ethnically· fragmented stations.   See Veciana-Suarez,
*Hispanic Media, USA: A Narrative Guide to Print and Electronic Hispanic
News Media in the United States* (Washington, D.C., 1987),   pp. 75-80, and
Salazar, "Salsa Losing Popularity...", pp. VL-48, VL-67.

more airplay. In particular, Coca-Cola, which owned Columbia and other labels until 1987, successfully pressured WJIT and other SLR stations to promote Iglesias and other Latin pop singers at the expense of salsa. Needless to say, it is only the large, diversified corporations like CBS and Coca-Cola, rather than small, independent producers, that are able to exert pressure on radio stations through sponsorship of advertisements. Thus, for example, by the mid-1980s, Columbia was spending nearly $13 million annually on promotion -- more than twice the amount of its closest competitor; a considerable portion of these funds are alleged to have gone into payola.[23]   Meanwhile, since outright purchase of blocks of air time is no longer legal, independent record companies have no means of influencing playlists, except through payola (which, according to informants, remains widespread).

The hegemony of the sentimental ballad, and the absence of any station devoted solely or even primarily to salsa or *merengue,* are particularly remarkable in view of the popularity of these genres in New York. The tri-state metropolitan area is home to at least two million Puerto Ricans and Dominicans, and has played a central role in the evolution of salsa itself; a large portion of the more recent immigrants from Panama, Colombia, and elsewhere are also avid salsa fans.[24] Aside from hosting innumerable summer street fairs and festivals featuring salsa, the New York area contains roughly twenty-five clubs offering live salsa or *merengue* (the "cuchifruto" circuit), and not a single club specializing in Latin pop ballads[25]; in between playing ballads and Latin soft rock, SLR stations routinely broadcast advertisements for salsa per-

---

[23]Salazar, interviewed in 6/90, and Larry Rohter, "Payola Trial is Opening Today For Successful Record Promoter," *The New York Times,* 8/21/90, pp. C13, C16.   Several Latin musicians have assured me that payola is common in SLR radio.

[24]Guzman (*op. cit.*) estimates that roughly half the current salsa fans in New York are neither Puerto Rican or Cuban, but rather Dominican, Panamanian, and Columbian.

[25]In Salazar, "Salsa Losing Popularity...", p. VL-48; also interview with Salazar in 6/90.

formances. Moreover, salsa and *merengue* record sales continue significantly to surpass sales of ballad records. Thus, it is clear that on the grassroots level, salsa and *merengue* are considerably more popular than are ballads. It is also evident that although spokesmen for New York's SLR stations often insist that they are giving the public what it wants,[26] their policy of seeking a musical common denominator is in fact significantly at odds with grassroots taste -- except, of course, insofar as the steady diet of sentimental ballads may tend to *create* a mass, homogeneous audience for that music. The hegemony of the ballad on the radio thus clearly illustrates the tendency of the corporate mass media to promote homogeneity at the expense of ethnic diversity.

Given the importance of airplay to record sales, and the fact that 98% of Hispanics in the US listen to more than thirty hours of radio a week,[27] it is not surprising that salsa record producers and musicians have vehemently and consistently denounced the SLR stations' ballad programming. Combo Records distributor Bobby Rodríguez, for example, states that Puerto Rican rock fans "were salsa fans until the radio started playing rock. If the radio played Chinese music, then they would listen to Chinese music."[28] While Rodríguez is clearly exaggerating the manipulative powers of the radio, innumerable market research studies as well as common sense do indicate that radio airplay strongly influences tastes. Accordingly, Puerto Rican salsa musicians and promoters deplore the fact that most of the island's ninety-plus radio stations follow similar formats as their US counterparts, devoting roughly 75% of their music. programming to rock and ballads.[29]

Moreover, within these stylistic formats, commercial SLR stations, like their English-language counterparts, tend to restrict their playlists to a small number of top hits, thereby

[26]See statements by WJIT and WKDM spokespersons in *ibid.*, p. VL-48.
[27]Poll cited in "Latin Notas," 8/31/85.
[28]In Simpson, *op. cit.*
[29]Tony Sabornin, "Latin Notas," 7/4/87.

further limiting the choice of musics available to listeners. The standard radio programmer's argument -- that they are satisfying the public by playing only the most popular songs -- is naturally circular, insofar as radio play is a key determinant of popularity.

The lack of diversity in SLR programming is directly related to the oligopolistic concentration of ownership of radio stations; indeed, only eight Anglo-owned corporations control over half of the nation's SLR stations, and the trend toward "networkization" has increased in recent years.[30] Several studies have demonstrated a close relationship between concentration of ownership and homogeneity of popular music broadcasting, showing that genuinely varied programming is achieved only through diversity of ownership or, in some cases, public ownership.[31] Advertising reinforces the trend toward blandness and homogeneity, through the sponsors' goal of a unified mass market, and their general desire to target more affluent listeners.

Many commercial SLR stations, aside from downplaying salsa, have deliberately blacklisted certain performers. Rightwing Cuban exiles, several of whom are powerful figures in radio broadcasting, have effectively banned the music of Oscar d'León, Rubén Blades, and Willie Colón from the airwaves in Miami and elsewhere -- d'León, for visiting Cuba in 1983, and Blades and Colón for the anti-imperialist message of some of their songs. As mentioned above, other stations have chosen to shun the music of singers like Blades simply because it is too

---

[30] Carlos Agudelo, "Latin Notas," 3/31/90, and Jorge Reina Schement and Loy Singleton, "The Onus of Minority Ownership: FCC Policy and Spanish-Language Radio," in *Journal of Communication* 31/2, 1981, p. 80. The latter also note that over 75% of Spanish-language radio stations, and 90% of the larger such stations, are Anglo-owned.

[31] See, e.g., Eric Rothenbuhler and John Dimmick, "Popular Music: Concentration and Diversity in the Industry, 1974-1980," in *Journal of Communication* 32, winter 1982, pp. 143-49, or Ben Bagdikian, "The U.S. Media: Supermarket or Assembly Line?," in *ibid.*, 35/3, summer 1985, pp. 97-109.

"controversial" -- i.e., because, unlike most American popular music, it does attempt to address social reality.[32]

While commercial, corporate-owned SLR stations have tended to neglect salsa in their search for a homogeneous, apolitical mass audience, alternative listener-supported stations have not been constrained by any such policies and have in fact played important roles in promoting salsa. In New York, WKCR (Columbia Univ.), WBAI (Pacifica), and WBGO have all featured influential and sophisticated salsa and Afro-Latin programs for many years. In Los Angeles, where there is virtually no salsa on commercial radio, the non-profit college station KXLU broadcasts extensive, ad-free salsa programs.

In late 1988 the amount of salsa programming on a few New York SLR stations increased somewhat, partly, according to Carlos Agudelo, because of a "campaign" waged by critics, non-profit stations, and the public.[33] Meanwhile, however, it is significant that much recent salsa, as released on recordings, has been stylistically evolving in the direction of the sentimental ballad, in the form of the so-called "salsa sensual" popularized by Eddie Santiago, Lalo Rodríguez and others. Such music often consists of salsa-style versions of pop ballads, retaining the latter's sentimental texts, intimate vocal style, and essentially European formal structure, in which the responsorial, more Afro-Cuban *montuno* section is dropped, leaving only the "song"-like first section. The "salsa sensual" piece thus loses much of its improvisatory, Afro-Cuban flavor and approaches

---

[32]Thus, for example, Blades' LP "Buscando America" enjoyed prodigious commercial success despite being avoided by commercial radio stations. See "Latin Notas," see E. Fernandez, 6/1/85, and C. Agudelo, 5/20/87. Right-wing Cuban-Americans in Miami have also banned local performances of Blades and *salseros* Pete "el Conde" Rodriguez and Andy Montañez for visiting Cuba.

[33]Interview, 1/89. Shortly thereafter, the AM station WKDM switched to FM format, and in April 1990, WJIT, due to declining audience, changed to English-language "Z-Rock," playing heavy metal rock music. Salazar (interviewed in 6/90) attributes WJIT's downfall to its neglect of salsa.

much more closely the standardized song format representative of Euro-American bourgeois aesthetics.[34]   At the same time, commercial salsa texts have continued to shun social commentary and references to community concerns in favor of expressions of sentimental love and nostalgia more typical of romantic ballads (thereby leading many young Newyoricans to turn to genres like rap which remain more rooted in grassroots barrio culture).[35] Both these developments must be seen in the context of the commercial radio stations' policies of favoring the pop ballad over standard salsa.

The same dichotomy between corporate homogenization and grassroots, ethnic diversity can be seen in the operation of the Latin record industry in the 1980s.   We have outlined above some of the distinctions between the operating principles of major and independent record companies, and discussed the interaction of these tendencies with regard to salsa in the 1970s.   As we have mentioned, between the 1950s and 1980s, the majors did not aggressively involve themselves in Latin music, leaving much of the market to the more roots-oriented, specialized independents.   However, Fania's success in the 1970s had led it to operate as a major in its own right.   More importantly, in the early 1980s, the majors -- especially RCA/Ariola, CBS, A&M, and EMI -- energetically entered the Latin music industry.   While signing contracts with a few salsa groups, the majors have on the whole concentrated, like corporate radio stations, on common-denominator genres whose appeal transcends ethnic and regional markets.   Thus, they have focussed investment on pop balladeers, Latin soft rock, and "crossover" artists with both English- and Spanish-speaking

---

[34]Note that in live performance, *montunos* are invariably included. For further discussion of this aesthetic and its relation to salsa, see Peter Manuel, "Formal structure in popular music as a reflection of socio-economic change," in *International Review of the Aesthetics and Sociology of Music* 16/2, pp. 163-80.

[35]Record producer Rene Lopez, in an interview with John Murphy. Salsero Eddie Zervigón, in an interview with Murphy, characterized the current sentimental salsa texts as "*telenovelas* set to music."

audiences.[36]   The majors, as Enrique Fernandez notes, "have
brought sophisticated marketing, larger production budgets,
rapid international connections, and aggressive promotion to
the Latin scene."[37]   Such "aggressive promotion," as has been
suggested above, may well include pressuring commercial radio
stations to favor romantic ballads over salsa.

As a result, the 1980s have seen the perpetuation of the dichotomy between the homogenizing, corporate major record
companies, and the roots-oriented, specialized independents.
With the decline of Fania's monopoly and its purchase in 1980
by South American investors, regional genres like salsa,
cumbia, and *norteño* music have tended to return to the do-
main of small independent companies.   Despite airplay problems and competition from the majors, the indies have benefited in the 1980s from technological developments; the most
important of these has been the lower price of recording and
pressing technology, such that while the *average* cost of producing a record has risen, the *minimum* possible cost has fallen
substantially.[38]   Production of cassettes is even cheaper.

In the realm of salsa, the most important and successful in-
dependents in the 1980s and early 1990s have been the
Venezuelan TH ("Top Hits"), which has come the closest to re-
placing Fania's predominance, and Ralph Mercado's RMM.
Smaller independents abound, such as Montuno, RL, Lo Mejor,
West Side Latino, Ritmo, Perico, Caiman, Sarava, Vaya, and

[36]Successful "crossover" acts include crooner Julio Iglesias (who has
recorded in English), Latin rock group Miami Sound Machine, Los Lobos
(of "La Bamba" fame), and the manufactured teen fanzine band,
Menudo.   Rubén Blades has also entered the field, by singing in English,
and collaborating with Linda Ronstadt, while dramatizing the pressures
and contradictions of the entire phenomenon in his 1985 movie
"Crossover Dreams."   More recently, David Byrne and Paul Simon have
both produced salsa-style LPs.
[37]"Latin Notas," 9/1/84.   A representative "crossover" production was
CBS's Julio Iglesias-Stevie Wonder LP "Non-Stop" (1988), which, costing
over three million dollars to produce, was one of the most expensive LPs
ever made.   The album flopped.
[38]See Frith, *op. cit.*, pp. 155-56.

Pa'alante; the indies include some labels, like Bobby Valentin's Bronco and El Gran Combo's Combo Records, which are owned by artists themselves.   As noted above, the indies continue to suffer from parallel imports, Latino poverty, and the radio stations' discriminatory policies against salsa and independent labels in general.

Finally, mention must be made of Spanish-language television, which has, in the 1980s, come to include a considerable amount of music programming.   Although some salsa and *merengue* can be found on cable TV programs in New York and elsewhere, the large networks -- notably SIN-TV (Univision), which accounts for 82% of Spanish-language broadcasting in the USA -- and programs like "MTV International" have tended to favor pop ballads and Latin rock over "tropical music."   Independent salsa labels, with their regional audiences and smaller budgets, are in no position to invest heavily in the production of expensive music videos.[39]

Conclusions

Our sketch of salsa's relationship with the capitalist music industry has endeavored to suggest how the mass media have not functioned simply as neutral disseminators of music which "give the people what they want."   While responding to or exploiting popular demand are important goals of the music industry, inherent features of the industry -- and of modern capitalism in general -- have led it to promote certain genres or styles at the expense of others, thereby actively shaping mass

---

[39]In "Latin Notas," see C. Agudelo, 7/30/88, and E. Fernandez, 10/11/86.   Meanwhile, the two major Spanish-language television networks, Univision and Telemundo, have been criticized for their allegedly assimilationist, bourgeois, passively racist, and politically conservative orientation which, while reflective of the views of their Cuban-American managers and Anglo corporate owners, is markedly inconsistent with the values of the working-class Chicanos who constitute their largest single nation-wide audience. See Seth Mydans, "Spanish-Language TV Called Biased," in *The New York Times*, 7/24/89, p. C16.

taste. The industry can be seen as a site of negotiation of two opposing tendencies, with the key determinant being the control of the means of production -- in this case, the mass media. On the one hand is the *potential* for the mass media to respond to and represent all significant sections of a diverse listening public, and thus to serve as a vehicle of grassroots, democratic communication and empowerment rather than of corporate manipulation. On the other hand, the media may function in the classic manner of monopoly capitalism, wherein a few dominating corporations -- here, e.g., the major record companies -- seek to tap and, to a large extent, to *create* a homogeneous mass audience in order to achieve economies of scale on their products, or, in the case of radio stations, to attract sponsors. At the same time the corporate media may promote idolization of superstars, and song texts based on sentimentality, nostalgia, and in general, *fantasy*, rather than active expressions of the full spectrum of community and individual concerns. The net result, in such a situation, can be the exacerbation of a profound, if somewhat intangible *alienation* from one's sense of community (whether in the sense of region, ethnicity, gender, class, neighborhood, etc.).

The contradictory role of the mass media in simultaneously promoting and combatting such alienation in music is particularly evident in the case of salsa. We have seen how the corporate-controlled media -- commercial radio stations and multinational record companies -- have tended to promote common-denominator music styles, especially the pop ballad, at the expense of salsa, which is disseminated more energetically by independent record companies and non-profit radio programs. The corporate goal of tapping or creating a large, homogeneous market, although often denied by spokespersons, is occasionally articulated, as by one executive who noted, "The romantic ballad unifies the market, and salsa divides it."[40] Such practices illustrate the observation, taken as axiomatic in communi-

---

[40]In "Latin Notas," E. Fernandez, 3/3/84.

cation studies, that oligopolistic concentration of ownership of the mass media leads to homogeneity and blandness of content.

Salsa is, of course, a commercial, standardized popular music, and the small record companies promoting it are capitalist enterprises just like their rivals, the majors. As with other pop musics, only a minority of salsa songs assume socio-political stances or address controversial topics. At the same time, salsa, unlike the ballad, is a roots-oriented, regional genre intimately tied to its particular constituency. While *salseros* often endorse commercial products, there is little attempt to build superstar images around the performers; rather, the prevailing image is of unpretentious "men of the people." Live performances at dance clubs remain the heart of the salsa scene, and many salsa album covers routinely give the telephone numbers of the group's booking agent, reflecting the local orientation of the production. Moreover, despite the textual blandness encouraged by the larger record companies, many salsa texts, especially in the early years of the genre, have concerned local events and served, in their own fashion, to reiterate and strengthen a sense of local ethnic community.[41] Yet, as we have seen, the more that salsa has been dependent on large record corporations rather than grassroots indies, the more the music industry -- including Fania in its peak years -- has attempted to obscure the social origins and topical contemporaneity of salsa, preferring to promote the music as a bland, decontextualized pop genre.

Salsa in this sense may be contrasted with the pop ballad, whether in Spanish or English. Ballads are generally accessed through the media rather than in live performance. The genre is designed to appeal to an amorphous, homogeneous, international mass audience rather than a unified, local community, while listeners are further alienated from the performer by the

---

[41]See, e.g., statements by Rubén Blades and Felipe Luciano in Jeremy Marre and Hannah Charlton, *Beats of the Heart: Popular Musics of the World* (New York: Pantheon, 1985), pp. 80, 82.

aura of glamor and fashion woven around the superstar. Ballad texts, dealing exclusively with sentimental love, are oriented toward fantasy rather than any sort of social commentary or sense of community. The members of the pop ballad's listening community, indeed, are related to each other only indirectly, in their adulation of the stars. The genre as a whole could be said to promote "passive listening" which requires little aesthetic effort on the part of the listener, and is not associated with dance or any kind of group activity. In more than one sense, then, the ballad is the archetypical favored genre of a capitalist music industry which seeks at once to homogenize and atomize its audience, to cultivate passive consumers rather than active community participants, and, like bourgeois ideology in general, to obscure class antagonisms.

The data in this article thus corroborate the argument that diversity of ownership and media control is the only reliable source of diversity in content; thus, the more that the mass media are in genuinely public hands, whether via public/state control or grassroots ownership, the more will the media be potentially able to represent the ethnic and class pluralism of a given society, and the less will corporate marketing policies be able to prevent popular musics from serving as vehicles of social identity.

III

Socialism, Nationalism, and Music in Twentieth-Century Cuba

9

The Problem of Music and its Dissemination in Cuba

*It is a common assumption in the capitalist West that commu-
nist societies have never tolerated any degree of public dissent
or criticism of state activities.   Whether or not this belief has
been accurate elsewhere, such extreme censorship has never
prevailed in revolutionary Cuba.   Indeed, while public denunciation of the basic premises of the Revolution is explicitly for-
bidden, the Cuban media -- and especially the print media --
have always hosted lively debates on numerous domestic policy issues, often with trenchant criticism of bureaucratic inefficiency, mismanagement, corruption, and the like.   The Cuban
music industry has been the object of much public criticism
and discussion since its nationalization in the early 1960s, and
the following article by Leonardo Acosta is among the most articulate and balanced of such critiques.*

*On the one hand, Acosta wishes to see the Cuban music in-
dustry achieve the efficiency and responsiveness of its commercial capitalist counterparts, and he laments the tendency of
the state bureaucracy to inhibit rather than promote musical
development and vitality.   On the other hand, Acosta makes it
clear that the needed reforms should take place within the socialist framework of a state-run, albeit decentralized music industry that remains free of the evils of commercialism, corporate manipulation of taste, and the artificial promotion of fads
and superstars.   Moreover, Acosta retains a nationalistic, anti-
imperialist commitment to the revival of Cuban music and the
discriminating rejection of what he sees as the more decadent
and commercial forms of foreign popular music (such as the
sentimental ballads crooned by Julio Iglesias and his counterparts throughout the West).*

*This article, together with the preceding one, could form the
starting point for a comparison of some of the respective ad-*

vantages and disadvantages of capitalist and socialist mass media, particularly, of course, in regard to the dissemination of Cuban-style popular music in the USA and Cuba. If the corporate mass media, as in the previous essay, have often been accused of alienating consumers by promoting bland, fantasy-oriented musics aimed at a homogeneous mass market rather than localized grassroots audiences, an examination of the Cuban music industry serves to suggest some of the advantages and disadvantages of socialist media control as an alternative.

Culture industries in developed capitalist countries exhibit the four standard features of the capitalist mode of production, viz., mass production and distribution of commodities, capital-intensive technology, managerial organization of specialized divisions of labor, and maximization of profit as the criterion of success. The first three of these features are also common to developed socialist culture industries, including the Cuban music industry. The significant difference, of course, is the relative absence of profit incentives in Cuban socialism, allowing the Cuban music industry to avoid some of the evils of commercialization, while exposing it to other problems of motivation, efficiency and the like.

The state-run Cuban mass media are certainly no less centralized in ownership than the North American media. As Acosta points out, management of many aspects of the music industry is also highly centralized, leading to various sorts of bureaucratic hindrances and problems. State ownership of the media, on the one hand, can lead to repressive censorship of the arts or, alternately, to the implementation of enlightened cultural policies; as Acosta notes, some of the policies of the Cuban music industry -- such as the promotion of Afro-Cuban musics -- have been both laudable in intent and successful in realization. Further, freed from overt market pressures, the socialist media have no inherent need to fabricate superstars, to promote homogenization rather than diversity, or to cheapen and commercialize authentic folk or minority musics. By the same token, however, as Acosta observes, the lack of profit in-

centives hinders the motivation of the media to respond to public taste and leads to a pervasive inefficiency; similarly, he illustrates how the lack of accountability, coupled with bureaucratic sloth and condescension, can even lead to a sort of "commercialization" and facile promotion of superstars -- phenomena reminiscent of the capitalist media, even though the causes for their appearance in socialism may be different.

While a few of the details in this article are dated, Acosta feels that, as of mid-1991, the situation and problems he describes herein are essentially the same as they were a decade before. While his digression regarding the role of music in cinema and television may be of only indirect relevance to a study of the Cuban mass media, Acosta's article is well worth reading for its insightful and representative Marxist perspective on the problems and prospects of the Cuban music industry as of 1983.

9

The Problem of Music and its Dissemination in Cuba

Leonardo Acosta

Since more than a decade there has been much written and
said in our country about a crisis, alleged or real, in the realm
of popular Cuban music.   On various occasions I have commented on this question, arguing initially that this "crisis" was
more apparent than real, and that it derived largely from
problems of dissemination and organization and not from a loss
of creativity, or a paralysis or decline in the quality of our musicians.   I also asserted that this apparent crisis was most acute
in the years 1967-73.[1]   But some of my conclusions of that
period are no longer totally valid and must be revised.   Let us
recapitulate.

The years between 1959 and 1967 were musically very
rich.   In the realm of popular music, we may recall that those
years served to do justice to many talents that before the triumph of the Revolution had not received the opportunities

---

[1] I have addressed this question particularly in the work "Eterna
juventud de nuestra música popular," in *Revolución y Cultura* (66),
2/88.   Nevertheless, at the time that article was written (1978), we were
not witnessing the danger that now seems very real, i.e., the possibility
that many musicians, facing the prolongation of situations which we
are describing here, may sacrifice creativity for convenience and
conformity.   That is, they may waste their talent in a music which will
be (and in some cases already is) equivalent to the "commercial" music
in the capitalist countries.

they deserved, because of the commercial and discriminatory mechanisms of the capitalist disseminating apparatus, that was itself dependent on the Yankee "entertainment industry." (For example, it was in those years, specifically the late 1940s, that the genre *filin* [sentimental songs, from "feeling"] arose in proletarian circles.) Furthermore, in the years following the Revolution, there arose a number of influential "new rhythms," namely, the *mozambique, pilón*, and *pacá*. At the same time there appeared new foreign trends, above all, the international success of the Beatles in 1964, although they were scarcely heard in Cuba until 1970, when a new generation, with new demands and tastes of their own, arose as a listening public.

It was precisely around 1967-70 that this discussion of the supposed "crisis" arose, which I attributed, as far as I could ascertain, to two basic factors: the "self-blockade," which made us deaf to what was going on abroad, and the creation in 1968 of a centralized system of contracting which disjointed musical development and destroyed the normal forms of contact between the public and the popular musicians. The other aspect of this situation -- that is, the scarce dissemination of our music abroad, and its consequent loss of weight in the international market -- was due, as is worth repeating, to the cultural blockade imposed by the Yankee capitalist consortia, which, before 1959, controlled our musical production, in the process helping themselves to most of the profits.

Nevertheless, I insist that it was inappropriate to speak of inertia or a crisis, as 1967 saw the creation of the Orquesta Cubana de Música Moderna (from which emerged Irakere [a highbrow dance music group]) and other similar ensembles in the provinces. Two years later came the group Van Van (preceded by Revé), which would come to introduce important rhythmic and timbral changes in dance music. And in the same year (1969) commenced the work of the Grupo de Experimentación Sonora [GES], whose influence on subsequent music has been greater than is generally acknowledged. In connection with this group, the subsequent initiators of the *nueva trova* movement were already creating a new style of *canción*, and from this period would come some of their most renowned songs.[2]

The problem then was essentially that the musical mass media -- radio, records, and TV -- were not understanding what was happening and were continuing along the old schemes and styles; meanwhile, the national cinema (ICAIC, which was now allied with *nueva trovadores* and had organized the GES) could only confirm that film was the least suitable mass medium for the dissemination and popularization of music (except for in cases like the Yankee industry, as we will discuss). We can even affirm that, inherently, music plays an essentially marginal role in this medium. The proof of this is that GES itself failed to achieve significant popularity during its creative peak -- much of which was devoted to creating scores for dozens of ICAIC films --, and was already dissolving by the time it started to receive recognition via records and the radio.[3] Other new groups emerged a little later, which could be called "modern," "experimental", or "contemporary" (labels which can be regarded as questionable); these received no more attention than did the GES from the mass media, or from nightclubs, live variety shows, and the like (although these latter are not strictly mass media).

Around the first half of the 1970s appeared a number of different groups: Los Dadas were the most distinguished interpreters of rock music, although they offered nothing new in terms of Cuban music; Irakere, by contrast, introduced substantial innovations without abandoning the essence of our music; the vocal quartet Tema IV, who were *nueva trova* participants, joined the group Síntesis, which added electronic sonorities to our *canción*. Also appearing at this time were other, quite different groups, such as Algo Nuevo, Opus-13,

---

[2] Leonardo Acosta, "Presencia del Grupo de Experimentación Sonora," in *El Caimán Barbudo* (89), 4/75.

[3] See, in Acosta, *Del tambor al sintetizador*, "La música, el cine, y la experiencia cubana."

Arte Vivo, Afro-Cuba, Girón, Yaguarimú, and Septiembre 5, among others.   The publicity which these groups received, with the exceptions of Algo Nuevo and Irakere (after remarkable international successes), has been scanty if compared to that received by more traditional interpreters of our music.   And in spite of the fact that the most distinguished groups and soloists have made important foreign tours, there still exists a serious problem in terms of the contact our musicians have with *their natural public*, which is that of our own country.   We may also recall that there have been many recordings of these groups, but they have generally been too late in coming, too expensive, and of poor quality.   And radio and TV?   The question is obligatory, and the general opinion appears to blame everything on these two media, and particularly on TV, which has become a scapegoat for our musical problems.   There are those who believe that television is a sort of panacea which can resolve everything (or, by contrast, ruin everything), and who ignore the fact that the basis of the mass media is the interaction between them.   These media form a sort of network or chain in which each link transmits to the others the tensions originating in any one of them.

The "Chain" in Capitalism; Possibilities in Socialism

In capitalist countries, and especially in the USA, where the mass media are almost totally in the hands of large corporations, the interaction between the different media assumes characteristics of a veritable chain or network, in which each medium plays a specific role of greater or lesser importance in a given realm.   For example, the norm is that musicians, singers, and other figures of the entertainment world start their careers in nightclubs, musicals, or other nocturnal performances.   The trial by fire which determines the leap to popularity is the recording of the initial disc (first a single, then an LP).   The record's success, at the same time, will depend on the dissemination it receives on the radio, and, of course, on the publicity measures undertaken by the promoters.   The record-radio interrelation is the most important, and is the crucial link in the chain, and accordingly, there is already a long history of shenanigans between the record producers and the disc jockeys, due to the practice of bribing in which even some government officials have been involved.[4]

Such expensive media as cinema and television, with rare exceptions, constitute the last steps in the musical idol's ascent to fame in capitalist society. Due to the commercial risks inherent in the high production costs, cinema and television prefer to run the minimum risks possible by using figures whose popularity is already established and guaranteed. Television is particularly conservative in this respect, for two reasons: (1) as opposed to cinema, which initially had to create its own stars, television emerged at a time when all the markets in the entertainment world were full, such that its only resource was the novelty of the medium itself, and (2) the television programs, situated in more or less "strategic" time-slots, had to contend with fierce competition, such that any error of judgement could result in a loss of viewers and a subsequent decrease in the sacrosanct rating. We may recall, as an example of the extreme conservatism of TV, the case of the superstar Elvis Presley, who could only make his debut on television after becoming the hottest item in the other media, i.e., records, radio, and, soon after, cinema.[5]

The primacy of the record in the Yankee music industry (as in other capitalist countries) is indisputable, and corresponds to the displacement of cinema by music as a center of popular or pseudo-popular culture. In 1973, an important pivotal year, the sale of records and tapes in the USA reached two billion dollars, while the profits of cinema were only $1,600,000, and those of sports, that other staple of entertainment, only

---

[4] See Steve Chapple and R. Garofalo, *The history and politics of the music industry* (Chicago: Nelson-Hall, 1977), and John Morthland, "The payola scandal," in *The Rolling Stone illustrated history of rock and roll* (Rolling Stone Press, 1976).

[5] I have discussed the early years of Elvis's rise in "Los inicios de rock," in *Revolución y Cultura* (68), 4/78.

reached $600 million. But what happens if we compare music with television, the strongest medium? In the first place, we see that television's profits from commercials rose in 1973 to $4.4 billion, that is, surpassing profits of records and tapes. Nevertheless, this figure does not indicate that aside from dramas, serials, films, and telecomedies, television also broadcasts music, and many of the commercials are for musical programs. Nor does the figure take into account that the Yankee radio broadcasts news and recorded music almost exclusively, because of which the vast majority of radio advertising is connected with music programming.

Apart from the aforementioned, other data indicate that music surpasses cinema, *including television*, as the main vehicle of popular culture, particularly among the young. This is especially clear if we look at the *commercial indices*, although we recognize that, at least potentially, television can remain the most influential at the time of determining guidelines of behavior, due to its much broader informational range and the inherent power of the visual image. But economically, we repeat, music still surpasses TV if we take into consideration not only the sale of tapes, records, and cassettes, but also other items: thus it is that the data of 1972 show $1.9 billion in sales of tapes and records; $1.5 billion in related advertisements; $861 million in sales of recorders; $577 million in sales of record players; $983 million in sales of radios, and one billion dollars in sales of instruments. That is, without counting sheet music and other minor sectors, music totaled profits of $7.376 billion in the USA in 1972 alone.[6]

Since then, as we can show, music has constituted a highly complex industry, diversified and compartmentalized in the modern Yankee "society of consumption." Within this industry, the key factors are the agents and managers, the concert promoters, the critics, the specialized music press, the retail stores, the distributors, the regional programmers, the talent scouts,

---

[6] In Chapple and Garofalo, *op. cit.*

and record producers -- in sum, all a jumbled human conglomerate forming part of an interlocking industry concentrated largely in a country where monopolies tend continually to dominate all sectors of production. And we can also show now that it is the recording companies that dominate this network of businesses. We may consider a few examples. CBS includes radio and television networks, record and tape recording, the manufacture and sale of musical instruments (including a chain of stores), and music publishing houses. This musical emporium also operates Pacific Stereo hi-fi stores, the production of Fender electric guitars, of Steinway pianos, of Rhodes electric pianos, of Rogers drums, and above all, of Columbia records and tapes. The latter accounts for less than a quarter of CBS's global earnings, but remains the pivot, and the central factor, of CBS's musical activity. Other record companies (Capitol, Polygram, MCA, ABC, Warner, RCA, etc.) have distinct characteristics which space does not allow us to explore here, but all are distinguished by being diversified conglomerates, and at the same time by the condition of being companies emerging from the fusion or acquisition of other companies. But, above all, they depend more and more on the sale of records, especially in terms of their "prestige," that is, their public image.[7]

In contrast with capitalism, music in the socialist mass media need not follow the dictates of the network or "chain" we

---

[7] Capitol, for example, is today the younger sister of the British EMI, and sustains itself primarily by the Beatles and other English groups; Polygram arose from the merging of the British electronics conglomerate Philips, Deutsche Grammophon of Germany, and various American record companies like MGM, Mercury and Polydor; MCA arose from a merger of Decca and Kapp Records, but today forms part of a corporation dedicated to the "entertainment industry" and includes, among other concerns, Universal Films and TV, the Spencer Gift chain of stores, Yosemite National Park, the third largest music publisher in the USA, and the cemeteries (!) of Arlington and Mount Vernon, Virginia. ABC, now a vast conglomerate, originates from the fusion of various small record companies; but perhaps the most complex and diversified conglomerates are Warner Communications and RCA, which include everything from radar to refrigerators, and, of course, all types of music. [Ed.: Columbia Records has since been bought by Sony.]

have discussed, although some aspects of these latter do pertain, with some differences. Records (and cassettes), like radio, continue to account for most of mass mediated music, especially among the young. But radio depends to a much lesser degree on the record industry, and is not subject to its manipulative effects, thus allowing a consequent increase of recording possibilities by the radio stations themselves. Cinema, for its own part, can attempt new forms and depart from the routine of "film music" of capitalism, as has been done in the USSR, Poland, East Germany, Czechoslovakia, and Cuba, for example. Meanwhile, television, like radio, is able to take its own initiatives by, for instance, highlighting young artists not yet established by the other media. All of this, of course, within certain limits.

The Cuban situation presents certain special characteristics. Budgetary problems of infrastructure have restricted the principal mass media (especially the record industry); but not all of the problems encountered in making the best use of musical activity can be attributed to limitations in the material base. There has been a failure to achieve, as indicated above, the level of international dissemination of our music that existed in the 1950s, due to the role played then by the Yankee corporations, which later joined the blockade. What is less easily explained is that the Cuban record industry has not even succeeded in establishing a thriving market in its own country.

Adventures and Misadventures of the Cuban Record

Apart from the factors mentioned above, such as affect the material base of the record industry, there exist others which have had a negative impact on the industry, which happens to be the heart of the music dissemination in any country, and of the music of that country in the international market. As it is, a national industry like ours cannot aspire to compete with the gigantic multinationals referred to above, which, in the course of diverse mergers and acquisitions with other companies internationally, have come to enjoy a complete monopoly in the capitalist world. But there does exist an international market for our music -- with different demands according to the area in question -- which has not been satisfied to its potential, due to failures on our part. What is especially deplorable is that even the internal demand has not been satisfied -- a factor which has hurt the entire situation of the other mass media.

One factor which has impeded our record production has been the loss of the ratings and surveys -- however imperfect their results may be -- established by capitalism to determine the popularity of a performer, genre, or any musical entity, and by extension the tastes, preferences, and habits of the public. If indeed these ratings, based on surveys, sales figures, and methods typical of Anglo-Saxon empiricism, are neither entirely trustworthy nor suited to the standards that should prevail in a socialist society, neither is their complete rejection beneficial, inasmuch as such a policy does not sufficiently root out the criteria used in those old methods. Perpetuating those criteria -- without relying on the more or less "objective" bases of empiricism -- leads to pure subjectivity, and can be still more harmful when it is directed by those in charge of production. But if we entirely reject surveys and the like, we deny ourselves the positive contributions, however relative, which could be found in them. This loss becomes worse when we do not substitute anything for the surveys; it would be best if we were to complement those methods with others, such as the establishment of quality indices, technical levels, etc., which would require genuine collaboration between the art schools, conservatories, evaluation committees, teams of specialist assessors, and other entities.

Of course, none of these measures would constitute in itself a panacea: the establishment of an evaluation system, for example, which has already been done fairly successfully, is only the first necessary step, whose results always would be provisional and subject to change, although they would certainly afford some useful indices. In all, the record industry can not rely only on a device like that, nor can it use a single criterion to establish a policy which would satisfy all demands. We have referred also to material problems in the infrastructure. On top of these are problems like the marketing and distribution of the product, which for a long time has been out of the control of the record industry, although this problem may be in the process of resolution. There also exists the question of pricing the records, which are generally too expensive; this problem, of course, tends to be aggravated by the scarcity and high price of record players -- a dilemma which, even if it could be at least partially solved in the next few years, has already contributed to the visible decline in the image of records and record players in face of the growing appeal and prestige of cassettes and tape players. The rise of cassettes, although acquiring special dimensions in Cuba, is a universal phenomenon, and we can prepare ourselves to face reality: the tape recorder and cassette are increasingly turning records into "collectors' items" around the world.

So far, most of these problems have to do with a set of factors which are external to and not within the direct control of our record industry. Nevertheless, there are others which do depend directly on the quality of its management. For example, the process of releasing a record has been considerably shortened in recent years by eliminating bureaucratic obstacles (we have known cases in which two years have passed between the date of an album's recording, and its eventual appearance for sale -- a delay which, in the realm of popular music, is simply fatal). The record producers must also be faulted for the selection and, often, the realization, of music. The selection of performers and of music has, in general, maintained a frankly conservative direction, although we should admit that in recent years there have been attempts at renovation and even experimentation. Also, it is certain that this conservative line, that is, the tendency to disseminate almost exclusively traditional styles and "canonized" artists -- although in many cases nobody knows why or by whom they were canonized -- has not come solely from the record industry, but from the mass media in general.

The Interaction or Divorce of the Media

We have posited the interrelation between records and radio as the basic axis of the disseminating chain, especially in capitalism, but also to a large extent in socialism. The significance of this axis is evident in the fact that in Cuba, the occasions when musical dissemination has been worst have been characterized by a general absence of collaborative ties between the different media. Contacts between record producers and disc jockeys have not been lacking, but they have not had the weight which they should have. In general, it is the record industry which would profit the most from collaboration, since the radio always has the possibility, however under-utilized, of doing its own recordings. But the radio, for its part, could also significantly benefit by the often exclusive broadcast of recordings about to be released by the record companies, or of recordings which have exceptional quality or a special historic quality. In the last instance, this sort of collaboration will always avoid a useless duplication of works.

Such considerations can apply equally, with some qualifications, to television and cinema, and even to live performances in theaters or nightclubs, because these contexts, although not mass media, share the quality of being audio-visual, while not being restricted to the simple emission or transmission of music. Therefore, radio has the possibility of transmitting either recorded or live music, as opposed to the record (whose merits are obviously of another sort: preservation, ability to be repeated, etc.). The potentialities of television are similar to those of radio, although greater: live broadcast, or live with recorded background, videotape, etc. And in cinema, as we have noted, music still maintains only a marginal position, and if it is true that cinematic documentary and reporting has achieved remarkable levels in Cuba, there remains the ineluctable fact that the public rarely attends cinema to hear music.

Television and radio, furthermore, must be distinguished from live, *in situ* music programs which are not transmitted or reproduced by the mass media.   It is useful to regard television and radio as the final links of the network or chain, of which the live performance constitutes the first link, and is at the same time the principal practice school in which traditionally singers and popular musicians are shaped, although -- we repeat -- this is not an absolute rule, especially in a socialist society.[8] What is essential is the *interaction* of the different media to effect the greatest dissemination of the best in our music. In capitalism, this interaction often signifies subordination or absorption of one medium by another, and sometimes includes practices like bribery; in our society, by contrast, interaction should be able to be based on collaboration, rather than on the separation of or mutual ignorance between the diverse media.

Examples of this lack of cooperation abound: we have noted how around 1970, perhaps the most fertile period of *nueva trova*, the genre's most creative exponents were marginalized by the principal mass media.   We can also recall two equally negative phenomena, whose consequences we are still suffering, and which are to some extent complementary: on the one hand, the "dislocation," around the same time, in the functioning of nightclubs, and, on the other hand, the nearly permanent separation of this circuit from its principal stars, who performed, during this period, almost exclusively abroad.   Thus it was that a set of musicians, singers, and groups remained isolated from their natural media, which denied the public the .possibility of seeing their performances in person and thereby limited the size of their audience, especially among the young.[9]

---

[8] Let us not forget the busy regional concourses for amateurs in capitalism itself.   With a different conception, there exist television programs in the socialist world (for example, in Hungary) to give recognition to new values in music.   Cuban television has achieved undeniable success in the program *Todo el mundo canta*, even if other similar programs have been less successful in this regard.

[9] With the creation of this circuit of foreign performances, and artists who spend part of the year abroad, there only remained the opportunity of seeing them in brief, and often poorly-produced

Meanwhile, there was the attempt to meet the needs of the nightclubs and other activities by means of an office which centralized all contracting, like a sole corporation. The creation of this central body had a markedly unfavorable effect on the development of our popular music. Indeed, this office's management -- despite the apparent rationalization of the process through its centralization -- was converted into an entity even more irrational than the artistic personality itself. Thus, in spite of the many decentralizing initiatives adopted since around 1977, this agency tediously goes on conducting evaluations today as if it were issuing tickets of passage. In many cases, bureaucratic attitudes and procedures have impeded the formation of new musical groups with real creative potential and solid technique; such red tape constantly obstructs musical innovation, while further hindering the granting of formal professional status to groups (even when all the individual members possess such status) and the switching of musicians from one group to another; in general, this office obstructs the dynamic processes which has made possible the development of vital movements of popular music in Cuba and other countries.

One can add to the above the problem -- somewhat improved as of late -- of the many professional musicians who managed to remain inactive, while still collecting their salaries, with the consequent damage to the economy and to musical development in general. Further, in the absence of indices of popularity -- with their attendant implications regarding demand in the artistic sector --, and the impossibility of direct hiring by the tourist *empresas*, the mass media, or other organizations, sometimes one used to encounter the worst groups or soloists working, while others much superior (including high-level graduates of conservatories) remained inactive. Particularly damaged by this situation were live performance venues and nightclubs, many of which often found themselves unable to present live music. No less affected were radio and

moments on television, or hearing them in recordings subject to all the discographic problems we have discussed here.

television, which also depended on the central contracting agency to offer their daily musical programs. The same has not happened with the record industry, whose only advantage consists of being able to make arrangements for any musician without significant red tape involved.

Television: Scapegoat or Prime Offender?

For reasons which merit a separate study, television occupies a large part of the leisure time of our people, such that it has tremendous impact in some circles, including music. And by the importance it has for us, it can serve as an index, a barometer, a mirror (or perhaps a mirage) of Cuban musical activity, with the result that the viewer is accustomed to judge, however erroneously, our musical progress by what he hears and sees on television, and, conversely, he judges television in terms of what is happening with Cuban music. This situation has become frankly harmful for television, for various reasons.

Being situated in the center of public attention, the "mass medium *par excellence*" of our time can be regarded equivocally as that of greatest importance in musical activity, and is, as such, the object of the most lavish praise or pointed criticism. In my case, it has been criticisms which have prevailed, for various reasons, some of which I have outlined, *viz.*: (1) the "crisis" of the period 1967-74; (2) the coalescence of music programs into formal stereotypes (hence the comment that "they all look alike"), and (3) the reiteration of the same "renowned" artists, although the means by which they achieved this "renown" may be genuine or dubious. The increasing role that television has come to play in Cuban leisure time has changed its programming in such a way as to lead critics unanimously to denounce it, often justifiably, though superficially. Superficially, because television *is not an autonomous, closed entity*, as bourgeois sociologists have held it to be, but rather *the simple reflection of a much larger socio-cultural reality*. And if we accept that it is to be the ultimate link in the chain of musical dissemination, we need to assess it as part of a global context in which our country is involved.

Two of the primary criticisms of television have been fair: all the music programs have resembled each other in terms of format and style, and the artists are invariably the same, presenting, one time or another, the same items of their repertoire. The first problem resides exclusively with the TV producers, who follow tired formulas, in a situation which has started to be remedied with the emergence of new programs, especially youth programs and participatory ones, although decisive steps in other directions are still needed.[10]   In contrast, the second criticism -- the reiteration of the same artists and songs -- is only attributable to television producers in the final stage. Even if we do conclude that our television has established a star system, analysis would reveal that the charmed circle of stars consists of the same artists who represent our country in international events (as chosen by the Agéncia Cubana de Artistas); the same who perform in big concerts and on prestigious occasions (as chosen by the Centro de Contrataciones and the Dirección Nacional de Música); the same whom we see on the covers of records in our country; and, finally, they are the same whom we hear daily on the radio.   Our television, in a word, *does no more than reinforce the images and situations created by other media and in other spheres.*

We should also note that television finds itself dependent on other institutions for contracting singers and musicians.   This dependence affects not only TV programming, but the other factors mentioned, like the repetition of the same songs of an artist's repertoire, inasmuch as the decisions in this regard are not entirely those of the television producers, which provide a

---

10 In my opinion, the program *Te doy una canción*, based on a *nueva trova* which has been going on for years behind the scenes, has been one of the most consistently creative and ground-breaking shows, in spite of having to deal with the hostility of some of the performers themselves to television as a medium.   In terms of popularity, there is no doubt that the top show is *Para bailar.*

mere service, but of the *empresa* to which the artists belong. Nevertheless, our press appears to believe that it is the directors of the music programs who are guilty of the decisions and control all aspects of the music shows. In fact, these producers have little to do with promoting stars or hits, and instead of condemning them as if they were omnipotent, we should question the attitudes of all those people who *really* determine, in greater or lesser degree, these matters, from those who decide -- or used to decide -- which group or musician should receive what professional grade (*plantilla*), to those who determine which artists should represent us in foreign concerts, or which should be permitted to record an LP, while not excluding, of course, the directors of musical programs on radio and television. The problem is that the practice of making decisions without relying on parameters or definite indices, as we have seen, tends to result in decisions being taken just on the basis of personal preference, or even worse, guessing who or what should be "catchy." The latter practice is a commercial and patronizing attitude, and constitutes a dangerous leap of faith, as the taste of the public can vary and fluctuate constantly, while that of a particular individual tends to stabilize itself over the years, or even to *atrophy*. We must remember that *the individual gets old, while the public always rejuvenates itself.*

There are other problems specific to television, regarding its technical aspects and its expressive language, which demand detailed consideration. Although television is characterized as an audio-visual medium, like cinema, this term can be misleading, since the visual aspect -- the immediacy, expressivity, or peculiarity of the image -- undoubtedly occupies the primary position, at the expense of the audio part. Elsewhere we have addressed the secondary role of music in cinema (and of the soundtrack in general), a subordination which starts with the productive process itself and is reflected in the final product, including the credits.   Something similar happens in television, with some differences.[11]

The Program vs. the Sound:
"Musicalization" and "Representation"

The phrase "TV enters through the eyes" is not gratuitous, but rather is a simple and graphic way of reiterating that the language of television, like that of cinema, is above all a language of visual images.   For this reason the term "visual arts," as opposed to plastic arts, has come into common usage, to include media like photography, cinema, and television, that have become so important in our epoch.   But if so far the subordination of music -- and of sound in general -- to the visual image is a phenomenon common to cinema and television, the problem is very different in each case, because the methods of production and realization produce not only different results, but contrary ones.   In a dramatic film, the music is entrusted to the composer at the last hour, being added in the final editing process of the film, when the soundtrack is added, and the music will be mixed -- sometimes in a conflicting way -- with the dialogues, effects, and all sorts of sounds.   In television the problem is more complex, except when broadcasting films or material already filmed.   For example, in a teledrama produced in studios, one already uses canned music, or music specially composed and previously recorded; the director concentrates, as ever, on the visual aspect, the image and movement, and the sound plays an even more secondary role than in film, especially when its emission is simultaneous with the camerawork, instead of resulting all together in an *a posteriori* montage.[12]

---

[11] Since the beginning of television, the first writers who have addressed this problem have been those conscious of these phenomena, such as Richard Hubell, in *Television: programming and production* (New York: Rhinehart and Co., 1945).   In footnote 3 above I have cited my own work on this subject.

[12] L. Acosta, "Consideraciones sobre dos medios masivos: el cine y la TV", in *Verde Olivo* 20-22, 1977.

We might think that in musical and variety programs on television the situation would differ, and in some ways it may. Nevertheless, any attentive listener can note the difference between the version of a piece on a record and its equivalent on television. This is not only because of the infinite resources which a modern recording studio has (multiple tracks, playbacks, echo effects, etc.), but also because of another factor which practically no one takes into consideration: the TV program itself. The inherent structure and the dynamic of a television program, with all the factors that go into it (cameras, lighting, set design, scripts, animation) and which affect the proceedings in the studio along with the sound, all conspire against the fidelity of the sound. For example, if we take into account that the area in a studio is limited, and that only part of that (the so-called "useful area") will appear on screen, we can deduce immediately that an orchestra or musical ensemble should have a location which, if ideal from the point of view of the visual image, may well conflict with that needed for proper sound, with the correct positioning of microphones and other audio equipment.

Another matter is the intrinsic power of the televisual image, which has come to be called "hypnotic," although exaggeratedly so, by sociologists and mass media theorists, and which undoubtedly insures that the impact of the visual image prevails over the sound. This dominance creates a situation, as for the interpretation of music, which is generally ignored as a secondary factor in concerts and other live performances on television (a bit less so in cinema) and which doesn't pertain to performances on radio or records: we are referring to the need to *use all the inherent resources of the image in order to strengthen the impact of the music*.[13] That is, in a televised

---

[13] We are not referring here to the technical and acoustic factors which also contribute to the differentiation of the phenomena of musical reception that can obtain with different mass media, because we regard these as factors which are continually being diminished by technical advances, while the aesthetic and psychological indolence remains intact.

music program one finds an extreme situation which comes to be the exact opposite of that which we encounter in a musical program on film, on a TV serial, or a theatrical work.

When a score is composed or an extant recording is used as incidental or background music, the music is used to strengthen or complement the effect of the dramatic scenes. In broadcasting live performances on TV, the process is the reverse, i.e., the visual image should be used to realize the music. If in a film or televised drama we have a problem of *musicalization*, now we find ourselves facing a phenomenon which we can call, for lack of a better term, *representation*. It becomes a more complex phenomenon than its opposite, i.e., when a dramatic work on film or TV has the image as its primordial element, and the music as an accessory. When presenting a musical performance on TV, we find that, in contrast, *the principal factor, which is the music, competes with the visual image*, as it is the latter which is the predominant factor in television, and that with the most importance in programming, independently of the type of program. To apply this concept to a concrete situation, we can imagine a singer, instrumentalist, or ensemble in front of the cameras, with the television audience at the other end of the informational circuit. If the image on the television screen remains static, one's interest wanes rapidly, influencing even the appreciation and perceived value of the music itself. It thus becomes imperative to vary the camera angles in order to maintain the attention of the spectator at its optimum level (which implies that too much camera motion can also be counterproductive for the music's transmission, since it would tend to cheapen the music, as happens in some Western European short films). The televisual language itself, in any case, must adapt itself faithfully to the requirements of the music, following closely its internal rhythm and playing the role of a silent part, a silent counterpart.

If the medium itself tends thusly to separate the visual image of a singer, we can take as an example, over its interpretive quality or *sonic image*, especially when it comes without accreditation, before other media (radio, records), the director of the program finds himself obliged to use all his skill and resources to reduce this contradiction to the minimum. This is a most arduous task, especially in countries like our own, where a tendency to overvalue the visual image of an interpreter prevails, to the detriment of his or her genuinely important qualities.

The Crisis of Classical Music

In accordance with the above, it should be obvious that the music which stands to suffer most in its transmission on television or cinema is classical music, whether choral, symphonic, or chamber music (opera and ballet are exceptions), since televised music programs are performances conceived in terms of music and the image. Conspiring against this music are two main factors, namely the *stasis* (of the image) attending a string quartet, symphony orchestra, etc., and the *duration* of the most important works in the international repertoire, which are considerably too long, according to the standards and habits of television viewers -- standards which are promoted by the medium itself. Even in the developed countries with high musical and cultural levels, art music broadcasts are generally found only on educational or cultural channels; in countries where commercial television dominates, air time devoted to such programs is negligible, except in some government or university channels.

Symphonic music, furthermore, presents particular difficulties for televisual realization, whose proper execution requires familiarity with the work being broadcast, such that the cameras follow the lead parts (highlighting the flute during its solo, the horns or woodwinds during their parts, etc.). Accordingly, the musical material itself of a symphonic work is weakened and diluted by the lack of correspondence with the image. Two solutions to this problem would be the presentation of works rehearsed especially for the medium itself, and the presence of a musical director during the television production, who is familiar with the score and works alongside the camera director at every moment.

In our country the dissemination of symphonic, choral, and chamber music has suffered incessant decline and has come to fall into a general crisis. This crisis of art music cannot be attributed to television, since live concerts and music ensembles themselves were already in short supply, as were adequate education and serious and didactic criticism, among other things. The only medium which has responded to the need to promote this music has been the radio, thanks to the station CMBF.[14]

What are we Importing: The Genuine or the False?

Solid bases for the development of music in our country have been created in the last two decades. The greatest achievement lies, undoubtedly, in education, in the system and level of conservatories and schools. There remain details to be resolved, particularly the fundamental matter which has been tackled in symposia and other events sponsored by UNEAC, Casa de las Américas, and other institutions: namely, the systematic teaching of popular music as part of the curriculum, and conceding it the status it deserves, as we are confident will be done in the next few years. Another transcendental step for musical development has been the establishment of ideological and aesthetic bases, starting from the First National Congress of Education and Culture, and the First Party Congress, especially regarding the delineation, research, and rescue of our most valuable and genuine cultural roots, such as the documentation of our ties with other Latin American and Caribbean countries. Also established have been general lines for determining the correct assimilation of musical elements of other cultures, distinguishing the healthy influences and those which would serve

---

[14] For an appreciation of the situation of symphonic and chamber music in Cuba from 1970-77, see that written by Manuel Duchesne Cuzán in his response to a questionnaire of mine (in L. Acosta, "Con Manuel Duchesne Cuzán," in *Revolución y Cultura* (60), 8/77).

as vehicles for the penetration of neocolonial culture. At the same time, the bases for serious, scholarly, and objective music criticism have been established, in accordance with our fundamental ideological principles.

Quite clearly, the vicissitudes of our music and its dissemination show that in many cases the application of a correct policy has been inadequate, incomplete, or superficial. Some difficulties present themselves at the time of evaluating a given music, but they are those which, as with our deficient music criticism, have to do with problems discussed above. Meanwhile, meriting special attention in the realm of dissemination, is the problem of the correct discrimination between the genuine and the false in a given type of music and its eventual repercussions in our society. In this sense, we have made a correct revaluation and dissemination of traditional Latin American musics, of North American jazz, and of past and modern art musics. Nevertheless, we have failed to distinguish genuine from false on many other occasions. For example, Brazilian and Caribbean music have not been disseminated enough, and rock music has only received adequate critical treatment in a few recent radio programs.[15] As for the rest, there has been a lack of selective and informed criteria for establishing which musical products are authentic and which are simply commercial creations, fads, or by-products artificially created by the capitalist music industry.

The case of North American music has been typical, but one like it has been that of Brazil, although little attention has been paid to it. For years we rejected a lot of the best rock music -- even the Beatles; instead we were disseminating inferior commercial imitations (a situation which has subsequently improved, as mentioned above), or, even worse, we were broadcasting the worst Yankee pop music of the 1940s and '50s,

---

[15] Among these we may cite *Encuentro con la música*, from the channel Radio Progreso; in general, this station and Radio Liberación are those which have best responded to the need to disseminate good quality popular music.

which, disgracefully, we are still doing. As for Brazilian music,
we have broadcast the most contemptible kinds of pop music --
the worst examples of cultural colonization, like Nelson Nedd
and Roberto Carlos -- instead of the progressive, genuine modern music of that people, which in the last twenty years has
produced such creative artists are Vinicius de Moraes, Chico
Buarque de Hollanda, Antonio Carlos Jobim, Baden Powell,
Gilberto Gil, Edu Lobo, Caetano Veloso, María Betania, Milton
Nascimento, George Bem, Elis Regina, and many others.

Nevertheless, the most extreme and serious case, in my
opinion, is that of music from Spain, which in recent years has
exhibited a clear differentiation, although not as clear as that in
Brazil, between genuine popular music and that which I call
pseudo-pop music (commercial or stylistically dependent on
Yankee fads). The fact is that Spain, inheritor of such a rich
and diverse cultural patrimony, and tied so closely to our own
roots, is currently suffering a total penetration of the worst
Yankee pop, and has converted itself into a re-exporter of these
genres to other Spanish-speaking countries. And one of our
greatest errors has been to give carte blanche to the entrance
and dissemination of this mediocre music. Naturally, we aren't
referring to authentic artists like Paco de Lucía, Joan Manuel
Serrat, Paco Ibáñez, and others who have visited our country.
But we must note that Spanish pop performers -- from the
relatively good artists like Rafael or Nino Bravo to the worst
ones, like Julio Iglesias (who, unusually, became known first
through cinema, and only then through radio), Camilo Cesto,
Luis Gardey, La Pequeña Compañía and many others not worth
mentioning -- have exerted a nefarious influence on a number
of performers in Cuba itself. A few critics have sounded the
alarm about this, but many others start from the false thesis
that everything Spanish forms part of our own heritage, without noting that the commercial music which Spain produces
and exports today is nothing but a mediocre imitation of the
spurious products of the Yankee culture industry.

The fact that singers who follow such fads can now be found in Cuba has had negative repercussions on our radio and television broadcasts. Singers who follow this line and who sometimes are selected to represent us in international festivals obtain a certain preference in the "taste" of record, television, and radio producers. And when someone protests against the uniformity of such programs, in reality he is protesting against the practice of some director who is guided by these questionable criteria, who converts into "stars" whatever performers adapt passably to these international fads and sometimes even win prizes (generally "golden") in some event or other. It is clear that if a variety program restricts itself to such "artistes" who all sing the same (and it is impossible to distinguish any such singer as Mexican, Spanish, Italian, or French), the result can only be an monotonous atrocity. Also conspiring against the same concept of *varieties* is another tendency, very common among us, to pigeonhole every kind of music and disseminate it in autonomous programs: *son, danzón, trova tradicional, bolero, nueva trova, música campesina*, etc. This tendency contributes to the way a director of "variety shows" limits his options according to this compartmentalization, that is, by tending to highlight precisely this amorphous and impersonal terrain of commercial pop music.

When the Exception Conspires against the Rule

Musical activity is a daily event. The dissemination of our music should also be seen as a daily activity, which naturally includes major events like festivals, concourses, homages to composers or interpreters, international concerts and the like. Nevertheless, we have committed the error of concentrating our efforts on these "special" activities at the expense of our daily work, which has occurred also in other artistic spheres, but especially in music. This is an openly negative phenomenon, inasmuch as *the exception should become the rule*, and the special events should be *consequences and results of daily activities*, and not the reverse.

The carelessness and indifference toward the daily and multifaceted musical activities, and the subordination of this work to the celebration of special events harm our music. The various concourses and festivals are useful and necessary, but they remain essentially innocuous and bear a certain conventional falseness insofar as they don't correspond to a real base, from which they should emerge like the culmination of a sustained effort. They can also be converted into a more harmful than beneficial practice when they constitute a calender of events that distracts and distances those involved in various aspects of music production -- organizational functions, artists, producers, technical equipment, material resources -- from daily and normal activities. This subordination of the daily to the special can also provoke the hastiness and consequent failure of some of these events, whose success should develop, like a natural and organic result, from the solid base of whatever kinds of well-managed daily or weekly music.

The Roots and their Fruits

A positive development (but one which we must see as an ongoing, incomplete process) is that which we can categorize under the motto of "the rescue of our roots." There is no doubt that one of the fundamental premises of a cultural policy aimed at the maximum development of our creative potential and our musical identity, should deal above all with the revitalization of the most authentic national traditions. But we cannot lose sight of the fact that all of our music represents a dialectic process, and that the conservation and revival of the traditional and genuinely original are in direct accordance with the process of renovation, of creating of the new starting from the old. Defence and revitalization of the roots (liturgical music, *son*, *danzón*, *trova tradicional*), agreed -- but this diligent and even intransigent activity must have its necessary complement in the active support of innovation, and of the artists who work, as Edgar Varese used to say, "for the man of his epoch," and even for the future. In our fatherland we have, in the realm of music, the exemplary cases of intellectuals like Fernando Ortiz,

Juan Marinello, and Alejo Carpentier, who in their time not only reappraised our great traditional music, but supported equally and without reservations the aesthetic positions of Amadeo Roldán and Alejandro García Caturla, whose music was regarded as "experimental," if not "scandalous," by the musical reactionaries and academics of their time. Today the works of Roldán and Caturla, which are characterized precisely by a genuine respect and veneration of the most authentic of our popular traditional music, are an ineradicable part of our "classics." We should also remember the advice of Ilya Ehrenburg regarding tradition: "The blind acceptance of the past is as foolish as its baseless denial. . .We cannot receive the past indifferently; it is not an inert stone, but living earth."

At present, and especially in regards to our popular music, there is not enough just homage to our past artists and the styles they represented. Our homage to them would be much more fruitful if we tied it directly to the study and assimilation of that music by our young musicians, with the ultimate goal of developing new forms which at once maintain the essential features of our roots while incorporating new elements which define our contemporaneity. Naturally, we do not lack for artists who are following such lines. The *son* has been rejuvenated in the work of Pablo Milanés, Juan Formell, Juan Pablo Torres, Emiliano Salvador, and others, just as even the *danzón* has taken modern form in works like those of Chucho Valdéz. The imperative from this point is to support young musicians and new groups which are emerging -- a practice which disgracefully seldom happens. This brings us to the matter we addressed at the start: the difficulty of forming new groups, changing personnel, the bureaucratic red tape imposed on talented young musicians emerging with the best qualifications from our schools, the shortage of (non-bureaucratic) mechanisms which could channelize the energies of those who are called upon to perpetuate and rejuvenate our great musical tradition. Once we have obtained this state of mind and managed to make it materialize in efficient measures and practices, our mass media will naturally be influenced by the phenomenon. However, we repeat, the media are only a reflection of the state of our national culture in general, and especially our music, which is evolving and thriving constantly in plains and mountains, in conservatories and popular dances; when we attain a better management of our musical resources, we will have great need of the mass media, just as we need them now, however imperfect they may be at present.

10

Institutions, Incentives, and Evaluation in Cuban Music-Making

The preceding chapter offered an insider's appraisal of the Cuban music industry, criticizing its problems and inefficiencies, while also noting its achievements and implying that any reforms should take place within the context of the socialist and nationalistic policies of the Revolution. James Robbins' essay offers a complementary view of Cuban music-making. In capitalism, musical production operates by the workings of the market, with the numerous and varied aspects of production -- from manufacture of instruments, to formation of dance bands, and commercial dissemination of music -- establishing their own forms and interaction, in a relatively spontaneous manner, according to the "invisible hand" of profit incentives, with relatively little structural need for state guidance or regulation. In socialism, and especially in a relatively centralized communism like Cuba's, all such aspects of production, as well as many aspects of amateur music-making, are governed by state bureaucracies and formalized procedures. Robbins describes the primary institutions involved in Cuban music production, focussing on the musicians' organizations and the recording and broadcast media. He then outlines the various material and ideological incentives which are designed to replace the profit motive of capitalism; further, he discusses the procedures for evaluation of musicians, recordings, and the like, outlining the manner and extent to which these procedures are intended to and do in fact replicate the supposedly "natural selection" of the free market, while avoiding the sorts of corporate manipulation documented in chapter 8.

Robbins supplements this empirical description with his own balanced evaluations of the extent to which the Cuban institu-

tions and procedures succeed, both by their own standards as well as those of the capitalist world. He concludes that judged by relatively empirical criteria of efficiency, diversity, accessibility, and the like, the Cuban music industry and amateur organizations are neither utopian models nor abject failures. Perhaps most significantly, however, he notes that Cuban communism is not to be judged merely as an "inefficient but equitable way of producing consumer goods." For indeed, the most significant characteristics -- and, one could argue, achievements -- of music-making in communist Cuba are those which are ultimately subjective and intangible, having to do with the ideological effects of the substantial elimination of commercialism and profit motives from music-making. However extensive and frustrating the inefficiencies and bureaucratic impediments engendered by public control may be, the relative liberation of art from commerce remains a unique and fundamental attainment, and one that is inherently impossible in capitalism.

1 0

Institutions, Incentives, and Evaluation in Cuban Music-making

James Robbins

In Cuba, it is the institutions of socialism that must solve two central problems in the production of music: how to get people to produce; and how to determine who will produce. These were the problems which had earlier been dealt with, however inadequately, by vesting the power to determine social roles in a market. The termination of this power by socialism necessitates other means of selecting and rewarding musicians; hence the establishment of new institutional means of providing incentives for and evaluation of musicians.

Institutional involvement in musical life does not end with production. Cuban socialist ideology has not only inherited Lenin's vanguardist ideas, but also Guevara's concept of the "new socialist man." Both imply active support for certain kinds of activity deemed socially valuable, which in practice includes amateur cultural activities such as music making. Here too, support for amateur musicians is conducted through institutional channels.

The institutional structure in Cuba must therefore serve both economic and cultural purposes. As presently conceived, these purposes are not always congruent. Consequently, some institutions are at times at odds with others, or at times even at odds with themselves.

It is the purpose of this article to consider the following questions: How does this system work? How well does it work? And how different is it, in practice, from musical production in capitalism?

The Nature and Structure of Cuban Musical Institutions

For those readers who lack experience with presently (or formerly) existing socialism, it may be somewhat difficult to grasp two distinctive features of state institutions in Cuba: their extent, and their non-monolithic character. That is, Cuban socialism is at once more and less different from contemporary capitalism than might be expected.

Although almost the entire Cuban economy is controlled by the state (apart from illegal transactions), in the interests of both efficiency and democracy there has been a serious attempt at economic decentralization. Designed to engage in production and allowed a certain degree of autonomy, bodies known as "enterprises" (*empresas*) are expected to function like profitable businesses. Their operations are "auto-financed", i.e., economically independent: they (ideally) do not receive money from the national budget, they make deals with other enterprises, they have their own bank accounts, and they make their own plans. While the planning -- along with the market activities -- takes place within limits set from above, there is a complex arrangement of higher authorities who are themselves sometimes acting at cross-purposes, including the Central Planning Agency (JUCEPLAN), a multi-tiered set of legislative bodies, and different ministries. The autonomy of "cultural enterprises," which includes enterprises pertaining to music, is indicated in the criticism directed at them by Castro:

> We have seen strange things such as, for example, a state- administered school [which] had to pay 30,000 pesos to a cultural enterprise of the socialist state in order

for the little girls to be able to exercise themselves in dancing, such phenomena ... And every moment the fact appears everywhere that the interests of the system based on enterprises conflict with the interests of society ... [C]learly the cultural enterprises are enterprises; so an individual decides where to organize a show, where it will produce the most profit, which country to go to, and not to the country where it should go for cultural reasons, for political reasons ... [1]

Auto-financing represents one pole in Cuban economic planning; the other is represented by centralized budgeting, or "budget-financing." The so-called "great debate" of the 1960s concerned the choice between auto- and budget-financing; the former now predominates. Because budget-financing is the result of deliberations concerning allocation of resources for the social good, the distinction between budget- and auto-financing resembles the distinction of subsidized and market activies in capitalist countries. Accordingly, there remains a certain amount of budget financing, for unprofitable services deemed socially valuable.[2]

Employment

In music, there is a mix of budget and auto-financing. There are, for example, two types of "Cultural Institutions" (IC's) which handle the employment of musicians: auto-financed enterprises and budgeted IC's. As I have described elsewhere,[3]

---

[1]Fidel Castro. "En el V Congresso de la Unión de Jóvenes Comunistas," *Cuba Socialista* 3, May-June, 1987: 1-35 [14-15].

[2]See Bertram Silverman, ed., *Man and socialism in Cuba: The great debate* (New York: Atheneum, 1973) on the polemics of the debate. Andrew Zimbalist provides a historical overview of post-revolutionary economic planning in "Incentives and Planning in Cuba," *Latin American Research Review* 24/1, 1989: 65-93.

[3]James Robbins, "Practical and abstract taxonomy in Cuban music," *Ethnomusicology* 33/3, 1989:381-83, and "Making popular music in Cuba: A study of the Cuban institutions of musical production and the musical

this distinction by subsidy corresponds to certain distinctions
of musical types. For example, performers of classical music
and *nueva trova* predominate in the budgeted IC's, while performers of *música bailable* are found largely in auto-financed
enterprises.[4]

A similar distinction is found in the history of state employment of musicians. In 1962, the Music Directorate of the
National Cultural Council (the predecessor of the Ministry of
Culture) "established the plan of contracting performers, con-
verting Cuban performers into permanent artists of the people
. . ."[5] These appear to have been primarily or entirely classical music performers. Other performers were working for "the
private initiative of some artistic centers" referred to by Pérez
Blanco and Oliva López in 1963.[6] While at some point in the
early 1960s the state assumed responsibility for booking of
foreign tours and musicians through the Empresa Cubana de
Artistas,[7] it was not until 1968 that a centralized contracting
system was established which included popular musicians.[8]

---

life of Santiago de Cuba," Ph.D. dissertation, University of Illinois at
Urbana-Champaign, 1990,pp. 89-96.

[4]*Nueva trova* is Cuba's version of Latin American "new song." *Música
bailable*, Cuban dance music, is an important generic label, whose social
connotations are not fully conveyed by its translation, or even by its
use in Spanish outside of Cuba. In some respects, it combines
implications of terms such as "commercial music" (in terms of breadth)
and "disco" as used in the late 1970s (in terms of partisanship).
Specifically, *música bailable* also shares with disco certain distinctions
of race, class, and "cultural capital," as discussed in Pierre Bourdieu's
Distinction: A social critique of the judgement of taste, trans. Richard
Nice (Cambridge: Harvard University Press 1984). See Robbins, "Making
popular music in Cuba, 1990. pp. 473ff.

[5]Harold Gramatages, "La música culta," in *La cultura en Cuba
socialista* (Havana: Editorial Letras Cubanas, 1982), p. 148.

[6]Armando Pérez Blanco and José Oliva López, *Farandula 1962-1963:
Las figuras mas destacadas de teatro, radio, televisión, cabaret y disco*
(Havana: Editorial Clase, 1963), p. 3.

[7]Gramatges, *op. cit.*, p. 148.

[8]Leonardo Acosta, *Del Tambor al sintetizador,* (Havana: Editorial
Letras Cubanas, 1983), p. 112, translated above on p. 188. The
contracting system mentioned by Acosta was reorganized by the

In other words, both the present form of financing and the history of state involvement in employment of musicians are based on a similar conception of musical types and their social value as that which informs subsidy structures found throughout capitalist Europe and North America, as well as pre-revolutionary Cuba.[9]

Recording

In the employment system, the contradiction between the "cultural" and the "economic" occurs between different kinds of institutions (the enterprises and the budgeted ICs).   In the recording industry, it takes place within a single one, the Enterprise of Recordings and Musical Editions (EGREM), which falls under the auspices of the Ministry of Culture.[10]   EGREM was founded in 1962, as a result of the nationalization of "three record pressing companies and a few other music printers, which -- with the exception of the press Musicabana -- were parts of foreign consortiums."[11]   It now has two recording studios, one, Areito, located in Havana, and another, Siboney, in Santiago. The studio in Santiago was built in 1980, to ease the pressures of the recording bottleneck in Areito studios, and to promote decentralization of the recording industry, redressing an imbalance, when, for the eastern groups, "it was very difficult to record in Havana."   Siboney and Areito studios have similar material facilities, which, if not state-of-the-art, never-

---

Ministry of Culture in 1978 to the present system of IC's; internal changes in IC rules were made in the early 1980s.   See Robbins, *op. cit,*,pp. 84-87.

[9] State subsidies of the Orquesta Filharmónica de la Habana began in 1956; see Maruja Sánchez Cabrera *Orquesta filarmónica de la Habana: Memoria 1924-1959* (Havana: Editorial Orbe, 1979), p. 8.

[10] See Cuba, Comité Estatal de Estadísticas, *Anuario estadístico de Cuba 1986* (Havana: n.p., 1987, p. 268).   Recordings are placed under the Ministry of Culture in export products listed by ministries.

[11] María Teresa Linares, "La música campesina, la infantil y las ediciones musicales," in *La cultura en Cuba socialista*, p. 180; also see *La política cultura de Cuba* (Havana: Cuba Ministerio de Cultura, Dirección de Divulgación, 1983), p. 32 [henceforth: "Cuba CEE"] .

theless suffice for international markets.[12]   EGREM's total production has surpassed pre-revolutionary record production in
Cuba; in 1983, its output (slightly over 1.5 million records) was
four times higher than that of Panart, the largest Cuban record
producer before the Revolution.[13]

Since EGREM is an enterprise, it is auto-financed. According
to the Ministry of Culture, in 1983, the only profitable cultural
industry is film,[14] so by implication EGREM fell -- and may still
fall -- into a category of auto-financed enterprises which do not
in practice show a profit, but are not let to go bankrupt.[15]
Unlike book prices, however, which are kept well below the cost
of production, record prices seem designed to make EGREM
profitable in the event of sufficiently high sales.[16]   However,
EGREM is not designed purely to make money from the sale of
records, however desirable such an end might be.   Rather,

> Its principal lines of work are directed towards national
> folkloric music, current popular music, music for children,
> so-called educated music, music of social and political
> content, literary *testimonios* [oral histories], music with a

[12]This information is from an interview with José Padilla Sánchez,
among whose many activities is the production of records for Siboney.

[13]Zoila Gómez García,"La actividad presupuestada y autofinanciada en
la música cubana," mimeograph (Havana: CIDMUC, 1986), p. 28.

[14]MinCult DiD, 1983, p. 19.

[15] Cf. Zimbalist *op. cit.*, p. 89, fn. 6, and Dirección de
Perfeccionamiento del SDPE de la Junta Central de Planificación
[JUCEPLAN], *El sisteam de dirección y planificación de la econmia en
las empresas* (Havana: Editorial de Ciencias Sociales, 1981), p. 7.

[16]A 'high' book price -- with the exception of art books -- for a
hardbound book of some 500 pages is $3.60 (here and elsewhere, "$"
denotes Cuban pesos unless otherwise specified); most records cost more,
with some as high as $10.   Since $10 is also the price of six packs of
parallel market (legally unrationed) cigarettes, or a fairly good
restaurant meal, including the customary two beers, in terms of buying
power a top-priced Cuban record would, in Canadian terms, cost over
CAN$20.   At the time of writing, this is still very expensive for a
domestic record in a Canadian store. For a discussion of wages and retail
preices in Cuba, see Jorge Pérez López, "Wages, earnings, hours of work
and retail prices in Cuba," *Cuban Studies* 19, 1989: 199-224.

didactic purpose, and various forms of international music.[17]

This policy of recording without regard to marketability is one of the reasons for poor sales and consequent stockpiles of certain records in record stores, according to "experts of EGREM" cited in a study of the problem of distribution and sales:

> [EGREM] has the historic mission of preserving all the values of Cuban music which are not yet totally recorded. Tastes and preferences cannot be the guiding force. Classical music is not the best-liked, but it cannot be left unrecorded for that reason.[18]

While the recording industry and the system of employing musicians are structured differently -- the latter centralized in one enterprise with only two points of production, and the former scattered throughout the country in a network of enterprises and budgeted IC's -- they both demonstrate a mix of the profitable and the culturally valuable which (it is assumed) must be budgeted.

Broadcast Media

Shortly after the revolution, changes were made in radio programming in at least some stations:

> I was designated Chief of Music of the radio station CMZ a few days after the triumph of the Revolution. Immediately, we planned to revamp the whole system that was in place, with respect to the music of the old commercial stations, trying to give cultural programs with revolutionary content, and, above all, to include in the programing a number of artists in classical music -- an

---

[17]MinCult DiD, p. 32.

[18]Zoila Gómez García, "Investigación sobre la comercialización del disco," mimeograph (Havana, CIDMUC, 1988), p. 41.

aspect practically ignored in the programming of the old stations -- and also artists of popular expression who were not usually broadcast.[19]

CMZ stopped broadcasting in 1963; but the broadcast of "classical music of all epochs and styles," with emphasis on contemporary music and "national creation," was taken over by the national station CMBF.[20]

Beyond this policy of encouraging classical music, which parallels the history of state-managed musical employment, the new government began to balance the geographical range of national broadcasting. In 1959 there were 156 stations in the country, but 32 stations, with 64% of the total power capacity, were in Havana. By 1962, there were only 51 stations, including five national, seven provincial and 39 regional, with 30% of power capacity in Havana. Although the number of stations had declined, total power capacity had more than doubled, from 348.1 kw in 1959 to 900.1 kw in 1962. [21]

A Cuban Institute of Radio-Broadcasting was created in 1962 to coordinate all Cuban radio; it was renamed the Cuban Institute of Radio and Television (ICRT) in 1976.[22] With television, the ICRT handles another important means of disseminating music; music programing accounts for 20.49% and 14.51% of respective broadcast time on Cuba's two national TV stations, including prime-time slots. Many kinds of music are represented, but most music programing on TV is of *música bailable*. Although the media have been chastised by various writers for undifferentiated, lowest-common-denominator programing,[23]

[19]Juan Blanco, quoted in Jorge Calderón, *María Teresa Vera* (Havana: Editorial Letras Cubanas, 1986), pp. 101-02.

[20]Gramatages, *op. cit.*, pp. 147-48.

[21]Cuba, [CEE], p. 544. There are now 31 municipal stations, 17 provincial networks, and five national networks.

[22]MinCult DiD, pp. 33-34.

[23]Sonia Pérez Cassola, "Iniciación al estudio de la incidencia de los medios de difusión en la formación estético-musical del niño cubano; la

they are not doing so out of any economic pressure -- there is no advertising on Cuban television or radio.   In fact, the ICRT has no potential source of income from the public; it is entirely budget-financed.

Thus, broadcast media are dealt with by an institution different in structure from those responsible for recording and employment of music: a budgeted "Institute" rather than an enterprise.   They differ also in their position within larger institutional hierarchies: the ICRT is subordinate to the Ministry of Communications; EGREM and the IC's to the Ministry of Culture.

Mass   Organizations

So far, the institutions referred to have been of familiar types -- government institutes, ministries, state enterprises which bear some resemblance to private businesses and even stronger ones to crown corporations.   However, the revolution has established institutions of a different sort, i.e., mass organizations whose closest analogies in capitalist countries, in terms of structure and membership (not -- or only to a limited extent -- in terms of function), are labour unions, political parties, and churches. In fact, one such mass organization is the Confederation of Cuban Workers (CTC), whose existence antedates the revolution; among its member unions is the Syndicate of Cultural Workers, formed around 1977.   Like other unions, the Syndicate's main functions are resolution of worker/management frictions and maintenance of worker discipline.   It also can provide a channel for grassroots input into policy.

The Syndicate pertains to all cultural workers in the broad sense of the term; it includes, for example, maintenance workers at sites of "cultural" events such as concert halls.   An organization which pertains to a more narrow conception of cultural worker, but which is far more important in shaping contempo-

---

televisión, II," *Música* 103-104 (Jul-Dec., 1984: 27); and Acosta, *op. cit.*, p. 126 (translated above, p. 202).

rary cultural policy and affecting musical life, is UNEAC, the Union of Cuban Writers and Artists.

UNEAC, founded at the 1961 Congress of Cuban Writers and Artists, was among the first post-revolutionary cultural bodies to be formed.[24]   It has four sections: one each for "literature," "plastic arts," "music" and "radio, film and television and scenic arts."[25]   Its functions as a national organization are to promote internal cultural activity, to facilitate international cultural contacts and to provide input into cultural policy making. Among the areas which fall within UNEAC's advisory realm are "Social Security for independent artists and writers"; "material incentives," including questions of salaries and contracts; and copyright.[26]   The music section, which "assembles the most distinguished musicians of the country (composers, performers, musicologists, etc.)," organizes national and international competitions and festivals, as well as visits by foreign musicians.[27]

The UNEAC centres found in each municipality, often housed in former mansions, provide a regular meeting place for local intelligentsia.   Scheduled activities include weekly readings of literary works of members, lectures, discussions and the like. Unscheduled activities include informal musical performance and jamming, encouraged by such facilities as a piano and a bar (open to members). Attendance is not restricted to professionals in cultural activities, nor is membership.   In short, UNEAC, with its youth wing, the Asociación Hermanos Saiz, assumes different

[24] Isabel Taquechel Larramendi et al, *Apreciación de la cultura cubana II: Apuntes para un libro de texto* (Havana: Empresa Nacional de Producción del Ministerio de Educación Superior, 1986), p. 152; Cuba MinCult DiD, p. 40;   Max Azicri, *Cuba: Politics, economics and society* (London: Pinter, 1988), pp. 186-87.

[25] Cuba, MinCult DiD, pp. 40-42.

[26] Unión de escritores y artistas cubanos [UNEAC], "Dictamen sobre asuntos de economía de la cultura," *La gaceta de Cuba* [Supplement]: *Documentos fundamentales del IV Congreso de la Unión de Escritores y Artistas* (March, 1988), pp.14-15; reports of Grupos de Trabajo, nos. 1,3, and 6.

[27] Cuba, MinCult DiD, pp. 40-41.

guises at different organizational levels: it appears as a powerful voice in the formation and execution of cultural policy; as a
coordinator and forum for local cultural activities; and as a kind
of social club for people with artistic leanings.

In 1961, the Cuban government initiated what is variously
known as the "Movimiento de Aficionados," "Movimiento de
Artistas Aficionados al Arte," or "Movimiento Nacional de
Aficionados."[28] The Movement of Amateurs is cited with pride
in almost every summary of cultural accomplishments since the
Revolution. However -- and this is perhaps the reason for the
terminological ambiguity -- its exact structure is elusive.

The Movement of Amateurs is a more concrete entity than
general cultural policy, as indicated by the availability of figures on numbers of amateurs.   The total number of members
has increased from 14,812 in 1965, to 919,138 in 1985; there
was a jump in participation in 1984.[29]   The coordinating agency
of the Movement is the Ministry of Culture.   Nevertheless, the
Movement is decentralized in what Culture Minister Armando
Hart has called "a vast network of cultural institutions."[30]   Since
at least as early as the mid-1970s, this network has included
"Casas de Cultura" along with the other so-called "basic institutions," and the "Consejos Populares de la Cultura."[31]   The latter

---

[28] The first is found, e.g., in Cuba, [henceforth, "MinCult DiC"]
Ministerio de Cultura, Dirección de Cultura Masiva, "Antecedentes de la
cultura popular másiva; Cuba: 1902-1978," in *La Cultura en Cuba
socialista* (Havana:n.p., 1983), p. 66; the second is in Taquechel
Larramendi et al, *op. cit.*, p. 195; and the third is in José Ardévol,
Introducción a Cuba: La música (Havana: Instituto del Libro, 1969), p.
170, as well as in Linares, *La música y el pueblo* (Havana: Editorial
Pueblo y Educación, 1981), p. 200.

[29] Cuba, MinCult DiC, p. 83; Cuba, CEE, *op. cit.*, p. 554.

[30] Cuba, MinCult DiC, p. 66; Armando Hart Dávalos, *Cambiar las reglas
del juego: Entrevista de Luís Báez* (Havana: Editorial Letras Cubanas,
1986), p. 26.

[31] Taquechel Larramendi et al, *op. cit.*, p. 195. *Casas de Cultura* are
community cultural centers.   Typical musical activities in the *Casas*
include workshops, artistic performances, the organization of choirs, of
amateur groups, festivals, short music appreciation courses, social

are arms of Poder Popular, the popularly elected branches of the State, and subordinate in some areas to the Ministry of Culture.[32]   The Movement also includes groups sponsored by various non-cultural organizations, including the CTC, the Revolutionary Armed Forces (FAR), the Committees for the Defense of the Revolution (CDR's, or neighbourhood watch programs) and student federations.

Among the services provided to amateur musicians by the Movement is the provision of public venues.   These include festivals devoted to amateur activities, media space, and other opportunities for live performance in and outside of Cuba.   As an example, in Santiago during the late summer of 1988, one amateur *nueva trova* group, Muralla, was preparing for a trip to Leningrad which took place in the fall of 1988; they had also had an LP recording in progress.   The Movement also manages to provide its members with a considerable amount of radio and television airtime.   Obviously there are not a million Cuban amateurs making records (or their equivalents in other arts) and touring abroad. The more typical function of the Movement is to provide contact between amateurs and professionals.   The latter act as teachers and evaluators,[33] bringing previously informal activities within the scope of state institutions.

In a similar way, the Movement of the Nueva Trova (MNT) provided an institutional identity to pre-existing activities in Cuba's version of the Latin American "new song":

---

clubs, etc. (Cuba, Ministerio de Cultura, Dirección de Orientación y Extensión Cultural, Documentos normativos para las Casas de Cultura [Havana: Editorial Orbe, 1980], p. 58 [henceforth, Cuba, DiOri]. They may also provide rehearsal and practice space for amateur musicians. The "ten basic institutions of culture," set out as requirements for every municipality by the Ministry in Resolución No. 38 of 1981, are: "A concert band [banda de música], a choir, a museum, a library, a Casa de Cultura, a store specializing in the sale of handicrafts, a theater group (amateur, if it is newly formed), a movie theater, a bookstore, and an art gallery" (Taquechel Larremendi et al, *op. cit*, pp. 200-01).

[32] Hart, *op. cit.*, pp. 58-59.

[33] Cuba, MinCult DiC, p. 66.

> In December of 1972, in Manzanillo, the Movement of the
> Nueva Trova was constituted, under the auspices of the
> UJC [Union of Young Communists], with the objective of
> forming a core, organizing and orienting the hundreds of
> young people who through the whole length of the island
> had taken their guitars, and, in proportion to their per-
> sonal potential and capacities, had begun to realize, spon-
> taneously, from the base, the work of creation and dis-
> semination of songs of the Nueva Trova.[34]

This support goes beyond the special treatment of the *nueva trova* within other institutions.[35] Nevertheless, the existence of a "Movement" with specific origins and a structural subordination to the youth branch of the Communist Party does not imply a rigid organizational structure or membership. One informant, a *nueva trova* musician, explained that the MNT wasn't an organization with a fixed membership, but rather an idea, a commitment. On the other hand, a non-musician from Santiago told me that one group which labelled itself as of the *nueva trova* wasn't really *nueva trova*; they played too much *son*. The only reason that they played as a *nueva trova* group was that the leader of the group happened to be the head of the local MNT. In other words, audience members may have ideas about the musical identification of *nueva trova* which they see contradicted by its institutional identification, implying that the

---

34 Víctor Casaus and Luís Rogelio Nogueras, *Silvio: Que levanta la mano la guitarra* (Havana: Editorial Letras Cubanas, 1988), pp. 41-42; see also Peter Manuel, "Ideology and popular music in socialist Cuba," *Pacific Review of Ethnomusicology* 2, 1985: 20.

35 Such special treatment includes the following: *Nueva trova* employment is handled by the budget-financed agencies (as is employment of musicians who play classical music). The salary structure is different (*nueva trova* musicians have a self-imposed ceiling on their salaries, like the quotas for classical musicians). Performance types are such that monthly quotas of performances are generally much lower than those for most musicians; performance venues are usually budget-financed. At one point, the *nueva trova* had a special record label.

MNT has an institutional existence beyond the ideas and commitments of individual groups or musicians.

These mass organizations -- the Syndicate, UNEAC, the Movement of Amateurs and the MNT -- vary in the coherence of their membership and structure, and the extent to which they demand active participation. With the exception of the Syndicate, there is a vague interface between membership and non-membership. Even in UNEAC, which presumably has a fixed membership, non-members may affiliate themselves with it by attending its functions and partaking of its social aspect. This looseness allows such organizations effectively to replace or incorporate loose or voluntary associations of the past, such as those responsible for carnival processions. The Cuban counterparts to garage bands, to coffee houses, to dances at community centres, to local commercial music schools -- in short, to a large amount of music making characterized by its "informalidad" -- are to be found in mass organizations. This accounts for the vastness of their scope, particularly in the case of the Movement of Amateurs, which includes almost one out of every ten Cubans.[36]

Production   Incentives

Employment of musicians takes place in a market, albeit one in which all the enterprises involved are state-run. Music enterprises "sell" their musicians' services to other enterprises, such as those running restaurants and nightclubs, who pay with receipts from cover charges and from the sale of food and drink. The customers can choose where to go; the clients of the music enterprises can choose who to hire, and so to the extent that there is pressure on enterprises to be profitable, there is consumer-oriented competition among enterprises.

The primary incentive for musicians to work is simple: they get paid for it. This, in Cuba, is known as "material" as opposed

---

[36]Not all members of the Movement of Amateurs are involved with music.

to "moral" incentive.   There are two forms of hiring of performers by enterprises: by *plantilla* (staff, i.e., on salary) and by contract.   There are as well two forms of contracts, "definite" and
"indefinite."   A musician on *plantilla* works exclusively for one
enterprise (although exchanges are possible in some cases).
They are hired on passing an evaluating board and are subject
to periodic re-evaluation to determine their rating.   The rating
system has six levels, "A" through "F", with "A" the highest.
According to informants, a "C" or better is required to attain
plantilla status, but according to written records, a small number -- 23 out of a total of 1695, or 1.4%- - of *plantilla* groups or
musicians are rated "D".   The majority of *plantilla* groups or
musicians are classified as "B."[37]   Ratings, along with the position of the musician (director, instrumental musician, singer,
etc.) and the type of group *(orquesta,* campesino group, duo,
etc.) determine salary and to some extent the type of gigs musicians are allowed to play.   Top (highest rating for a given position) wages vary from $400 for the director of an "orquesta
popular de concierto" to $250 for a "practical," i.e., self-taught
instrumentalist.[38]   The theoretical lowest monthly salary, for a
class "F" instrumentalist in a small group, is $128, but the low-
est paid class "C" musician receives $171 monthly; the wage
spread among *plantilla* musicians, excluding the anomolous "D"
class musicians, is thus from $171 to $400.[39]

---

[37]Cuba, MinCult DiOrg, pp. 28-32; Cuba,, Ministerio de cultura,
Departamento de programación,   Dirección de programación y extensión
de la música y los espectaculos, *Potencial artístico de música popular y
de concierto* (Havana, n.p., 1987)[henceforth Cuba, MinCult Dep], p. 2.

[38]Cuba, Comité Estatal del Trabajo y Seguridad Social, "Catologo de
Tasas," separately paginated appendix to: *Instrucción sobre las Formas
de Pago en los Géneros de Música Popular y Campesina* (Havana: Comité
Estatal del Trabajo y Seguridad Social, 1984), *passim.*

[39]*Ibid.*, pp. 1, 3, 27.   These are on the high side for Cuban salaries.
The wage spread since 1981 has been from $85 to $450 (Zimbalist, *op. cit.*,
p. 75).   The average monthly wage for the year of publication for my
source of figures on musicians' salaries (1984) was $186; in the sector to
which musicians belong, "cultura y arte," it was $227.   The most recent
available figures (for 1986) show little change: $188 and $224,
respectively.   In fact, "cultura y arte" is the highest paid sector of the

The salary paid to *plantilla* musicians may be pro-rated depending on compliance with *normas*,[40] but never drops below a guaranteed minimum.   Current rules allow *plantilla* musicians to be fired in the case of consistent noncompliance with *normas* (over a year at less than 70% compliance) but musicians over the age of 45 are exempt from this clause.[41] *Plantilla* musicians, like most Cuban workers, have paid vacations and retirement benefits.   Retired musicians may, if they so desire, continue to play.

Musicians on contract may work for any enterprise.   They are evaluated by their enterprises every three years in the case of indefinite contracts and every three months in the case of definite ones.   While musicians on indefinite contracts have vacation and retirement benefits, those on definite contracts do not.   Contracts handled by the enterprises include those for music teachers, at least those who teach particular instruments. It is common for musicians to hold more than one contract. When conflicts between different contracts occur, as, for example, when musicians with teaching jobs go on tour, the unfulfilled contract goes unpaid.   For long tours, substitute teachers are contracted from other schools.   Too many absences will result in the loss of a contract, but teachers may miss up to a year of classes without losing their teaching jobs.

Cuban   economy,   rating   above   even   "ciencia   y   técnica"   and "administración" (Cuba CEE, p. 198).

[40]For musicians, fulfilling the *norma*, or individual work quota, means playing the requisite number of gigs per month.   This number depends on the type of gig as defined by the music enterprise hiring the musician.   The enterprise, in conjunction with the provincial branch of the Syndicate of Cultural Workers, has the power to raise *normas*; lowering of the same requires the decision of national agencies (Cuba, Comite Estatal del Trabajo y Seguridad Social, *Instrucción sobre las Formas de Pago en los Géneros de Música Popular y Campesina* (Havana: Comite Estatal del Trabajo y Seguridad Social, 1984), pp. 25-26. This imbalance reflects general SDPE objectives for raising production levels per worker.   For details on *normas* and gig types, see Robbins, *op. cit.*, pp. 101-03, 532-33.

[41]Cuba, CETSS:6.

Apart from the relative lack of job security, it should be noted that since the "D,""E"," and "F" rankings do not pertain to *plantilla* musicians (with a very few exceptions for the D range), they presumably do pertain to contract musicians. In other words, contract musicians are potentially less well paid than *plantilla* musicians for the same work.

Bonuses provide further material incentives for musical work. The main rationale for bonuses is regional development, "to stimulate . . . performances in different areas."[42] Accordingly there is a scale of bonuses which are incurred by one-nighters and tours outside a musician's home region; there are further bonuses for performances in "places of difficult access." Additional bonuses are granted for occasional "performance of political, social and cultural interest," for which approval must be granted in advance by an agency of the Ministry of Culture.[43] The bonuses figure into the calculation of *normas*. That is, if a musician performs under conditions eligible for bonuses, fewer performances are required to comply with the norma. Overcompliance with the *norma*, either through bonuses or simply extra work, results in extra pay on a pro-rated basis for the musician.

Similarly there are material incentives for recording. Evidently, a flat rate was a common pre-revolutionary form of payment for recording.[44] This practice was changed temporarily after the revolution. A Cuban Institute of Musical Rights

---

[42]Cuba, MinCult DiOrg, p. 7.

[43]*Ibid.*, pp. 9-13.

[44]Miguel Matamoros relates that the Trio Matamoros was paid US $20 per side for their first records for Victor in New York in the late 1920s (in Alberto Muguercía, *Algo de la trova en Santiago* (Havana: Biblioteca Nacional José Martí, 1985), pp. 72-73). Sidemen with Duo Los Compadres, recording for the RCA affiliate Panart in the early 1940s each received $50 per side -- a substantial increase, but still a flat rate (according to former sideman Regoberto Echeverría, personal communication, 1988). Songs were also sold to publishers for a flat rate (Rosiendo Ruíz, quoted in Muguercía, *op. cit.*, p. 35). I have encountered no evidence of payment for recording by royalty.

was created in August, 1960. In 1965, María Teresa Vera, by
then one of Cuba's most distinguished singers of the traditional
trova, received royalties on a two-tier schedule of one or two
cents per LP sold.[45]

Currently musicians, arrangers and producers are paid a
flat rate (*tarifa*) which varies according to the complexity of the
work recorded. This rate need not be very high in order to
compensate musicians for work lost while recording, as the
normal period allowed for the production of a record is fifteen
days.[46] A rough estimate of the fees may be made from noting
that a producer used his *tarifa* to purchase and personally distribute copies of the record to friends, musicians, and researchers in Havana. If his fee covered all expenses, it must
have been several hundred pesos at least, i.e., a good monthly
salary for a musician.[47]While a copyright law was passed in
1977 granting royalties to members of UNEAC (and was still in
effect as of 1988), it apparently applies only to domestic
sales[48]; at any rate, it is commonly reported that musicians do
not receive royalties for music or recordings sold abroad,
whereas informants spoke of musicians "still receiving money"
from domestic use of songs they had written.

The incentive structure for the production of music differs
from that of capitalism in that musicians are treated much like
other workers, with regular salaries and a measure of job security. The tendency found throughout the world for musical
employment to be based on short term contracts is minimized

[45]Calderón, *op. cit.*, p. 193; note the letterhead of the statement of
royalty payments.

[46]Gómez, *op. cit.*, p. 41.

[47]J. Padilla, personal communication, 1988.

[48]This law did not yet apply to all kinds of "creación intelectual"
(UNEAC, *op. cit.*, "Grupo de Trabajo No. 6"). It did apply to painters (for
which see "Interview: Lisandro Otero," *Cuba Update* 8/5-6 (Winter,
1987), pp. 11-12) and writers (see Georgina Dopico Black, "The limits of
expression: Intellectual freedom in postrevolutionary Cuba," *Cuban
Studies* 19, 1989:107-142).

in Cuba. But there is still direct economic pressure on musicians to work.

Distribution   Incentives

Contrasts with capitalism are most evident in the system by which music as product, not service -- transubstantiated into vinyl or tape -- is distributed in Cuba. Here, while there are material incentives for any given employee to do his or her job, there is no overriding imperative to sell records or go out of business, to grow or die, such as exists in capitalism. The structure for distribution is basically as follows: EGREM produces records and delivers them to the Wholesale Industrial Enterprise of Popular Power, which then distributes them to Municipal Enterprises of Retail Commerce which in turn distribute them to retail stores. Employees of those stores will ideally comply with plans for sales, and there is control from above in the form of audits and supervision. But while a mechanism exists for the store employees to request specific records from the Municipal Enterprises, it does not actually work in the majority of cases, so that the stores have no say over what they stock.[49] The actual cost accounting does not take place in the stores, but rather in the Municipal Enterprises.

The financial or managerial repercussions of unsold stock are not felt by the stores themselves, but by the Ministry of Interior Commerce enterprises and by EGREM. But EGREM has no responsibility for marketing, and the enterprises have no say in what gets recorded. In other words, the economic pressures for the sale of records are extremely diffuse. It is bad for the entire system if records don't sell, but there is nowhere in particular to fix the blame, and no way of rectifying the situation, short of inspired guessing as to public taste by people who have no direct contact with record buyers. While this system

---

[49]Gómez, *op. cit.*, pp. 16, 28; Partido Comunista de Cuba, *Socioeconomic guidelines for the 1981-85 period* (Havana: Political Publishers, 1981), p. 128.

has the great advantage of sparing Cubans from marketing campaigns characteristic of the capitalist music industry (except via foreign media), it is not very efficient economically.

Evaluation: Recording

Selection is problematic in the area of recording, with its distribution network distancing record buyers from producers, and its mandate to record some music which is not especially popular. Decisions as to the amount of recording in a year, and some of its general characteristics, are made by the Ministry of Culture.[50]   Specific recording projects are decided through a process of institutionalized evaluation.

According to Linares, EGREM's "evaluation council" has thirty members, who are from "all realms" of music, including researchers like herself.[51]   The council, or a sub-committee of it, meets with all of EGREM's producers to plan projects; the plans are made a year in advance.   Each producer suggests projects which are then discussed by everyone.   The discussion includes questions of sales, production costs, and rotation of groups recorded, so that the same musicians are not recorded too frequently.   In 1987, a little over thirty projects were chosen to be produced, out of approximately ten times that many evaluated.   The meetings of producers with the evaluation council are monthly; they serve not only to choose projects but to evaluate projects in progress and resolve any difficulties that might occur in production.[52]

According to one musician, the evaluation system does not always operate in an even-handed way, at least in Santiago. He cited a group which had not been able to record because the director of the Santiago Cultural Directorate did not like the type of music played by the group, and exerted his influence on the EGREM council. Such criticism is not so much of EGREM's policy,

[50]Gómez, *op. cit.*, p. 41.
[51]María Teresa Linares, personal communication, 1987.
[52]J. Padilla, personal communication, 1988.

but of what is seen as the "low cultural level" of many func-
tionaries in positions of power, which impedes the correct application of policy.

The evaluation procedure, however fair or unfair it may be,
is limited in what it can accomplish. While it is likely to be
more catholically inclusive than the great patronage institutions of music history were or are at any given time -- the
church, say, or multinational record companies --, such objective standards of evaluation as may exist are bound to preclude
unexpected musical developments and produce a certain conservatism. The Ministry of Culture's categories within which
evaluation take place -- *música culta, música folclórica*, etc. --
are a futher source of rigidity. Most significantly, as Acosta has
noted, the evaluation procedure is unresponsive to consumer
demand. That means the council lacks a systematic means of
addressing EGREM's empresarial function, which is to finance
and ideally profit from a recording industry. Nor could the
evaluation council abide by the dictates of market research,
even if it wanted to, because, until recently, little or no effort
had been made to collect market data.[53]

This raises a question: What is known in a more-than-anec-
dotal way about the tastes of the Cuban public? According to
Padilla, the request shows on the radio are important in this
regard; they provide a "thermometer for the receptivity of the
public." Public dances, jukeboxes, and sound systems operated
in clubs by disk jockeys provide further information. None of
this, however, is collected systematically for the use of record
producers. There are no published radio "top ten request lists"
and only a very few record producers who, like Padilla, also
work in radio will have an accurate idea of what gets requested. However, some effort has been made recently to collect such data in order to analyse problems in the record industry and in the general dissemination of Cuban music. Such
studies are conducted under the auspices of the "development

---

[53]See Acosta, *op. cit.*, 119-20, translated above, p. 195.

department" of CIDMUC.[54] The utility of the studies are limited by two factors distorting the relations among popular taste, actual sales and potential sales in the event of higher production -- the volatility of public taste[55] -- and the economy of scarcity, where the infrequency of new releases may artificially enhance their appeal to the public as novelties, regardless of their content.[56]

Evaluation: Professional and Amateur

Selective mechanisms in the form of evaluation councils similar to EGREM's are used for hiring purposes. The institutionalization of evaluation councils was part of the general late 1970s institutionalization of the Revolution, which included the creation of representative political bodies (the *Asambleas del Poder Popular*), the Ministry of Culture and the current enterprise system. The initial formation of evaluation councils (*consejos de asesor*) was discussed by Culture Minister Armando Hart in 1977[57]; the councils are controlled by the Ministry and the Bodies of People's Power (OPP's).[58] The OPP's

---

[54]E.g., Raimundo Villaurrutía León, "Informe sobre la sustitución de talento artístico por música grabada," mimeograph (Havana: CIDMUC. Departamento de Desarrollo, 1988 [Written 1985]); and Gómez, *op. cit.*

[55]In 1984, La Orquesta Original de Manzanillo was cited as one of the groups whose records sold poorly (Gómez, *op. cit.*, p. 14). The release of their LP *Vía Libre* (Siboney LD-391) in the summer of 1988 prompted line-ups outside of record stores. On the other hand, a record may in fact be a radio hit and then lose popularity by the time it is released for sale (*ibid.*, p. 40; and personal communication with Raúl Díaz, 1988).

[56]It should be noted that imports are rare, because of Cuba's chronic shortage of hard currency. Contrast this situation with "a business that has long been organized around the vagaries of public taste and the problems of overproduction," as Simon Frith characterizes the capitalist recording industry ("Video pop: Picking up the pieces," *Facing the music*, ed. S. Frith [New York: Pantheon, 1988], p. 94).

[57]Armando Hart, *Del trabajo cultural: Selección de discursos.* (Havana: Editorial de Ciencias Sociales, 1978), p. 118.

[58]Hart, *Cambiar las reglas*, pp. 58-59; cf. Judith Weiss, "The emergence of popular culture," in Sandor Halebsky and John M. Kirk, eds., *Cuba: Twenty-five years of revolution, 1959-1984* (New York: Praeger, 1985), pp. 120-21.

have "Culture Directorates" at provincial and municipal levels. These bodies are among those which form the Culture Councils, which act as evaluation councils in addition to planning such activities as "culture weeks."[59]

The local Councils function at their levels as does the Ministry on the national level: both Ministry of Culture and Councils curb the independence of the enterprises chiefly in the matter of deciding questions of cultural and political value of performances which affect pay scales.[60]

The local Councils are further responsible for ratifying membership in the Artistic Councils of the enterprises themselves. These are the evaluation councils responsible for rating musicians, which not only affects their pay and the type of gigs they may perform, but also their status as professionals. It is through evaluation that a musician may get or renew a contract, or get on *plantilla*.

According to Guido Medina, the president of the Artistic Council of Santiago's enterprise, council members are chosen "among the musicians of the highest level, the greatest knowledge, so that they will have a well-known worker."   The enterprise makes a proposal, and it is voted on by the "directors of all of the orchestras, the secretary of the Syndicate, adminstrators, distinguished musicians," and other enterprise members. Following motions and a vote by this group, decisions are passed for approval to the Provincial Culture Directorate, which then passes them for approval to the Ministry of Culture.[61]

There are two forms of evaluation for the enterprises.   One is a graduation exam for music students, in the form of a public recital.   After completion of courses, a student is given six

---

[59]See article 10 of Cuba, Ministerio de Cultura, *Resolución no. 12/81 sobre las semanas y jornadas de loa cultura* (Havana: Dirección de Divulgación de Ministerio de Cultura, 1981), p. 3.

[60]Cuba, MinCult DiOrg, p. 13; and Gómez, *op. cit.*, p. 22.

[61]G. Medina, personal communication, 1988.

months to prepare a program; successful performance not only completes requirements for graduation but provides the student with his or her professional rating.[62] The other is evaluation of working groups. Groups which have already been evaluated are periodically re-evaluated. On re-evaluation, all members of the group are rated according to the new group rating. This provides a means by which young musicians may achieve *plantilla* status. They may join a group which is on *plantilla*, while they themselves remain on contract until evaluation. Also, new groups which work by contract, and are technically amateur groups, may be evaluated and thus attain *plantilla* status. However, this has been a rare experience in recent years; several musicians spoke of the difficulty of getting, much less passing, an evaluation. In certain groups, evaluation is made on an individual basis.[63] The enterprise's evaluation council is also responsible for continued maintance of standards of working groups, which is accomplished by giving technical advice on, for example, arrangements, or supervision of rehearsals.

Evaluation is also used as a means of raising musical abilities of non-professional musicians (those in the Movement of Amateurs) in the ideologically motivated quest for general cultural development. The institutional tool for the evaluation of amateurs is the network of Casas de Cultura. Casas de

---

[62]Silvano Mustelier, personal communcation, 1988. According to César López, of the Escuela Nacional del Arte, recent graduates are expected to teach for three years before becoming *plantilla*-status professionals. Evidently, some exceptions are made for musicians of outstanding ability.

[63]Cuba, MinCult DeP, *passim*. The potential rigidity of this close relation of education and employment is tempered by the existence of two educational streams which may converge at different points: one is for students who decide at an early age to become musicians, and whose secondary-level schooling specializes in music; the other is for "practical musicians," who go through a system of "Professional Improvement Schools." Students in the "Improvement" stream do not receive financial support, and generally work as part-time musicians or teachers; they are also generally older than their counterparts in the regular stream.

Cultura have a cadre of teaching and supervisory staff which forms a "Technical-Artistic Department" for the Casa, and works with the advice of the local Culture Directorate.[64] Frequent meetings and seminars are held with teachers "in order to analyze the fulfillment of the agreements, and revise or orient, according to the case, the work plan, and evaluate deficiencies and difficulties in the fulfillment of the plan."[65] The teachers are responsible for evaluation of amateurs.[66] Because there is no strictly economic reason for the evaluation of amateurs, it is not suprising that ideological concerns are stronger than they are in discussions of evaluation of professionals:

> Political, cultural and technical improvement [of teachers]: This revolutionary task is valid for all the art instructors and in their case should be a permanent incentive for the work. The Ministry of Culture has drawn up the training courses, and it is the responsibility of each instructor to attend regularly and study the materials which are taught. As well, each instructor should try to get involved in other types of courses for their cultural and political improvement. Not only is improvement achieved through courses, but also through participation in groups, conferences and seminars which are convoked by the Syndicate, the Party or the Administration, as well as through the reading of books and through speeches made by the directors of the Revolution, through attendance at cultural activities offered in the community, and other activities.[67]

The collective nature of evaluation and decision-making may extend to the internal structure of musical groups. While groups have directors, who receive higher salaries than other

---

[64] Cuba, MinCult DiOri, pp. 43-44.
[65] Ibid., pp. 44-45.
[66] Ibid., p. 46
[67] Ibid., p. 48.

members, the directors may be part of a "Direction Council" or "Technical Council," involving positions such as "Aesthetic Administrator," or in the case of groups with dancers (i.e., most *grupos folclóricos*), musical director and dance director/choreographer. Some groups (again, this seems to pertain to *grupos folclóricos*) have a researcher on the council. In smaller groups, one musician is the boss. Directors are chosen when necessary by the members of the groups themselves.

An Evalution of Evaluation

Both a centralized system of evaluation, and the collective and diffuse nature of decision-making are not without their attendant problems. The first could be called the *"quis custodiet"* syndrome. As has been seen, Casa de Cultura instructors are expected to be constantly upgrading their skills, as are members of evaluation councils, who attend seminars on musical topics involving top Cuban musicologists, teachers and musicians. This continuing education of evaluators is not always as thorough or as well-directed as it might be. The following is from a CIDMUC report on music in rural areas:

> As for technical evaluation, in general it is poor, unsystematic, and exhibits deficiencies in its theoretical focus, which results, at times, in the deformation of the musical expression of those groups on account of the ignorance of the instructor; which ignores the specific treatment that should be given to amateurs, especially those who are carriers of our popular-traditional music.
>
> We give the following example found in our field work in the province of Matanzas: in the locality of Pedro Betancourt, there was the Agrupación of Tambores of Makuta. Its members played drums of Congolese provenience and knew the patterns of *yuka* and *makuta*. The instructor of the Casa de Cultura who oversaw them got them a *batá* set -- of Yoruba provenience. The group ini-

tially rejected this "incorporation" and requested that
they be permitted to make their own drums with tree
trunks or play with conga drums. As the instructor did
not understand why, and anyway everything that might
sound "African" could be played with whatever drum,
there were problems and finally the group broke up . . .
We felt that this type of undervaluing affects considerably the movement of support and study of these groups
which possess scanty resources.[68]

This "undervaluing," as a function of a bias towards musical
literacy,[69] is somewhat mitigated in enterprise evaluations. It
is true that all professional musicians are expected to be more
well-rounded than amateurs, and ideally, literate. But the literacy requirement is waived sometimes in the case of percus-
sionists and singers, although it remains an ideal.[70]

Another potential problem of the evaluation system is that
of preferential treatment not based on professional criteria.
Cuba is not exempt from injustices effected by friends -- or enemies -- in high places. A case of personal factors entering into
recording policy, it will be recalled, was cited in connection
with EGREM's evaluation system. The problem is recognized by
members of evaluation councils, who strive to eliminate it:

There [in the Artistic Council] there can be no arbitrari-
ness, and much less partiality. One must do what is
just.[71]

Another form of bypassing quality standards in evaluation
procedures, according to one informant, is membership in the
PCC (Communist Party of Cuba) or the UJC (Union of Young
Communists; the youth arm of the PCC), which insures job

[68]"Investigación sobre la comercialización del disco." Mimeograph
(Havana: CIDMUC, 1988 (written 1984)).

[69]See Robbins *op. cit.,* chap. 3.

[70]G. Medina, personal communication.

[71]*Ibid.*

placement. As is typical of many young Cubans, this informant declared himself to have "revolutionary [i.e., socialist] feelings" but felt that many Party members were in it for personal gain, because it is easier to get into the Party than it is to become a good musician.

A further problem with the evaluation system has already been mentioned, namely the difficulty encountered by young musicians in arranging for an evaluation. Those musicians commonly complain of "fossilization" in the employment system. Older musicians take a different viewpoint on the large number of young ones who have not managed to get *plantilla* positions and consequently work by contract; they are "new kids" who need to get experience before reaping the full benefits of professionalism. Medina acknowledged that it was difficult to make the transition to professional status; and explained it as deliberate policy, to raise standards and to avoid having to dismiss incompetent musicians.

The great virtue of the evaluation system, apart from simply filling the vacuum left by the absence of market forces, is that it provides a means of integrating the institutional structure of Cuban musical life with local communities. The councils, from the Sectoral Directorates on down, are workers' councils; they are not composed of (or wholly composed of) bureaucrats, but of working musicians. Many areas of the institutional structure at higher or more remote levels are staffed by professional musicians: Argeliers León, heading the music section of Casa de las Américas, is a composer as well as a musicologist; Leonardo Acosta in the IRCT is a saxophone player; Leo Brouwer works in the National Film Institute, and the list of musicians -- especially composers -- to hold important administrative posts could be continued. This provides some personal contact between institutional structure and musical life, but in a rarefied way; and the positions mentioned are appointments, not elected offices. The evaluation councils create a more direct contact. The members of the council work locally as musicians; they work with local musicians in seminars and the sorts of continous supervision of standards mentioned earlier (e.g., at rehearsals), and they know local musicians socially. This is perhaps more the case in Santiago than in Havana; the latter's size precludes the kind of close-knit musical community that exists in the former. But in this respect, Santiago is more typical than Havana, as all other cities are even smaller.

The policy of evaluation of amateurs creates futher direct links between the institutional structure, established professional musicians and young aspirants, all of which come in contact in Casas de Cultura. Likewise, a by-product of the shortage of *plantilla* positions is the contact between work and education; many, and perhaps most music teachers have contracts as performers.

This interface of community and institutional structure does not mean that the structure *per se* will be responsive to community needs and concepts of music making -- the local council members might make local music history, but they do it in the circumstances chosen by policy makers at higher levels. But it does mean that those policies will be interpreted and executed in a way that does reflect local factors; because the interpreters and executors are local musicians.

Conclusions

Despite the critique offered by Acosta of the mass media,[72] the Cuban system of musical production and distribution is reasonably successful according to criteria of variety, accessibility and affordabilty offered to the consumer, and equity and security offered to the worker. Where the system most resembles capitalism -- where balancing the ledgers of auto-financed enterprises override other concerns -- chronic problems of capitalist musical production appear. For example, managers of auto-financed venues where music is played in some cases prefer canned to live music, because it is cheaper. They are thus at

---

[72]Acosta, *op. cit.*, translated above.

odds with the enterprises which make their money selling the services of musicians. However, such conflicts are resolved by discussion and arbitration with the assistance of political bodies, rather than by the direction of the market.[73]

Where decision making is centralized, and economies of scale dominate other concerns, Cuba's musical production leads in some cases to the same kind of standardization as in corporate music production. The music played on the cable radio station piped into restaurants and hotels by INTUR is of the same sort as that described by Manuel as promoted by corporate-controlled media: "common-denominator music styles, especially the pop ballad."[74] This is not necessarily what consumers are after, at least as evidenced by surveys of record-buying preferences.[75] By and large, however, there is a remarkable degree of variety of programming on radio and television, compared to commercial broadcast media, both with regard to the nature of the music and the format of the shows. This variety extends to the offerings of EGREM, where the deliberate attempt to produce a broad spectrum of music impedes the enterprise's economic performance -- a problem exacerbated by slow and inaccurate response to consumer demand. It should be remembered, though, that large capitalist record companies themselves are hardly clever at assessing consumer preference; a few hits pay for the losses on the many records which don't sell enough to recover costs. Their bad guesses lead to a reliance on the tried-and-true: "a company's stockpile of old material -- the back catalog -- may now be a more important form of musical capital than a roster of new acts."[76]

Discussing Cuba's musical culture in these terms is a bit like regarding socialism as some kind of non-profit version of capitalism. In some ways it is; it has been possible to talk about "production," "consumption" and "distribution" of music in rela-

---

[73]Villaurrutía León, *op. cit.*, pp. 16-17.
[74]See Manuel, "Salsa and the Music Industry, p. 170 above.
[75]Gómez García, *op. cit.*; see Robbins *op. cit.*, pp. 187-89.
[76]Frith, *op. cit.*, p. 105; see also p. 93.

tively familiar ways; i.e., where music is a commodity, the objectified labour of musicians.   But socialism is more than an inefficient-but-equitable way of producing consumer goods; it is also an attempt at redefining the relations of production and consumption as inherited from capitalism.   With respect to that attempt, one of the great achievements of Cuba has been the support and promotion of amateur music making.   Cuba of course was fortunate in having a good base of participatory musical activity to build on.   Where in capitalism, the direction of amateur music making is perhaps best symbolized by one of its more popular recent forms -- 'air guitar' --, in Cuba, an institutionalized amateur movement provides non-commodified music making with a new structural existence, and prevents its dwindling into a silent mimicry.

This is not to say that the music stays the same.   The example of the Makuta Drum Group shows some of the less happy effects of institutionalization on amateur activity.   In order to rectify such situations where resources -- in this case, drums, or the material to make them -- are allocated inappropriately, the integration of community and institution described in the previous section needs to be used systematically.   The problem here is not merely a badly trained functionary; it is a badly trained functionary with too much power vested from above. It is doubtful whether the 'expert advice' of musicologists, however excellent it may be, can provide solutions to this kind of problem.   Rather, the musicians, and others similarly affected, need greater input into decision making.   The point of socialism is, after all, that it is not the one who pays the piper, but the one who pipes, who calls the tune.

1 1

Regarding   Folklore

As communist governments and orthodox Marxist theory have in many cases been critical of religion, socialist states been faced with the problematic task of formulating coherent poli- cies toward traditional folk cultures which, although part of the patrimony of the common people in whose names revolutions were implemented, are nevertheless frequently inseparable from archaic religion and superstitions.   Rogelio Martínez Furé, in his own career and attitudes, reflects some of the ways in which Cuban socialism has confronted the nation's rich heritage of neo-African folk culture.   On the one hand, he is a Marxist, committed to historical materialism and the Cuban Revolution. At the same time, he is a Cuban black who, in his capacity as a leading director of the Conjunto Folklórico Nacional in Havana, has devoted his life to the promotion, preservation, and revital- ization of traditional Afro-Cuban dance and music -- including genres associated with neo-African religions.

In the following essay, which is fairly representative of Cuban cultural policy as well as the author's own attitudes, Martínez Furé presents a Marxist view of Afro-Cuban folk cul- ture, while surveying some of its affinities with other Caribbean traditions.   Some readers may well suspect an apol- ogy for authoritarian intervention when Martínez Furé speaks of the need to "cleanse" folklore of its "negative" practices and attitudes -- including religious beliefs -- in order to promote a materialist revolutionary culture.   Accordingly, there is no doubt that the Cuban government has had to make decisions about which aspects of folk culture should be promoted and which should be discouraged.   Of course, critical readers should remember that such practices as digging up graves and sacrificing animals are controversial, if not illegal, in most "free" Western countries; further, the Cuban government, as discussed in the final essay in this volume, has made no attempt to discourage Afro-Cuban religions (nor, unlike the USA, does it forbid rituals involving animal sacrifice). Accordingly, Martínez Furé's essay stresses less the reforming of folklore than its promotion and popularization and, indeed, the Conjunto Folklórico, with its regular and well-attended performances, workshops, and other outreach activities, has made a remarkable contribution in this regard.

Some readers outside Cuba will no doubt have mixed reactions to "Regarding Folklore," with its somewhat obscure citations, its denunciation of "bourgeois" attitudes toward folk culture, and, above all, its pervasive, vehement, and rather orthodox Marxism. At the same time, the essay should be viewed as a sincere articulation of a set of Cuban attitudes which have been shaped in reaction to a history of colonial and neo-colonial racism, North American political and economic domination, and the sense of rediscovery of Afro-Cuban culture that the state has attempted to foster since 1959. "Regarding Folklore," indeed, has been widely read and informally circulated, acquiring the status of a sort of manifesto on the progressive role of Afro-Cuban culture in revolutionary Cuba. Hence, aside from its intrinsic value or problems, the essay merits attention as a document of Cuban cultural policy, as articulated by one who is himself an artist, an intellectual, an inheritor of the Afro-Cuban cultural patrimony, and an active contributor to its perpetuation.

1 1

Regarding Folklore

Rogelio Martínez Furé

Folklore as Viewed by the Bourgeoisie

Folklore is a people's culture, as transmitted generally through oral tradition. It consists of the manners and customs of a society which reflect the group's experiences, tastes, aspirations, conception of life and death, and so on; the ways it builds and decorates its houses, its oral prose and poetry, remedies, home cooking, popular art, beliefs and superstitions, mythology, music, dance, holidays, traditional dress, and all that which scholars have called "popular knowledge" or "traditional popular culture." Folklore is the opposite of the official, the bookish, and the institutionalized. It is the product of the socio-economic and historical experiences which characterize that community as a social entity. Folklore is from the people, and for the people. It is anonymous, empirical, collective and functional.

In the hands of the bourgeoisie, folklore becomes something exotic and picturesque, a minor form of culture suitable for exhibiting in festivals and shows for idle tourists, but segregated from the great currents of contemporary civilization. It is treated as a museum curio, a diverting object, a quaint fossil belonging to an infraculture incapable of achieving the so-called "universality" of the great works of bourgeois art. At the same time, groups that conserve these forms of traditional popular culture live on the margins of this class society, as victims of every kind of exploitation and prevented from participating in its technical and scientific progress.

In most American countries, "folklore" is the name given, with a certain pejorative meaning, to the survivals of Indian, African, or Oriental cultures; these have often been preserved by some groups as manifestations of the existing class struggle and as forms of resistance to the culture of peasant groups of European or mestizo origin. The ruling capitalist political system has regarded these genuine subcultures as marginal and backward entities which will eventually be eradicated from the ethnographic map, just as ethnic minorities or even majorities disappear, becoming assimilated, like simple wage earners or crude labor power, into the prevailing system of exploitation. These subcultures are seen as devoid of culture and incapable of contributing any valid elements to the creation of a modern national culture, since, for the oligarchies in power, such creation is possible only within the boundaries of Western capitalist culture.

Folklore in a Socialist Revolution

Folklore, that is to say, the most authentic manifestation of traditional popular culture, as opposed to the culture of the dominant classes or "official" culture, is viewed from a different perspective within the context of a socialist revolution. In the first place, it is seen as the genuine creation of the masses, and as a refuge for some of the best traditions of a people in struggle against cultural penetration by foreign-inspired national oligarchies serving imperialist interests.

The objective in the new society is to integrate the best of the traditions, while eliminating the "negative" aspects of folk culture (superstition, antisocial behavior, ignorance, erroneous perceptions of reality, etc.). After being subjected to objective, unprejudiced, scientific criticism, folklore's positive values should be adopted and, together with the values of contemporary civilization which haven't been corroded by capitalist conceptions, a new national culture can be created in which folklore plays a part and which is made available to all those sectors of the population traditionally denied access to such education by the interests of the exploiting classes.

These positive traditions must be made known to those social groups who were unfamiliar with them because of the previous class divisions. This education would contribute to the subsequent development of the population, since traditions are the living forms of a people's culture, subjected to the processes of change in a society. Folklore should not be seen as a museum piece, a "frozen" culture, or a quaint fossil. Its organic development should be stimulated and directed toward the goals of socialist construction, by, for example, improving techniques of building musical instruments, or scientifically analyzing the values of traditional pharmacopia, or enriching indigenous choreographic forms, and finally, in expurgating harmful ideas and habits contrary to a materialist conception of the world and integrating all of this national property into the grand current of universal revolutionary culture.

This process should not be forced, but should occur dialectically in the course of development. In the same way that the whole society transforms itself, folklore, its most pristine product, develops with it. For this reason, there is always a current folklore and a historical folklore.

It is essential to approach folklore with maximum respect and with solid judgment. We should reject as superficial a picturesque appreciation of folkloric culture and, at the same time, a static vision of this phenomenon. It is the mine of vital forms which will allow us to battle victoriously against ideological diversionism. Folklore does not disappear but transforms itself and nourishes our true revolutionary culture.

In present revolutionary society, one has to be careful not to stylize, in a way which falsifies, the truth of folklore.   One shouldn't try, with class-based criteria, to somehow make more "artistic" the people's art forms which have been created by thousands of persons over the course of generations.   Such attempts could be reflections of bourgeois conceptions concerning what is "art" and what is "beautiful."   Folk art has its own laws, which don't necessarily correspond to academic criteria or those of "connoisseurs," who are accustomed only to the art forms of the dominant classes.   The popular artist should be encouraged to make himself more skilled in the mastery of his own techniques and to enrich himself with an understanding of the valid cultural traditions of humanity; he should not try to impose artistic criteria which often correspond, in most of the Americas, to cultural conceptions which originated in different civilizations.

Bourgeois Influences in Cuban Folklore

In a class society such as colonial Cuba's, when our folklore took root, it was impossible not to have a dialectical process of reciprocal influences between the culture of the exploiting classes of European origin and that of the exploited classes, made up largely of Africans and their descendants.   As early as the sixteenth century, free blacks and mulattos began to imitate the dress, habits, and dances of the classes that held economic and political power in the island.   These dispossessed peoples erroneously believed that by such imitation they could join the affluent social strata which benefited from the privileges conceded by the Crown.   At the same time, little by little, music, dance, and clothing of European origin were modified, and assimilated to a system of new values different from what they had possessed in the milieu which had created them. They were "creolized,""mulatto-ized."   Thus, cultural practices that had originated at the base of the social pyramid were being surreptitiously adapted and integrated into the habits of the slave-holding classes.   In effect, there was transcultural movement in both directions (from below to above, and from above to below), facilitated by the productive relations and by the social and political structure of the type of slavery in which Cuban culture originated.

However, in this process of national development, which included the emergence of our folklore, truly popular features asserted themselves, creating a language, various musical and dance forms, oral literature, and strong and original visual art forms, all of which showed the creative genius of the masses. Many of the best traditions of the humble ancestors were preserved -- in some cases by African captives, as in the case of the traditions which were "Cubanized" and perpetuated through rumbas, *congas, sones,* proverbs, legends, food, and so on.   In other cases, the humble people of Spanish origin contributed popular features, as happened with the *punto guajiro,* the *zapateo,* or children's folklore.   Although this traditional popular culture almost always managed to win out in confrontations with the foreign customs imported by the slave-holding bourgeoisie, some of our folk culture does owe a debt to elements carried to us from European salons; but in such cases, the borrowed elements were incorporated into folk culture only after our people had made them their own, giving them new content and uses.   As examples, we can mention the so-called *tumba francesa,* whose costumes and, in some cases, dances remind us of rigadoons and quadrilles; similarly, the *décimas* used by our *guajiros* have roots in the "cultivated" tradition of Espinel; or the robe of the black and mulatto women -- today a national Cuban dress -- which is simply a folklorization of the slave-holding lady's negligee.   We can even include the so-called "cycle of the *contradanza,*" which comes from the music and dance introduced from the French salons of Haiti and Louisiana and was crucial in the evolution of our own "salon music" (the Cuban *contradanza, danzón, danzonete,* etc.).

The most unfortunate bourgeois influence which persists in our folklore is exactly in the conceptions the so-called middle classes have of traditional culture, i.e., regarding it as backward and barbaric, consisting of coarse and uncouth forms that should be swept away; such attitudes were increasing until the revolutionary triumph which, fortunately, stopped this process of disintegration of national values. This reactionary view of folk culture contributed to the exploitation of poor by the middle classes, which thus served the haut bourgeoisie as *aides-de-camp*, without understanding that, at the same time, they too were being exploited by them. Thus it was that this ideology came to penetrate several sectors of the populace -- urban and rural -- causing people to feel ashamed of their parents' customs and to reject their own traditions. Their negative attitude, indeed, resembled that of the free men and former slaves of the colonial period, which prevented people from recognizing the positive aspects of these traditions.

It is in this area where the Revolution has achieved its greatest victory, in recovering the valid, positive traditions created by our people, whatever their antecedents, for the new socialist culture that we are building; the Revolution has made these traditions known for their true worth, contributing thus to our people's assumption of their true ethnic identity, and to the disappearance of any vestiges of ideology developed in the capitalist epoch or influences of imperialist penetration. In this way, our people's cultural heritage will be enriched and people will become aware of its traditional sources, a legacy whose strength and diversity reflects the great ethnic variety that shaped us. Ours is a living culture, by no means fossilized, which, from the moment we Cubans began to guard it until the present, has fulfilled an important social function; were this not so, it would long ago have passed into the category of history, of dead folklore.

Further, we must go on to destroy totally the final vestiges of the obscurantist ideology promoted, since the nineteenth century, by the bourgeoisie, which tried to set in opposition to one another the two fundamental [racial] roots of our nationality, presenting them as incompatible, or attributing integral Cubanness only to those cultural manifestations of Spanish origin and considering those of more obvious African derivation

as only slightly less than foreign.   Currently, both traditional
streams exist in Cuba and the greater or lesser degree of purity
is not important; both streams are the natural result of the
historical process lived by our people, of the socio-economic
and political relations that have existed in our island for more
than four hundred years.   As our Revolutionary government
has clarified in speeches and meetings on many occasions, our
culture is an "Afro-Hispanic culture of the Caribbean area."   The
African contribution, as Don Fernando Ortiz aptly observed, did
not inject itself into an already pre-existent Cuban culture; on
the contrary, Cuban culture arose from the marriage of Spanish
and African, through a long process of transculturation.   The
process of synthesis still goes on, and we can help accelerate
that process in a revolutionary way.

The "clash of civilizations" originated through the class
struggle that began when the exploiting Spanish and the exploited Africans arrived, and through the diverse subdivisions
of these two large groups which resulted from the complex
cross-cultural influences, social and racial, between all colonial
castes.   Since that clash, we can affirm that all of our folklore
has been mestizo in greater or lesser degree, and this process
of blending, which increased with the coming of the pseudo-
Republic, has become irreversible with our triumphant
Revolution.

The "Mulattoization" of Cuban Culture

As an example of the process of "mulattoization," which is the
general rule for our whole culture, we can cite the *punto guajiro*, which, over the course of centuries, added to its instruments the *güiro*, which came from Africa, and which now is accompanied by bongos and drums in many rural areas; the same
has happened also with Cuban ritual songs of African descent -
- such as the ritual songs called *changani* and *kimbisa*, or those
of the *lucumí "cruzao"* -- which for many decades have been
influenced by Spanish language and music.

Static and Developmental Features of Folklore

One characteristic feature of folklore is tradition, which in its turn, is one of the inherent elements of culture, since it transmits uses, customs, beliefs, and techniques from the past to the new generations which, thanks to tradition, sing songs, perform dances, eat food, repeat stories and proverbs, etc., which arose in earlier eras and sometimes belong to a level of socio-economic development different from the one in which they survive.   These so-called "survivals" are the static elements present in folk culture.

Tradition transmits, a "survival" fixes.   Both prevent civilization's values or folkloric entities from disappearing with the passage of time.   They are preservative and tend to freeze cultural manifestations in the form practiced by the ancients. However, as we have observed, folklore is the product of society, and as such, it develops and is conditioned by all those processes of change that affect social life.   Folklore is a living form, and it dialectically opposes dynamic elements to the static ones.   Thus, folklorists write of the transformation, variation, or, alternately, extinction of folkloric entities or practices.   In accordance with these tendencies, folkloric phenomena passing from one generation to another, or from one social stratum to another, or from one region to another, undergo modifications and adaptation, from which variants arise; finally, when such a folkloric phenomenon ceases to have a function in the community, it is transformed into a different one.   Thus as Lizcano said, survivals do more than survive, they are reborn; that is, they are transformed into "life experiences."[1]

The development of a country's folklore can be promoted in an intelligent and scientific way, gradually eliminating what we have called its "negative" aspects (superstition, taboos without

---

[1] Juan Lizcano, *Diccionario botánico de nombres vulgares cubanos* (Havana: Editorial de Consejo Nacional de Universidades, 1965)

scientific basis, medical quackery, coprolagia, xenophobia, magical conceptions about supernatural forces which govern people's lives, etc.) while enriching and using its positive ones. These would include everything that could aid the harmonious development of society, that contributes to reinforcing the bonds of solidarity between people, and which exalts the tradition of struggle against oppression; they would further comprise the folklore of games, beneficial folk medicine, and all artistic forms that flourish around popular religious conceptions but which possess cultural values independent of their religious content, of which they can be cleansed by being given a new social revolutionary function in music, dance, visual arts, and so on. Indeed, we can find many such examples of grand manifestations of human culture which arose in their own epoch, supported by an ideology which we today consider negative, but which, in their own day, performed a positive social function and which, in turn, were impregnated -- in the best cases -- by folkloric elements of their time.

For example, the works of Johann Sebastian Bach, created to be played in churches and the great cathedrals, are today treasures for all of working humanity; nevertheless, not a single case can be documented of conversion to Christianity through the act of appreciating their aesthetic values which today function in the cultural interests of the masses. We can also cite the case of ballet and opera, which, in the past, were privileges of the exploiting classes and vehicles for reactionary ideology, but which, since the beginning of the October Revolution, have become artistic forms with a new social function, which has nothing in common with the elitist conception from which they were created. Similarly, the critical selection, use, and enrichment of folklore must be made based on a profound and dynamic understanding of the laws which govern cultural phenomena and the science which studies them. Finally, all such efforts should be based on a solid, scientific methodology -- in our case, Marxism-Leninism -- with care taken not to kill folklore by applying erroneous criteria which are often nothing but

leftovers of a Eurocentric, capitalist, petty bourgeois conception
of folk culture and its role in civilization.

As Mostefa Lacheraf says, tradition must be revitalized, so
as not to turn into a prisoner of the past. Further, the decay
and loss of tradition should never be revived artificially in the
form of pseudo-folklore. This regressive policy of inventing
folklore has always ended in failure, since authentic folklore --
anonymous, collective, functional, traditional, and empirical as
it is -- is the only kind that really exists.

Pseudo-Folklore in Cuba

We can remember the sad attempts in our country to create a
siboneyista and white pseudo-folklore in the nineteenth century, intended to obscure the real problems of our national
culture; such, for example, was the function of the character of
Liborio, which was falsely intended to epitomize a Cuban national identity. As Argeliers León has said, "The vernacular
theater exalted an astute *guajiro*, a non-Cuban kind of character called Liborio, which was labelled a representative of the
people,"[2] and in this way the African contribution to our nationality was excluded.

Folklore should be the source and inspiration for new works
of art; to quote Lacheraf again, "Folklore, rationally explored
and appraised in a selective sense, will have to enlighten popular culture, becoming accessible to all, such that it converts itself, at the same time, into a reservoir of fresh inspiration,
stimulating the creative appetites of the artist, writer, and
scholar." But in underdeveloped countries this will only occur
"when there is universal education, and when a genuine cultural consciousness replaces the rough sentiments of popular
traditions which are in the process of decomposition or painful

---

[2]Argeliers León, *Del canto y el tiempo* (Havana: Editorial Letras Cubanas,
1984), p. 99.

survival, and are subject, because of this decadence, to dishonesty, abnormal exaggerations, and artistic demagoguery."[3]

Because of this, [Lacheraf continues] it would be useful to act with extreme care and separate two quite distinct planes, namely:

> Folklore as popular culture, adjunct of written culture and national aesthetics (quality craftmanship, developed music, oral literature of the highest standards, domestic painting in good taste), as opposed to folklore as makeshift diversion bearing impurities of inspiration and of non-cultural influences (ballet of dubious quality, inauthentic costumes, exhibitions without style, contrived orchestration, and sugary songs that betray the most elementary rules of the national language and of simple melodic composition).

Common Elements in Cuban and Caribbean Folklore

There are notable affinities between Cuban folklore and that of other Caribbean countries, since our economic, historical and social development share a great deal. The Indo-Antillean cultures which extended throughout the majority of our islands came from the same geographic regions. All evidence seems to indicate that the Siboneys, Tainos, and Caribs were originally from South America and emigrated in successive waves, departing from the coasts of Venezuela. Each new emigration imposed itself on the already-established populations and contributed its respective technology. For this reason, agriculture, ceramics, and the kinds of housing, boats and tools, are similar in almost all of the Antilles; although more developed in some areas that in others, all belong to the same civilization complex (an offshoot of the Arawak).

---

[3]Reference not given.

Western Europeans set themselves up on the remains of these populations exterminated by the conquistadores. Subsequently, because of the need for labor required in the mines, gold beds, and plantations, African captives were brought from almost every corner of that continent (although we should remember that the first blacks who came to these lands arrived together with the conquistadores and were Spanish blacks, servants rather than slaves).

Centuries later, the expansion of the sugar industry and the subsequent labor shortage led to importation of Chinese, Hindus, and Malayans to work in the cane fields; we should also mention the assorted North Americans, Lebanese, Syrians, Jews, and others who were cast on our shores by a variety of circumstances. For more than four hundred years our ancestors were depositing and mixing their varied cultural forms in one of the most complex and violent processes of transculturation in world history, where dozens of cultures corresponding to different levels of development were fused in a new kind of civilization. This new society was originally based on a plantation economy (the cultivation of sugar cane), forced African labor, and a colonial social hierarchy which has been called a caste system based on color.

In the beginning of the colonial period, all the Caribbean belonged to Spain. From the end of the sixteenth century and above all the seventeenth, after innumerable wars, many islands and parts of the continent passed into English, French, Dutch, or Danish hands. But all of these variants of Western European culture adapted to the system of slave-based production, creating an Antillean lifestyle characteristic of the Indies. Centuries of struggle between the European powers for domination over the Caribbean and the sugar islands greatly contributed to shaping the profile of our peoples. Jamaica, discovered by Columbus, was conquered by England in 1655. The Western region of Santo Domingo was snatched from Spain by the French in 1697. Havana, which was in the hands of the English for almost a year, was returned to Spanish hands only in exchange for Florida in 1763. The island of Trinidad was declared a British possession in 1802. Later, independence struggles, abolitionist conspiracies, or successful revolutions threw waves of immigrants from one island to another, or to the coastal regions of the continent. These immigrants carried and transmitted many of the elements of their civilization.

As for the substratum of African origin, forcibly removed from its birthplace and established in captivity in this part of the New World, it has a common origin. Although one or another African culture may predominate in certain regions (Yoruba here, Dahomeyan or Fanti there), the pre-eminence of one ethnic group does not exclude the influence of others on a secondary level. For example, in French possessions, captives of Ewe-Fon origin predominated; however, Africans from this ethnic group could also be found in former Spanish colonies such as Cuba, Venezuela, or Colombia. We can say the same about the Bantus who left their imprint in almost all regions, or of the Fantis and Ashantis, preferred by the English, but who also came to Cuba and Haiti.

An Antillean Civilization

The Antilles have thus hosted an ongoing "clash of civilizations," of reciprocal influences between the cultures of Western Europe and Africa (plus the contributions of a few Asian cultures) being fused together on Indian soil. Conditioned, as discussed above, by a slave economy based on the sugar industry, the entire process has created historically cultural bonds which are expressed in musical and dance traditions, popular arts, oral literature, dietary habits, religious beliefs, and common superstitions, to the point where we can speak of an "Antillean civilization." This civilization presents local variants -- determined by the presence of the dominant culture (Spanish, French, English, etc.) -- but still reflects much coherence at the level of folk culture, in spite of the diversity of languages or of official cultural forms. Even the languages have been affected by the Indo-Antillean and African languages, creating creole dialects in all of our islands.

Thus, the Cuban *son* has its counterparts in the calypsos of Trinidad, Jamaica, and the Bahamas, in the Martiniquean *biguine* and *lagghia*, in the *plena* of Puerto Rico, the Haitian and Dominican *merengues*, and in the round-dances of the Caiman Islands. The dances of the Cuban *tumba francesa* and its rhythms, which have had strong influence on our folklore (*tahone, cocuye*, etc.) came to us from Haiti, but also find counterparts in Martinique and Guadeloupe, and even in the Dutch West Indies, where one of the most popular rhythms is known as the *tumba*. The solo-chorus structure (which, in the particular forms adopted among us, is unquestionably of African ancestry) is one feature that characterizes almost all musical genres of the Caribbean countries. The collective processional dances with poly-articulated movements in the style of our *conga* are equally prevalent (for example, as in the Martiniquean *videe* or the Trinidadian *camboulay*). Our colonial *caringa* of Congo origin is the *calinda* or *calenda* of the slaves of Haiti, Martinique, Trinidad, and New Orleans. The Cuban dances with Yoruba influence (from ancient rituals to the more modern *mozambique, pilón*, and *koyudde*) share origins with the dances of Shango in Trinidad, and the *diablitos* dance in Cuba, Venezuela, and Panama. The plucked string present in the guitar, *tres, triple, cuatro, requinto, mejorana*, and other instruments of Spanish origin, can be found in peasant hands throughout the Antilles and in the coastal countries of the Caribbean. Similarly, the *marimbula, maracas, güiro*, drums, cowbell, jawbones and many other African instruments flavor the music of the New World, by way of *rumbas, cumbias, bombas, malembes, porros, sangueos, tamboritos, limbos*, and *mambos*. The carnivals and masquerades are together the most spectacular exhibitions of people's popular art, where its collective genius comes out in masks, variegated clothing, body painting, pantomime, popular street theater, and extemporized poetry. Various styles of French, British, and Central European music enjoying great popularity since the end of the eighteenth century have also influenced ballroom music throughout the region, producing African-influenced *contradanzas, lanceros*, quadrilles, polkas, waltzes, rigadoons, and mazurkas, and bringing to us the whole musical richness of violins, flutes, clarinets, *figles*, pianos, and cornets, which today are part and parcel of Antillean music. The *zapateado* and a singing style influenced by Semitic music -- which came to us by way of Andalusia and which is found in the sources of the *punto guajiro* and the Cuban *zapateo* -- we find also in the *mejorana* of Panama, in the Margaritan *puntillano* and *punto cruzado*, the Venezuelan *joropo*, the Columbian *sanjuanero*, and in the *mediatuna, mangulina,* and *zapateo* of Santo Domingo, and so on.

To conclude, it would take forever to enumerate the elements we share, and the degree of correspondence between our popular cultures. We share everything from food dishes to proverbs, stories, riddles, biases, and historical misfortunes. Above all, we share a tradition of struggle against exploitation, symbolized by the *palenques* [isolated hideaways] the Indians built, and continued by the runaway slaves, whose struggle assumed nationalistic form in the *mambises* (liberation armies in the anti-colonial wars), and revolutionary form today.

Knowing each other better will make us aware of the cultural patrimony that unites us, and it will help us to confirm our uniqueness within the American context. At the same time, our shared culture will be a powerful barrier against imperialist penetration and a stimulus to struggle victoriously in those countries that today still suffer from colonialism or neo-colonialism. This Antillean uniqueness will not isolate us; on the contrary, it will reinforce bonds that are historic, cultural, and the result of revolutionary struggles, bonds which unite us and make us an integral part of our America.

Havana, 1973

1 2

Of the Axle and the Hinge:
Nationalism, Afro-Cubanism, and Music
in Pre-Revolutionary Cuba

One of the significant developments in art music of the decades around 1900 was the emergence of musical nationalism in the various countries situated, geographically or culturally, on the periphery of the Western European powers. Such trends also emerged in Latin America, where composers, as in other regions, self-consciously sought to express a national identity by synthesizing European and indigenous stylistic features. Cuban nationalism and its expression in art and salon music were colored by historical circumstances -- especially, the late persistence of Spanish rule, its replacement in 1902 by a thinly disguised North American domination, and above all, the ambivalence toward nationalistic struggles on the part of the Cuban bourgeoisie.

In the following essay, Argeliers León divides the efflorescence of Cuban musical nationalism into two stages, which he likens to the leaves of a great hinge. The first stage occurred primarily in the late colonial period, when a distinctly Cuban light-classical music arose, which borrowed, albeit in a gingerly fashion, from native folk and incipient popular musics. Vernacular musical theater and stylized versions of rumbas and campesino music played a part in this movement, although its most prominent manifestations were the contradanza (or habanera) and, from the 1880s, the danzón.

The replacement of Spanish colonial rule by North American economic and political hegemony occasioned a reorientation in Cuban nationalism. Further, as electoral democracy and free-market capitalism came increasingly to be seen as vehicles for North American domination and interference, the nationalist movement naturally became fused, for many artists, intellectuals, and others, with socialist goals. A turn to proletarian, non-European artistic sources was thus a logical step. If in Mexico, painters and classical composers looked to Indian culture for inspiration, the most influential Cuban artists turned to urban Afro-Cuban culture, using the Cuban black not only as an inspirational source, but as a symbol of exploited Cubans in general. The subsequent rise of a sophisticated "Afro-Cubanism" was inaugurated, in literature, by the poetry of Nicolás Guillén (d. 1990), and in music, by the works of Amadeo Roldán (1900-39) and Alejandro García Caturla (1906-40). It is the initial appearance, in the mid-1920s, of the seminal works of these two composers, that León has likened to the axle of the hinge, dividing the first "leaf" of Cuban musical nationalism from the second, animated by Afro-Cubanism and Marxism. As one of Cuba's leading art music composers, Argeliers León himself played a role in this movement, and was thus uniquely capable of documenting it.

1 2

Of the Axle and the Hinge:
Nationalism, Afro-Cubanism, and Music
in Pre-Revolutionary Cuba

Argeliers   León

"The national accent discovered
with the help of the living document..."

Alejo Carpentier

The years from 1925 to 1927 constitute the moment in which Cuban music incorporated, with a leap and a visible break from the previous situation, a contemporary cultural movement that would bring it up to date. While this movement was clearly assuming features distinguishing it from the dynamic vanguards emerging in Brazil, it was nevertheless part of the same long process of forming nationalist consciousness in Latin American countries -- a process which we can better perceive in historical perspective.

The incorporation of the music of the common people as material for the composer had commenced in the nineteenth century, coinciding precisely with the process of defining American identity occurring then.   This process involved the incorporation into our music of the most crucial elements in our historical trajectory.[1]

Although Cuban art music underwent a brief and belated phase of Europeanization around the close of the nineteenth century and in the first decades of the capitulationist Republic, producing works (such as those of Sánchez de Fuentes, Arizti, and Tomás) which still command attention, the cultural movements of the 1920s were opposed to the goals of the latter. The earlier Europeanized art music, indeed, was defended more by cliques and literary polemics than by a confrontation of the two musics, and even less by a confrontation with an audience, which would have been the appropriate judge. We may recall that some of Amadeo Roldán's works were debuted only after the triumph of the Revolution, and that others which were performed before were executed so precariously, with such minimal rehearsals and audiences, that we could consider them as remaining virtually unperformed and unpublished -- especially since the editing and recording of these pieces have yet to be undertaken in such a way as to consolidate them as public cultural assets.

The goal of this later movement was to bring artistic creation in all fields up to date. "But that goal appeared at a time troubled by urgencies of another order, which eventually left their mark."[2] The movement of the vanguard in music yielded to the force of Afro-Cuban music, whether vocal or instrumental. In this it resembles the interest contemporary Brazilian composers were taking in their own neo-African. music, especially samba. Aesthetic interests were thus reoriented toward the living and the immediate, such that man became their document. Diego Rivera and José Orozco [Mexican muralists] showed how to speak a national language with a new art, and

---

[1] Juan Marinello, "Sobre el vanguardismo en Cuba y en la América Latina," in *Los vanguardismos en la América Latina.* Havana: Casa de las Américas, Serie Valoración Multiple, 1970, p.329.

[2] *Ibid.*, p. 331.

Fernando Ortiz battled colonial prejudices against the black man.[3]

Roldán, born in 1900, was only six years older than Alejandro García Caturla, so that he falls within the fifteen-year period which, straddling the turn of the century, situates them in the second generation of the Republic, and in the generation which gathered around the "Grupo Minorista" ("Minority Group").[4] That the nationalist movement in question only consisted of these two musicians, even after their deaths -- which were incidental: an incurable disease in one case, and a murder, in the other -- is explained by the low status of the profession of music, the feeble state of musical training, and the narrowness of the music ambiance. It was only during this period that two stable symphony orchestras were formed, after the futile efforts of Guillermo Tomás many years before; even then, the early life of both orchestras was endangered by conflicts more provincial than aesthetic.

This is not the place to delve deeper into the situation of the earlier music, which resembled the leaf of a hinge which was on one side, the side which remained behind. Roldán, born in Paris and musically educated in Spain, collided with that rotting leaf that was rusting completely away, with its screws falling out. Caturla, who had lived in these surroundings, and who came from the prudish environment of old, small-town families, showed himself from his earliest years to be opposed to the virulent racism clearly reflected in the shining floors of the colonial mansions, which were always polished by black servants.

The political frustration already producing outbreaks of crisis manifested itself in rebellious movements which strove to

---

[3] Alejo Carpentier, *La música en Cuba*.   Mexico: Fondo de Cultura Económica, 1946, p. 236.

[4] That is, if we view the situation from the perspective expressed by Roberto Fernández Retamar in his study of the Cuban poetic vanguard. In Marinello, *op. cit.* , p. 311.

unite certain sectors of the population, in worker agitation which sought to organize labor unions, and in student demands that shaped the revolutionary attitudes of young people. But above all, the Cuban vanguard, together with a liberal creole bourgeoisie, arose from the fervor for the national independence that had been denied to us. The new dominant class, trying to guard the public treasury against penetration by Yankee monopolies, pampered itself with patronage, sophisticated magazines, aristocratic sports, and the like. But after the second decade of the century, a period of action began, in which political philosophers and creative artists were moved by an anxious search for new direction. "Paths were opening up, although their precise course could not yet be determined."[5]

The Yankee policy of cultural domination was not yet developed, such that the creole bourgeoisie was able, at least for a while, to cozy up to the vanguard manifestos, especially those that it considered sufficiently elitist and that did not threaten their interests, such as *Cantos para soldados y sones para turistas*, Nicolás Guillén's poetry volume *West Indies Ltd.*, or the paintings of Carlos Enríquez.

The musical atmosphere during these twenty years was miniscule, feeble, and weak. A few small businesses had emerged, pompously calling themselves conservatories, which focussed all attention on the piano, harmlessly but ingloriously rehashing old colonial methods and an antiquated repertory. Only the one established by Hubert de Blanck was founded on a broader base. Blanck struggled for the official government accreditation that would allow him to use the name of National Conservatory; meanwhile, he incorporated a few more contemporary elements, and strove to develop concert activities, including invitations to foreign musicians, alongside teaching. Alberto Falcón gave a few chamber music sessions in the auditorium of his conservatory, which were attended by a small

---

[5]*Ibid.*, p. 330.

group of his friends and students.   For the rest of the population there was a free Municipal Conservatory in Havana,
founded in 1911, which was the product of the zealous efforts
of Guillermo Tomás.   Some businessmen went bankrupt from
engaging performers for concerts in the National Theater.   Even
the companies that performed Italian opera left much to be
desired in their performances, and urban folk music saw the
appearance of some Afro-Cuban songs, *carabalí* songs, and
slave laments that represented, for the public, the sugary
sweetness [*melcocha*] of the period.[6]   Facing this situation and
the scandal which the debut of Caturla's *Obertura cubana* produced in the small groups of those involved in one side or the
other, the slogan arose -- at the time it was called "the cry" [*el
grito*] -- of "Down with the lyre, up with the bongo."   [Novelist
and music historian Alejo] Carpentier, who was very involved
in this movement of the Cuban vanguard, and especially its
musical aspect, must have been the author of the slogan, or at
least so it seems judging from the paternal pride with which he
continued to repeat it.

Roldán and Caturla also operated outside of these worn-out
schemes.   The two of them had very different backgrounds,
and in this they conform to the model of Patterson (*Las gen-
eraciones literarias*), who applies and analyzes Retamar in respect to Cuban poetry.   Roldán's training was academic and
European, following every step of a prescribed curriculum, receiving the corresponding prizes at each level, beginning his
studies comfortably at the age of five.   Caturla represented the
other side of the coin, that of combative autodidacticism.   His
passage through Paris, working with Nadia Boulanger, and earlier in Havana with Pedro Sanjuán, must have been a rough
trial, more for the severity of the former and the professorial
condescension of the latter than for his innate perfectionism,
the work piling up on his desk, and the enormous demands he
made upon himself in terms of the acquisition of technique.

[6]Alejo Carpentier,   "La música cubana en estos últimos 20 años," in
Conservatorio. Havana: Conservatorio Musical de Música, 1944, v.1, no.2,
p. 6.

Moreover, since his training did not include   childhood years, and since he then had to alternate his musical work with college preparation for a career off which he would later live -- and die -- it was a struggle for him to find time for music. Roldán had to look after himself, so after taking his last class with Conrado del Campo in Madrid, he   played violin in a small ensemble whose members eked out meagre livings entertaining in the early mornings at a seedy cabaret at the corner of San José and Amistad [in old Havana].

It should be noted that at this moment these were only two composers who were capable of joining the vanguard. A situation had not emerged in which a group could have formed whose members would coexist with composers from the generational group immediately preceding them, or from the one born right after them. The vanguard movement in literature, on the other hand, included a considerable number of poets, who emerged because of its mobilization and were able to build upon the contribution made by poets who had been trained earlier.[7] Aside from Roldán and Caturla, the other Cuban composers followed the more decadent currents from Europe, while at the same time perpetuating, quite successfully in some cases, the currents handed down in the form of a drawing-room nationalism that stemmed from the old *contradanzas*, with a superficial incorporation of the folk genre later to appear in the capital, namely, the *son*.

Some works of greater length and elaboration within this nationalistic current were written by Eduardo Sánchez de Fuentes, Tomás Casas, Ernesto Lecuona, and [Gaspar] Agüero; this period of our musical history ends with the work of Roig, Prats, Valdés, and Castellanos. I mention these data in order to clarify what is meant by a musical vanguard consisting of only two musicians, who occupy the axis of a hinge in history. Two Spanish musicians also appeared on the scene of the Cuban musical vanguard: first, Pedro Sanjuán, who carried out an in-

---

[7]Fernández Retamar, "La poesía vanguardista en Cuba" [publication data not given], p. 317.

tense educational effort in his brief stay; and later, José Ardévol, whose entry into the Cuban scene lent support to the work of Roldán and Caturla.

It must be left to other studies to consider the ways in which our two musicians subscribed to the social and political theories[8] which were spread as a result of the Mexican Revolution of 1910 and the Russian Revolution of 1917. However, their affiliation with the aesthetic theories of the vanguard was evident.   I am sure that if broad studies were conducted, it would be possible to trace the idiosyncracies of Roldán's and Caturla's relationship to politics, social renewal, and the polemical and militant importance of culture.   Such a study would also clarify the extent to which these two musicians incorporated the various extramusical pressures (or extra-poetical demands as far as Retamar's work is concerned) in their historical context.

A more in-depth analysis could also explain what we have suggested on other occasions with no more evidence than a brief retrospective glance from the point of view of the circumstances existing in Cuba today.   The fact is that for the dominant classes, the implications of literature and music were handled with different strategies: the word was more dangerous; sounds, a melody, a theme, and rhythms were less so.   In order to be seen as threatening by the elite, music would have required a combative text, or would have had to accompany an act of protest, as in *El milagro de Anaquillé* (1929), with its Yankees and sugarcane fields; thus, *Ebbelí*, with its American plantation owners, and its peasants turning in desperation to witchcraft, could not be shown on stage until after the triumph of the Revolution.

On the other hand, militancy in reformist political action was more easily stifled if expressed in the context of a concert given by the Philharmonic Orchestra, with its upper-class patrons who would smile unenthusiastically, and with an audi-

---

[8]*Ibid.*, p. 312.

ence that on many occasions numbered no more than twenty. In other words, the social demands of a musical vanguard could be tacitly neutralized by the actions of patrons and societies with a few pros and many cons, offering performances by the great soloists booked by the contracting agents. In this way, aesthetic appetites were satisfied and there was a bit of democratization. Literature was harder to control, so it required different tactic. The two fashionable magazines which covered the vanguard groups -- *Social* and *Grafos*, and also the supplement to *Diario de la Marina* -- owed their existence to the tactical differences as to the solution, by the dominant bourgeoisie, of the problems posed by the relationship between social pressures and literature.

How far-reaching vanguard music was, or how far the vanguard went in music, with Roldán and Caturla as the two isolated names, within the limits of the opportunities allowed by the dominant class and those that could be eked out of it, is a matter that deserves examination by historical musicologists in Cuba.

It is necessary to go as far as the appearance of *Musicalia* (1927), the magazine edited by María and Antonio Quevedo, to find another magazine that was enthusiastic about the new aesthetic ideas and was supported by private sources and friendly businessmen; these were magazines that responded to the need for the collective mobilization of aesthetic unrest, for personal community, and for participation in world movements. Because the vanguard artists were committed to fighting for change, they sought and found communication and camraderie. Roldán and Caturla had such a rapport, and it was broadened to include the musicians who would arrive later, notably Sanjuán and Ardévol, by means of the vanguard work carried out by María Muñoz and Antonio Quevedo through *Musicalia* and the Society for Contemporary Music. A full analysis of these circumstances must be left for a study of the overall historical evolution of music in Cuba, which would consider the work of other musicians, in addition to the two focussed on in this study.

The need for communication was related to the state in which Roldán and Caturla found themselves. Aside from their individual economic circumstances, which we've discussed above, as members of the same generation they together confronted the same general socio-economic situation of the country. The economic crisis called for a radical change in the overall cultural situation. There was no shortage of ephemeral vanguard publications, and the enthusiasm for founding institutions that would serve as philosophical platforms, barricades for action, and frames on which to hang pamphlets calling themselves manifestos. Most of these efforts, however, were titanic individual efforts which would disappear without a trace like futile shots against official inertia.

These actions, however small, were signs of a revolution which was desired, although at times it was not very clear what was to be the relationship between artists and the people. Hence the drifting of many artists toward abstruse elitist politions. In Cuba, some of these innovations remained on the margins of history; others, precisely because of the support of the people, contributed, for example, to the Universidad Popular, or to the overthrow of the Machado dictatorship, but all of them petered out on their own. Thus, events ocurred in the 1920s which were decisive in creating an awareness of the need for social change: the establishment of the Communist Party of Cuba, the outbreak of the university revolution, the protest of the Academy, the publication of *Venezuela Libre*, *América Libre* and *La poesía moderna en Cuba*; the positive transformation of *Social*; the development and failure of the Movement of Veterans and Patriots, the manifesto of the Grupo Minorista, and the appearance of the *Revista de Avance*.[9]

It is important to mention Caturla's efforts to maintain a small symphonic orchestra in Caibarien and to note the quality

---

[9]Marinello, *op. cit.*, p. 330.

of its programs and the material conditions in which its performances took place.   For his part, Roldán was responsible for
founding the Conservatory of the Philharmonic Orchestra, with
fees of two pesos per month, as well as for founding, together
with Sentenat, the association called *La Obra Musical*, and for
his own work which he carried out from the offices of the orchestra.   Roldán participated with great interest and hope in
the plans for the creation of a national school of music once its
fruition seemed possible, lending the same vigor and enthusiasm   as   he   put   into   the   organization   of   the   Municipal
Conservatory.   These   institutions   made   it   possible   to   link
Roldán and Caturla with subsequent composers, such that the
link survived Roldán's death in 1939 and Caturla's the next
year.   I might add (again in accordance with Retamar's work)
that the demand for action was a constant tension, and it required   a   talent   for   participating   in   every   undertaking   that
would imply a change.   This might explain for us certain incon-
gruities which, after the triumph of the Revolution, we see today in the social participation of the men of those generations,
and in particular in our two musicians, and how a talent for
contributing to change could lead to contradictions which at
that time could only be overcome with certain concessions.   In
any case, a strict accounting would leave a considerable positive balance, so that today the works of both are gaining in importance.

With these   two   names,   which   are   the   framework   upon
which the two large leaves of the hinge in our history are hung,
there was no question of guidance, or even of a kind of collective tyranny which petered out on its own.   Rather, music's at-
tachment to the vigor of literature would lead it to   seek in
poetry a guide which had found the proper weapon for action.
I can state unequivocally that in this sense the key individual,
both in music and poetry, was Nicolás Guillén.   The time that
separates   the   inaugural   works   of   Roldán   and   Caturla   --
Obertura   sobre   temas   cubanas (1925) and *Tres   danzas   cubanas*
(1927) -- from those of Guillén in 1930-31 and 1934 (*Motivos
de son, Songoro cosongo*, and *West Indies Ltd.*, respectively) did

not prevent the latter from exercising unquestionable influence on the final works of Roldán and Caturla.

Guillén had found the synthesis of a Cuban language in the *son*, and he had given it back to the people in a vigorous oevre subsequently reflected in Caturla's *La Rumba* (1933-34) and *Berceuse campesina* (1939), and in Roldán's *Tres toques* (1931-32) and in *Motivos de son* (1931), the latter of which were logical successors to his *Rítmicas* (1930-31). What had happened was that a musical development which took its own dynamic and vigorous Cuban roots for granted was consolidated through the work of a poet; this consolidation of a new musical language, however, took some time. I now believe that it was a question of attitude and environment. Those of us composers who followed would continue to insist on themes of *contradanzas* and *habaneras*.

It is true that Caturla and especially Roldán used second-hand materials in many of their creations.[10] Roldán turned to what Adolfo Salazar has aptly called the music of the "fritas," -- referring to the urban music enjoyed by the petty bourgeoisie which flocked, together with an occasional pimp and the attendant prostitutes, to the kiosks of La Playa [a beach suburb outside Havana], where there was an abundance of stands selling fried foods [i.e., *fritas*]. In the small dance halls along the avenue leading to La Concha beach in La Playa, popular musicians performed with informal combinations of instruments; aside from a singer of more or less ordinary merit, these invariably included congas and bongos, *claves, maracas, tres*, and perhaps a few other instruments. But this music of the "fritas" was an urban product that arose from the popular stylization of indigenous elements of the two sources of our musical identity, i.e., Spanish music and African music. Moreover, both Roldán and Caturla had made excursions into this music -- Roldán via the ensemble of the Infierno cabaret, and Caturla by composing for and taking part in small bands which played *danzones* (of

---

[10]Carpentier, *La Música en Cuba*, p. 239.

which he has left quite a few), boleros, and various types of urban folk music.

The development of their creative capacity led the two men to feel the need for this investigation into the more traditional elements of our music, such that they sought to incorporate the subtleties of the rhythms of *abakuá* drums and the complexities of the *bembé* beat.   Hence the significance of the role played by the scholarly work of Fernando Ortiz, not only for the Afro-Cuban movement as the *color* of the Cuban vanguard, but also for Roldán and Caturla.   While Guillén showed the way for a creative synthesis, Ortiz alerted them to the fact that the rhythms of the blacks were not monotonous, that their music was not mere noise, and that in place of the *variations* of Western European music, black people used *phrasing* that allowed them to change a rhythmic figure successively until they hit upon a new one; he also alerted them to the fact that the closed phrases of European music were transformed in these musics into a more loosely structured expressive form whose segments could conclude simply with the exhaustion of an idea, without the dominant-tonic relationships or the voice-leadings being of any importance.

In addition to the extant references to the works that they left unfinished -- e.g., Roldán jotting down rhythms, working with an *abakuá* drummer, and having two drums made (a *bonkó-enche-miyá* and another of the *biankomeko* group) -- other references made by their acquaintances have been collected which show their shared preoccupation with this Afro-Cuban ritual music which at that time was still guarded with natural precaution from the eyes of whites and unbelievers.

On various occasions we have said, and still believe, that the nationalist current which began together with the vanguard movement lacked and still lacks (since we are not yet dealing with a distant past) a good command of these fundamental elements [i.e., Afro-Cuban music]; that is, it needs to delve more deeply than was done with the music of the "fritos."

An understanding of these elements, taken from that second-hand product which is urban folk music, appeared in the last works of Roldán and Caturla. In the *Rítmicas*, and in the two piano pieces *Canción de cuna del niño negro* ["The Black Boy's Lullaby"] and *El diablito baila* ["The Little Devil - or *abakuá* supernatural personage - Dances"], structural elements of earlier black music were put into play.[11] The same things happen in later works by Caturla, as in the *Berceuse* and in a *Son* written the same year.

"With the death of Roldán and Caturla, Cuban music was decapitated. A harmonious transition from one generation to the next became impossible."[12] And this difficult transition from one moment to another has been one of the tragic aspects in which Cuban music has existed; it has been due to a complete absence of the mechanisms that Europe and North American had found for their music, namely, popularization by means of the mass media, creating for itself, through the media, an audience of consumers. We have lacked the creator-audience situation for obvious historical reasons which would only explain the phenomenon, but would not be sufficient to justify it.

Roldán and Caturla had to sip the few drops of Cuban music they found in old editions that were already out of print, and which were not placed on students' music stands for them to study. The historiography of music -- which already included such world-famous names as those of Fétis and Ritter (Federico Luis), to mention but two in passing, one in France, the other in the USA -- had no counterpart in the works that had been written in Cuba; the studies by Laureano Fuentes Matons and Serafín Ramírez lacked the most basic musicological research methods which were already circulating worldwide, and their works had little to offer to a composer who wanted to consiously link up the cart of Cuba's music history. Because of

---

[11] Argeliers León, "Las obras para piano de Amadeo Roldán," in *Revista de Música*. Havana: Biblioteca Nacional José Martí, 1960, a. 1, no. 4, p. 120.

[12] Carpentier, "La música cubana," p. 7.

that, a new historiographic vision had to wait until the work of Alejo Carpentier.

Once Roldán and Caturla had died, their music was left in their manuscripts; it took a real struggle to manage to study them, and they are still unedited. Even after the existence of the phonograph record, their music did not achieve more than very sporadic publication, and even then, in editions so small that the few copies available were barely enough to pass from hand to hand.

"Caturla," to conclude now with Carpentier, "together with Roldán, was another decisive factor behind the Cuban musical orientation toward works of greater importance. Thanks to the sojourn of those two among us, higher credentials are required in order to qualify as a real composer in Cuba. Across the border raised between the two centuries, Ignacio Cervantes, Roldán, and Caturla stretch out their hands to each other."[13] And so the thread of Cuban cultural tradition has been repaired.

---

[13]*Ibid.*, p. 7.

1 3

Musical Pluralism in Revolutionary Cuba

Insofar as Cuba, in recent years, has become one of the very few remaining communist countries on earth, the study of its contemporary culture has acquired particular importance. The world is now permeated as never before by capitalist social, economic, and cultural relations, such that Cuba has come to serve as one of the only examples of a surviving society providing a heuristic alternative to the hegemony of bourgeois ideology and the commodification of all aspects of life, including music. An examination of Cuban musical culture and its controlled pluralism may further help explain why Cuba has so far resisted the social, political, and economic changes that have transformed most other communist countries. Although Cuban socialism is in many respects quite rigid, the degree of ideological and stylistic diversity tolerated, if not encouraged, in some of the arts, and above all, in music,. has no doubt contributed in its own way to the flexibility, adaptability, and persistence of the Cuban Revolution. This musical pluralism derives from the idiosyncratic nature of Cuban communism, which, in Revolutionary ideology, is at any rate regarded as secondary in importance to nationalism. Further, given the importance of music in Cuban culture, both past and present, it is not surprising that a festive and tolerant approach to music -- in Ché Guevara's words, "a Revolution with pachanga" -- should underlie the relationship between official and popular cultural attitudes. The following article explores some of the complexities of this relationship, and the means by which diverse music forms are incorporated into the fabric of Cuban revolutionary ideology.

1 3

Musical Pluralism in Revolutionary Cuba

Peter Manuel

The development of music in Cuba since 1959 can be seen as the lively interaction of inherited traditions and trends, external influences, and significantly, the changes wrought by the Cuban Revolution itself. These changes include both the direct impact of cultural policy (as practiced and as articulated) and, in a more general sense, the ways in which the creation of a new and different social, economic, and political milieu has influenced music. The musical developments shaped by these processes include not only overt, concrete trends (e.g., nationalization of the music industry) but also the more subjective changes in the ways that music is perceived by a population conditioned by three decades of communism.

The study of modern Cuban cultural policy and attitudes as they pertain to music can serve to deepen our understanding of the impact of the Cuban Revolution as a whole. While music genres such as *nueva trova* that have evolved since 1959 clearly reflect certain recent developments, a different sort of insight may be gained by the study of the role played by pre-Revolutionary musics in modern Cuba. The function of such genres as Afro-Cuban cult music and European classical music raises questions of musical meaning and the extent to which it is conditioned by social context. In particular, the hermeneutic study of musical life in revolutionary Cuba poses with special clarity the relations of musical meanings -- past and present -- to contemporary socio-political realities; it may further clarify the nature of the problematic interrelationship between form, content, and context in music, while contributing to an understanding of the kinds of roles music, and art in general, can play in socialist societies.

This article focusses on certain aspects of state support for music in Cuba in order to explore the ways in which this patronage conditions musical production and consumption. Such features as the generous state expenditure on music, and the pluralistic embracing of a wide variety of music genres can be seen clearly to enhance the quality of Cuban musical culture in several ways; at the same time, they may also be said to subject it to a set of limitations and problems quite different from those besetting music in capitalist societies.

Musical production and consumption in Cuba are not conditioned by the same class interactions that characterize capitalist societies. Cuban society is classless in the sense that almost all adults are wage-earning proletariat employed by the state. Thus, while there are distinct *levels* of income, wealth, and power in Cuba, the members of these levels do not constitute *classes* with structurally distinct relationships to modes of production. Because basic levels of nutrition, housing, education, and medical care have been maintained for all citizens, Cuban musicians, like all on the island, have enjoyed a cradle-to-grave security which they regard as a responsibility of the state. Thus the Cuban professional musician has been free from many of the adversities, as well as incentives, that affect his counterparts in the capitalist world. His problems and complaints also tend to differ. Aside from the austerity caused by the recent disruption of trade relations with the erstwhile Soviet bloc, many Cubans in general have been dissatisfied with the quantity and quality of consumer goods available, with the level of bureaucratic intervention in various aspects of life, and with the restrictions on structural criticism of the Revolution. Exposure to affluent North American and European culture via tourism in Cuba, the media, and visiting relatives contributes to frustration with communism and its problems. Musicians themselves complain of bureaucratic inflexibility, limited access to imported instruments and accessories, and other problems.[1]

Most Cubans enjoy a relatively high amount of leisure time. The average worker receives a month's vacation every year. Many Cubans make their lives even more leisurely, as officials often lament, by rampant absenteeism or simply phlegmatic work patterns. The many professional musicians who manage to acquire *plantilla* status are particularly fortunate[2]; a typical *plantilla*-level musician of average competence can support himself adequately by playing two or three hours at a hotel or club in the evening. The stability enjoyed by such musicians contrasts markedly with that of their North American counterparts, over ninety percent of whom, according to most estimates, are obliged to supplement their income with non-music-related work in order to survive.

The undemanding work hours of musicians and others may be seen as a form of disguised unemployment, for the Cuban economy has traditionally been unable to absorb its workforce, except during cane-harvesting seasons. (The same, of course, is true of Puerto Rico and the Dominican Republic, which have partly "solved" the problem by massive emigration to the USA.)

---

[1] While some leading musicians have defected, most have clarified that they have done so not for political reasons, but because they wanted greater opportunities to perform abroad, and particularly (in the case of jazz musicians) in the USA. Restrictions on the free travel of performers between Cuba and the USA have been imposed by Washington, not Havana. One might say that it is Cuba's misfortune that it continues to produce such brilliant musicians, who inevitably seek international careers hindered by the USA's cultural blockade of Cuba.

[2] Musicians not on *plantilla* status are employed by contract (*contrato*) according to their demand; since the late 1970s it has been increasingly difficult for younger musicians to achieve *plantilla*. *Plantilla* musicians' base salaries, set according to the artist's rank, are roughly as follows: A-grade artists: 340 pesos monthly; B-grade, 310; C-grade, 280. Musicians can of course augment their earnings by working more, if they are in demand. The average Cuban salary is around 180 pesos. See Robbins' essay in this volume, p. 231.

The leisurely life enjoyed by many *plantilla* musicians is also disparaged by some as another example of the "institutionalized indiscipline" which restricts Cuban productivity, insures dependency on foreign aid, and breeds cynicism and demoralization in the workplace. A Cuban emigre composer derisively commented that "anyone who can shake a maraca can support himself playing music." In fact, while musicians' salaries are well above the national average, a fair amount of talent and skill are indeed prerequisites to employment as a musician, and *plantilla* status has become increasingly difficult to achieve since the late 1970s. Once established, however, the musician enjoys a security that frees him from the constraints of the market and the struggle for mere subsistence that characterize the lives of so many artists in the capitalist world.

The security enjoyed by such Cuban musicians reflects the high priority accorded by the state to music in general. This priority is also evident in the impressive achievements in the realm of music education, radio transmission, publication of scholarly and lay books on music, and the democratization of access to performances of all manner of traditional, elite, and popular musics. Given the persistent shortages of consumer goods and the general stagnation of the Cuban economy, the heavy state subsidy of music would seem to require some explanation. Fidel Castro has repeatedly asserted that "cultural level is part of the standard of living" and thus should not necessarily be seen as a luxury. Moreover, as one musician explained to me, revolutionary Cuba is renowned for its achievements in three fields: health, education, and music, and it is partly to perpetuate this international prominence that music continues to receive such lavish state support.

Cuban musical life thus operates in an ideological and economic milieu quite distinct from that of capitalism. Music is never subordinated to use in advertisements, nor does the state force performers to overtly politicize their art. There is no superstar hype creating auras of fantasy and glamour around musicians.   Unlike their capitalist counterparts, the sectors of the state-run record industry are not engaged in cutthroat competition to outdo each other by manipulating tastes and seeking or creating lowest-common-denominator mass audiences for their "product."[3]   Rather, the Cuban music industry and mass media have a different set of problems, relating primarily to budget limitations, lack of incentives, sluggish response to demand, and, as mentioned above, bureaucratic inefficiency and inflexibility.

Charles Keil has observed that the variety of musics flourishing in Cuba can be seen as presenting a set of dichotomies, including black/white, African/European, capitalist/communist, pre-revolutionary/revolutionary, foreign/Cuban, and proletarian/bourgeois.[4]   How   are these dichotomies and the musics embodying them dealt with by the state, which determines cultural policies and operates in an explicitly Marxist-Leninist ideological framework?   To what extent does the existence of musics of such diverse social origins constitute a contradiction with the reality and morality of Cuban socialism?

Official Cuban policy, both in theory and practice, is to promote a cosmopolitan diversity of musics, including modern and traditional Western art music, Afro-Cuban cult music, regional folk genres, and all manner of local and foreign popular musics. (Punk rock, with its nihilistic and violent ethos, is to my knowledge the only music genre to be officially discouraged.)   Cuban musical pluralism presents a marked contrast with the more restrictive policies of the Soviet Union under Stalin and Andrei Zhdanov, or of China during the Cultural Revolution.   Indeed, official patronage of such diverse and seemingly non-socialist genres as rock, bourgeois art music, the sentimental ballad, and Afro-Cuban cult music (whether in folkloric or sacred contexts) would

---

[3] Again, see Robbins, and Acosta, "The Problem of Music..." in this volume.
[4] Personal communication.

seem to require some explanation in a communist state which practices in some respects an extremely orthodox brand of Marxism-Leninism, and whose political culture is not necessarily intended to be pluralistic.[5]

For most Cuban spokespersons, the original associations of musical genres with bourgeois, tribal, or imperialist societies do not disqualify them from state promotion. Nor, indeed, do such Cubans necessarily regard the "cultural baggage" attending such musics as posing profound contradictions for a modern socialist Cuban society. Instead, most of the numerous musicians, musicologists, folklorists, and bureaucrats I interviewed insisted on the ideology of musical pluralism, reiterating, in so many words, that whatever negative or anti-socialist character a music might have originally possessed would be nullified or negated in the modern Cuban milieu.[6] That is, the ideological content of music, it is argued, can be significantly altered by its context.

Thus, for example, musicologist and composer Argeliers León has denied that rock music has any inherent commercialism or capitalist character; such features, he argues, would be lost in the Cuban context, and thus the popularity of rock, or sentimental slow ballads in communist Cuba does not pose any contradiction with Marxist ideology.[7]

---

[5] As is well known, the Cuban government, at the time of writing this article, has entirely eschewed any sort of democratization or economic liberalization.

[6] Scholars and artists interviewed (to whom I am grateful) include musicologists Olavo Alen, Leonardo Acosta, Juan Villar, María Elena Vinueza, Jesús Gómez Cairo, María Teresa Linares, Argeliers León, Leonardo Acosta, folklorists and choreographers Angel Luís Servia, Rogelio Martínez Furé, and others. Three of these scholars, in response to solicitations by the author, agreed to write commentaries on this article, but unfortunately were too busy to do so; I was, however, able to discuss the article with them. Note that I am using the term "ideology" in a neutral rather than pejorative sense.

[7] Peter Manuel, "Marxism, nationalism and popular music in revolutionary Cuba," in *Popular Music* 6/2:161-78 (1987). Note that a few critics oppose the open dissemination of certain kinds of foreign

Such a stance might seem to be at odds with some varieties of Marxist aesthetics (and indeed has been challenged by a few Cuban critics). Scholars as diverse as Janos Marothy, Theodor Adorno, Stuart Hall, and Arnold Hauser[8] have insisted on the class and ideological character in music (and art in general) which is at some level embodied or encoded in the art work itself. Similarly, even non-Marxist ethnomusicologists have oriented studies toward the ways in which music reflects and mediates aspects of its social origins. Hermeneutic questions thus emerge: to what extent does the ideological character of music operate beyond its original audience and context? How can a new performance context alter the meaning of a music? And ultimately, we arrive Marx's oft-quoted question regarding the meaning of the persistence of art forms derived from a dead or alien mode of production.[9]

Prevailing Cuban attitudes toward this problematic, as articulated by a number of informants, are remarkably consistent, presenting a set of interlocking ideologies which reiterate and justify musical pluralism, tolerance, and a faith in the ability of social context to determine the broad parameters of

---

pop music in Cuba. Leonardo Acosta, in particular, denounces the importation of cheap, commercial Julio Iglesias-style sentimental ballads, whose dissemination in Cuba he attributes not to a healthy and reasoned pluralism but to a general lack of discrimination (in "The Problem of Music and its Diffusion in Cuba," translated in this volume).

[8]See, e.g., Janos Marothy, *Music and the Bourgeois, Music and the Proletarian.* (Budapest: Akademiai Kiado, 1974), and Arnold Hauser, *The Social History of Art* (New York: Vintage, 1960), vol. III, pp. 79-81, and Stuart Hall, "Coding and Encoding in Television Discourse," in *Culture, Media, Language,* ed. S. Hall et al (London: Hutchinson, 1973).

[9]"Is Achilles possible side by side with powder and lead? Is the Iliad compatible with the printing press and steam press?...The difficulty is not in grasping the idea that Greek art and epos are bound up with certain forms of social development. It rather lies in understanding why they still constitute with us a source of aesthetic enjoyment" (Marx, from the Introduction to *A Contribution to the Critique of Political Economy*).

artistic content. In a previous article,[10] I examined some of the official and informal attitudes toward the varieties of popular music in Cuba, *viz.*, rock, Cuban dance music, salsa, sentimental *canción,* and *nueva trova.* Some of the potential contradictions between musical meaning and Marxist ideology are even more apparent in the case of other music genres in Cuba, and thus merit some discussion here.

Afro-Cuban Religions and Music in the Cuban Revolution

Insofar as orthodox Marxism is a modern, secular, and predominantly atheistic ideology, the continuing importance of Afro-Cuban cults and their rich music and dance forms in Cuban society would seem to require some explanation. The Afro-Cuban religions (especially *santería, abakuá,* and *palo*) are syncretic faiths synthesizing diverse African and Catholic elements. Worship centers around ceremonies in which dance and music are used to invoke spirits which, in *santería* and *palo*, may possess participants. One widespread Cuban viewpoint, shared by Marxists as well as others, is that the cults are based on illiteracy, superstition, and lack of medical care, and that their eventual disappearance in Cuba is inevitable, given the progress in education, health, and other areas. Nevertheless, while it is possible that the cults are in fact gradually declining in Cuba, there is little evidence to that effect. Instead, all indications suggest that at present the syncretic religions are flourishing. Given the universal literacy and free medical care, the persistence of the cults would thus seem to be related to other factors. Clearly, they fulfill a spiritual need which secular Marxism does not at present satisfy; moreover, it may be argued that much of their appeal derives from the fact that they provide an entire social system -- a realm of belief, control, and human interaction -- which is wholly independent of the state.

---

[10]"Marxism, nationalism, and popular music..."

While some evidence suggests that the cults were regarded with disfavor, and to some extent actively discouraged until around 1971, state policy since then has been to tolerate the cults themselves, while vigorously promoting their music and dance on folkloric levels as vital and cherished parts of national culture. Official policy in this respect can be said to represent the views of the numerous scholars, artists, and Culture Ministry bureaucrats I interviewed, who, while affirming their belief in the eventual disappearance of the cults, insisted that Cuban Marxism is not fundamentally inconsistent with cult practice (except for obscure criminal black magic practices involving, e.g., desecration of graves), and that there is no repression of the syncretic faiths in Cuba. The perspective expressed by Rogelio Martínez Furé (in his "Regarding Folklore" in this volume and in conversations with the author) is typical. Martínez Furé feels that the state has a right to attempt to expurgate certain objectionable and antisocial practices from the cults, such as machismo, superstition, and religious chauvinism; at the same time, in Martínez Furé's opinion, while the cults may decline with education, they, like religion in general, are not inherently bad or undesirable, and certainly should not be actively repressed by the state. Rather, their positive values -- and especially their rich traditions of music and dance -- should be actively encouraged and preserved, as indeed they have been since 1959. Thus, student, amateur, and professional folkloric groups now perform cult music and dances throughout the country. Cuban ethnological scholarship, meanwhile, has concentrated its attention on the Afro-Cuban heritage (much more so, for example, than on the country's Hispanic roots). In doing so, Cuban scholars, and the Ministry of Culture in general are continuing the interest in neo-African culture which commenced in the 1920s, and was expressed in the nationalistic compositions of Roldán and Caturla, the poetry of Nicolás Guillén, and, above all, the scholarly works of Fernando Ortiz.[11]

---

[11]For further discussion of Afro-Cuban scholarship, see Jorge Duany,

While racism persists in Cuba, scholars I interviewed --
both black and white -- stressed that one of the foremost
achievements of the Revolution has been to discourage the
racist attitudes that had previously kept the cults underground; hence, the promotion of cult music and dance has
been an important part of reclaiming national heritage by
integrating them into the new socialist culture.   Martínez
Furé, for example, described the progress in such integration
by referring to the *batá* drum used in *santería* music: "A hundred years ago this was an African drum; fifty years ago it
was an Afro-Cuban drum.   Now it is a Cuban drum."[12]   Fidel
Castro himself has clarified that the conflict between religion
and   Cuban   communism   has   pertained   primarily   to   the
Catholic Church administration, which opposed the Revolution
(and   earlier,   the   struggle   against   colonialism),   had   relatively
weak roots among working-class Cubans, and remains tied to
a   reactionary   papacy.[13]   The syncretic cults, on the other

---

"After the Revolution: The Search for Roots in Afro-Cuban Culture," in
Latin American Research Review 23(1):244-55 (1988); Argeliers León, in
his essay "Of the Axle and the Hinge," translated in this volume,
discusses the use of Afro-Cubanisms by Caturla and Roldán. Note that I
am employing the term "cult" in accordance with Cuban popular and
scholarly usage.

[12]Personal communication, 1988.   Martínez Furé explicitly opposes
the view that the state should actively discourage religion; thus Duany's
identification of Martínez Furé with the extremist and unrepresentative
views of Isaac Barreal (in Duany, *op. cit.*, p. 254) is a distortion of
Martínez Furé's perspective; nor should Barreal's opposition to religion
be seen as representative of state policy.   Carlos Moore's study, *Castro,
the Blacks, and Africa* (Univ. of California, 1988), argues that the
Revolutionary government vigorously repressed the cults before 1971,
and that it remains profoundly ambivalent toward them.   While Moore's
volume constitutes the most exhaustive and detailed study of the
complexities of racial politics in modern Cuba, it is also heavily biased,
self-contradictory, and relies on secondary sources and interviews with
alienated expatriates for its assessment of the contemporary scene.   My
own   conclusions,   by   contrast,   are   based   primarily   on   extensive
interviews with blacks and whites in Cuba itself.

[13]*Fidel and Religion: Talks with Frei Betto* (Havana: Publications
Office of the Council of State, 1987); see p. 201 for the only reference to
syncretic cults.   For further discussion of the Church in Cuba, see

hand, lack ties to the imperialist West, have seldom militated against the Revolution, and are the patrimony primarily of the lower classes, in whose name the Revolution has been implemented.

Many Cubans -- whether on Marxist, racist or other bases -- regard the Afro-Cuban cults as primitive and backward. Nevertheless, Cuban Revolutionary ideology tends to celebrate many aspects of Afro-Cuban heritage, and especially the arts associated with the cults, as a vital part of national identity. Music plays an important part in this identity. Innumerable popular songs refer directly to this heritage, either by text references or by usage of musical elements derived from the cults (e.g., Irakere's "Misa Negra"). The Afro-Cuban heritage is unique to Cuba in a way that imported genres like rock and European art music are not; moreover, in contrast to the ever-dwindling Hispanic-derived folk music traditions, Afro-Cuban musics, from rumba to *santería* chants, remain flourishing and dynamic elements of grassroots culture, constituting, as in the title of folklorist Miguel Barnet's book, a *fuente viva* -- a living source.

Scholars and spokesmen do not attempt to draw sharp dichotomies between the folkloric and practical realms. Nor is it the policy of the state to coopt the cults by celebrating them as folklore while actively repressing cult practice itself. Accordingly, it is often difficult to separate the self-consciously "folkloric" recreations of Afro-Cuban culture from their grassroots, primary "folk" sources, just as the word *folklórico* is generally used in Spanish to denote both meanings.[14] Many members of professional Afro-Cuban folkloric

---

Margaret Crahan, "Cuba: Religion and Revolutionary Institutionalization," in *Socialist Cuba: Past Interpretations and Future Challenges*, ed., Sergio Roca (Boulder: Westview Press, 1988).

[14]Thus, the term *folklórico* (or *folclórico*) is often used in a manner more or less synonymous with the English "folk." In this article I am using the term "folkloric" to denote the deliberate, self-conscious endeavors, led by educated members of middle class backgrounds, to preserve and reproduce the artistic traditions of "folk" culture,

groups are at the same time actively involved, whether pro-
fessionally or not, as performers in the cults themselves.
Scholars recognize and do not appear to lament the overlap
between their research and the actual practice of the cults.
One musicologist, the producer of a scholarly record of *santería* music,[15] told me how pleased she was to discover that
the record was actually being used by *santeros* in ceremonies
where live musicians were not available.

Cuban scholars tend not to regard the persistence of the
syncretic cults as significantly contradictory with Cuban
Marxism. As one folklorist explained to me, "There is not
really a contradiction between Marxism and the cults; rather,
they just reflect the unequal development of our society."
Another scholar concurred (again in response to my query),
"There is not really a contradiction between secular Marxism
and cult worship, although eventually one or the other will
disappear." Miguel Barnet's remarks on the *abakuá* cult are
also representative. The exclusively male *abakuá* cult, he
notes,

> is a very macho society, and they practice a cult of
> machismo. . . Definitely it has [a reactionary element]. . .
> but anyway they exist, and their music is beautiful, and
> their dances are beautiful, and the Revolution cannot
> wipe out this [just] because it has reactionary elements.
> I mean, life is full of contradictions, and that is beautiful
> also. . .There are some people in life, even in socialist
> countries, that have a mystical way of seeing life. So it's
> very complex, because if you want to assume your cul-
> ture, if you want to really be a Cuban or a Caribbean,
> you have to assume all this [pointing to the cult idols
> and figurines around him], you have to understand all
> this, you have to live within all these elements.[16]

---

frequently with some government assistance, and on a more or less
professional basis -- as in the case of the Conjunto Folklórico.

[15] In the series *Antología de la música afrocubana.*

[16] From the film, "What's Cuba Playing At?" ("¿Qué se toca en Cuba?").

Thus, Cuban socialist ideology, while perhaps anticipating the eventual decline of the cults through education and material progress, nevertheless endeavors to preserve their vital elements (especially music and dance) and to affirm, on an unprecedented level, their role in national culture. The cults and secular Marxism are not seen as significantly contradictory, insofar as the Revolution provides a new social and ideological *context* which can alter the content and meaning of the cults and their associated dance and music. The argument, whether implicit or explicit, is that in a society which has overcome the worst aspects of racism, whites need no longer be threatened by such Afro-Cuban arts, while black practicioners need not feel socially marginalized. Similarly, the machismo in *abakuá* dance -- or for that matter, in the *rumba guaguancó* -- is disarmed and stripped of much of its malignance in the context of a society where male chauvinism, although still pervasive, is receding under a barrage of media propaganda and integration of women into positions of responsibility. Further, while the cults may reinforce machismo and religious obscurantism, these features are deemed less significant than the cults' positive values -- especially, their rich music and dance traditions, and the important role they play in national and proletarian culture in general.

Classical Music in a Classless Society

The role and meaning of classical music in socialist societies also present certain contradictions which have been the subject of much debate and comment. Art musics are invariably asssociated with elites. Appreciation of classical arts generally involves training and exposure to which only the upper classes in stratified societies have had access. Thus, the role of aristocratic arts in a classless society -- especially an envisioned "dictatorship of the proletariat" -- would seem to be ambiguous. Moreover, as has often been suggested, Western art music can be said to reflect its class character in its di-

chotomy between specialists and listeners, and in such features as the hierarchic roles of the symphony orchestra players led by a conductor.   A number of scholars have further
argued that the sonata form's use of long-range thematic development leading to definitive closure reflects aspects of the
bourgeois worldview, notably goal-oriented positivism, ratio-
nal control, and an individual-oriented conception of man in
relation to society.[17]

These considerations notwithstanding, the Cuban government has heavily subsidized classical music (and dance) since
1959.[18]   Symphony orchestras, conservatories, and music education in general have fared relatively well under the
Revolution.   In terms of quality, audience attendance, and
general extravagance, productions of light-classical *zarzuelas*
dramatically surpass their equivalents in, for example, New
York City. Alicia Alonso's ballet has achieved particular
renown internationally.

What, then, is the significance of Western bourgeois music
in a classless society governed by a Marxist ideology?   Why
does the Cuban government extend such generous support to
art music (in the form of maintenance of orchestras, training
of musicians, importing instruments, etc.), when such support
could be directed instead to more unambiguously popular and
proletarian genres (e.g., dance music, or *nueva trova*)?   Does
classical music constitute a Trojan horse containing elitist
bourgeois values?   Is the Cuban state merely vying for international prestige by producing and lionizing the renowned
Alicia Alonso ballet and a host of young instrumental virtu-
osi?

---

[17]See, e.g., Susan McClary, "A Musical Dialectic from the
Enlightenment: Mozart's Piano Concerto in G Major, K. 453, Movement
2." in *Cultural Critique* 4, pp. 129-70; and Marothy, *op. cit.*
[18]For a summary of classical music activity since 1959, see Harold
Gramatges, "La música culta," in *La cultura en Cuba socialista* (Havana:
Editorial Letras Cubanas, 1982), pp. 124-150.

There are several aspects to the attitudes toward classical music (and bourgeois culture in general). First, art music has a long history in Cuba, such that scholars and musicians can argue that it constitutes an integral and valuable part of national culture; light-classical genres such as the *danzón, habanera,* and *zarzuela* are viewed as especially important components of the Cuban musical heritage.

Jesús Gómez Cairo, music director in the Ministry of Culture, further articulated the importance and validity of state patronage of classical music. Gómez Cairo observed that bourgeois culture has generated much great art; moreover, he argued, Cubans should have access to such art and the education to understand it, such that they will then be free to make their own aesthetic decisions about it. Finally, Gómez Cairo, like León in regards to rock, argued that good classical music has no inherent bourgeois character and thus does not pose contradictions with socialist ideology. Similarly, Rogelio Martínez Furé stressed that classical music in Cuba has a different meaning and function in Cuban Revolutionary society, because it no longer serves the bourgeoisie alone, but rather the entire working class. Noting how Bach played in the eighteenth century differs from Bach as promoted by the Nazis, or Bach played in a modern factory, Martínez Furé insisted that the ideological content of music changes according to the social context in which it is performed and apprehended. Musicologist Olavo Alen echoed this viewpoint by observing that a Chopin Polonaise, once written as a symbol of Polish nationalism in the face of Russian aggression, now is associated by Havana citizens primarily with ice cream, as the piece is a regular part of the "mood music" tape played at Copelia, a central park and refreshment area.[19]

The meaning of music, indeed, is dependent on a complex code of learned responses which are shared by composer and listener. Ultimately, there is nothing in the notes themselves

---

[19]Conversations with Gómez Cairo, Martínez Furé, and Alen were conducted in 1987-88..

which is *inherently* sad, angry, or bourgeois, etc., except insofar as these meanings and expressive devices are accepted
and understood by audiences.   Thus, like Alen in reference to
Chopin, Susan McClary shows how there are many Mozarts,
from "Mozart's Mozart," to the nineteenth-century conception
of Mozart, to today's Mozart often recognized as "the soundtrack from 'Amadeus'."[20]

We should not assume, however, that the mutability of
musical meaning implies a complete break with the past.
Mozart's continuing popularity in Western bourgeois society
is due at least in part to the extent to which our society
shares aspects of eighteenth-century bourgeois ideology.   The
same might certainly apply to the appreciation of Mozart in
some circles in modern Cuba, especially since Cuban Marxists
themselves frequently note that bourgeois attitudes remain
strong in the country.   Moreover, performance norms (e.g.,
the aforementioned dichotomy between musicians and audience) must convey meaning in more explicit ways than the
music itself.

Aside from Khmer Rouge and Cultural Revolution fanatics,
spokesmen in communist countries have generally upheld the
value of classical art, while at the same time stressing the importance of educating the audience as to the class origins and
character of such art.   Thus, for example, Cuban writings on
classical music do not seek to denounce it, but rather to eluci-
date, in the course of discussing it, the relation between art
music and its historical context.   The educated socialist man
thereby learns to contextualize art music in a historical perspective, in a manner which need not diminish his enjoyment
of that music.   In effect, the Cuban Marxist hermeneutic em-
braces pre-communist elite arts, but with the understanding
that they are part of a Marxist meta-narrative, in whose
terms their meaning is rewritten.   Adorno's attitude regard-

---

[20]McClary, *op. cit.*, pp. 160-66.

ing such hermeneutic processes could be said to cohere with Cuban ideology regarding high art of previous period:

> Past art must not be abstractly negated, but consciously criticized from the vantage point of the present. In this manner, the present is constitutive of the past. Nothing is to be taken over uncritically just because it used to be highly esteemed and happens to be still around; but nothing is to be dumped, either, just because it waned.[21]

Similarly, Arnold Hauser's summary of the role of high art in socialism can be regarded as encapsulating, in a more general way, the current prevailing Cuban view:

> The way to a genuine appreciation of art is through education. Not the violent simplification of art, but the training of the capacity for aesthetic judgements is the means by which the constant monopolizing of art by a small minority can be prevented. . . Genuine, progressive, creative art can only mean a complicated art today. It will never be possible for everyone to enjoy and appreciate it in equal measure, but the share of the broader masses in it can be increased and deepened. The preconditions of a slackening of the cultural monopoly are above all economic and social. We can do no other than fight for the creation of these preconditions.[22]

While Hauser is clearly speaking of high culture rather than culture in general, his statement should be taken not as a denial of the vital role of proletarian culture in socialism, but rather as an affirmation of the role that high art could conceivably play in societies where education is not monopolized by an elite.

---

[21] Adorno, *Aesthetic Theory*, tr. C. Lenhardt, ed. Gretel Adorno and Rolf Tiedemann (London: Routledge and Kegan Paul, 1972), p. 60.

[22] Hauser, *op. cit.*, vol. IV, p. 253.

The Tropicana and 1950s Classical Kitsch

The pluralism of Cuban socialist aesthetics is also manifest in attitudes articulated toward the glittery cabaret shows offered primarily at the larger urban hotels. The cabarets first flourished in Havana in the 1950s, when they served as tourist attractions and adjuncts to gambling and prostitution. The most renowned and opulent has been the Tropicana, a largely open-air club in Havana which continues to feature a glittery, garish extravaganza of Cuban music and dance. The Tropicana show, like that of the other cabarets, overwhelms audiences with vignettes featuring rows of women in sumptuous, albeit scanty outfits, performing Rockettes-style dancing, alternating with wild "jungle" scenes, cult music, rumbas, Carnival processions, and the like, backed up by a live big band with continuous lighting and smoke effects. The character of the shows is joyously kitsch, incorporating everything from *santería* chants to the *chachachá* into a campy celebration of Cuban popular culture of the fifties.

Since 1959 the Revolutionary government, far from curtailing the cabarets, has expanded and extended them, especially into the provinces. The cabarets have been recognized, by the state and the public, as lively and important components of popular entertainment, which should be accessible to all, not just wealthy *habaneros*. Although incorporating more Cuban and Latin American folklore (as opposed to European themes) and some satires of capitalist vulgarities,[23] the content of the shows, with their emphasis on sensationalistic glitter, has remained largely the same as in the fifties.

The cabarets, like classical and Afro-Cuban cult music, might well be seen as anomalies in socialist Cuba. In the 1950s, they were disparaged, or celebrated, according to one's

---

[23] See, e.g., Peter Manuel, *op. cit.*, p.171, and the insightful and informative article by Graciel Oviedo Haza, "El cabaret: un centro de promoción cultural?", in *Temas* 16.

temperament, as the epitome of decadent entertainment. Oriented primarily toward North American bachelor tourists, the cabarets were marketplaces for prostitution, with the majority of female dancers routinely selling their services after the shows. Today, many observers, from North American feminists to educated Cuban women, disparage the perceived sexism of the shows, with their inevitable objectification of scantily-clad female dancers; in 1987, for example, the Tropicana's show featured a supposedly titillating vignette, certainly of questionable taste from a liberal North American perspective, wherein a white woman lost in the jungle was chased by black "savages." One would not need to be a dour and cynical Marxist to regard the entire extravaganza as decadent, pre-Revolutionary kitsch.

Santiago Alfonso, an assistant director of the Tropicana, explained his view of the show's relation to modern Cuban society. While the content and style of the cabarets have not changed markedly, their context has altered considerably. First, he noted, prostitution and the dire poverty which engendered it have been all but eliminated under the Revolution, and gambling has been completely terminated. Secondly, before the Revolution, admission to the cabarets was strictly for whites only. No such discrimination exists now; moreover, while admission is expensive by Cuban standards (about $20), it is not beyond the reach of the average Cuban.[24] The Tropicana's show itself, Alfonso argued, is "classical" in that it presents a charming, albeit dated recreation of Cuban pop culture from a particularly vital and lively period. Alfonso could also have noted that cabarets are now free of the pornographic content for which they were infamous in the Batista period.

As for the perceived sexism of the cabarets, it could be argued that objectification of women (and men) is to some ex-

---

[24]When this point arose in a conversation I had with one North American visitor, she pithily observed, "Great -- now even the proletariat can see objectification of women."

tent inevitable in modern society, and that it is only pernicious in the context of a harshly sexist society. While
machismo remains deeply ingrained in Cuban culture, as
noted above, it is increasingly on the defensive against an
extensive mass media campaign and, further, the increasing
equality of women in public life. (Moreover, were cabaret
dancers now required to dress more discreetly, bourgeois
critics would surely be quick to ridicule "Communist prudish-
ness.")

Thus, once again, the *context* of music and of performance
in general, is seen as redeeming whatever potentially negative or reactionary *content* such art might have. Pre-
Revolutionary kitsch, like nineteenth-century bourgeois music and animistic cult music, is thus tolerated, if not embraced,
by Cuban Marxism in the faith that its meaning is significantly altered by the socialist context in which it is recreated.

Musical Pluralism or a "Velvet Prison"?

We have seen, then, how Cuban attitudes toward cult music,
art music, 1950s kitsch, and imported genres like rock and
sentimental ballads form what Charles Keil has described as a
set of "interlocking ideologies which together constitute a
consistent aesthetic pluralism."[25]   Such a perspective recon-
ciles potentially reactionary art forms with Cuban Marxism
and nationalism by stressing the manner in which social context can negate or alter aspects of the art work's original
content.   The basis of the new social context, of course, is a
society which has eliminated desperate poverty, extreme in-
equalities of income, and the worst and most overt forms of
racism and sexism.   Only in such a society can classical music
cease to be entirely bourgeois, and neo-African cult music can
shed its disrepute.   Only in a society where racism and sexism
are under control -- to borrow Keil's words again -- can a
black girl play harpsichord "without embarrassment or sense

---

[25]Conversation with Keil, 1987.

of betrayal," and "whites can sing like Africans without feeling like thieves or appropriators, or dance 'down' without looking stupid."[26]

The relative vitality of Cuban musical culture owes much to the pluralistic cultural policy toward music, and, presumably, to the financial security enjoyed by the average *plantilla* musician. Such conditions are not, of course, unique to Cuba, and were found, with some differences, in other formerly socialist countries, particularly in Eastern Europe. In this sense these conditions may be taken as characteristic in a general sense of socialist culture in a certain stage of development. For the purposes of comparison and contrast, a particularly useful document is Miklos Haraszti's *The Velvet Prison: Artists under State Socialism.*[27] This book, written by a prominent Hungarian, formerly "dissident" intellectual, is an insightful description of cultural policy and practice in the author's homeland during the latter part of the socialist period. One of its basic premises is that, contrary to naive Western misconceptions, art in socialist countries like Hungary was generally not subject to crude and heavy-handed censorship, and that artists were not repressed, alienated beings perpetually at odds with their government. Rather, the pre-*glasnost* artists learned not to challenge the state or the system; like corporate workers in the West, they tended to accept, whether cynically or sincerely, the guidelines established by the state, their patron, and in exchange for their compliance and work they enjoyed security and a guaranteed income and audience. Thus, the "hard" and overt censorship and repression of the early socialist decades, or of the Stalin or Cultural Revolution eras, had given way to a more "soft", self-regulating, symbiotic process wherein direct state repression or censorship were seldom necessary. Haraszti argues, however, that despite, or perhaps because of the artist's comfortable

---

[26] Excerpts from Keil's field journal, 1987.
[27] Trans. Katalin and Stephen Landesmann (New York: New Republic, 1987).

position and the extensive state support of culture, the arts
suffered, even in this more tolerant phase, from a fundamental inertia, backwardness, and lack of dynamic creativity. *The
Velvet Prison* can thus be seen as a sort of sister volume to
Herbert Marcuse's *One-Dimensional Man*, which indicts the
self-censorship and false pluralism of contemporary bourgeois society.

Insofar as Haraszti is concerned primarily with the possibility of *dissent* in art, his book is only indirectly relevant to a
discussion of music in Cuba, since it is difficult to evaluate
music, the most abstract of arts, in terms of its oppositional
character. Nevertheless, Haraszti's sophisticated assessment of
late socialism does offer certain parallels with the Cuban
situation. Cuban cultural policy can be seen to have evolved
from an initially tolerant period in the 1960s, through a more
narrowly restrictive and stridently anti-American stage in the
early 1970s (heralded by the persecution of poet Heberto
Padilla in 1971), to the guardedly more relaxed pluralism of
the 1980s. Cultural policy in general loosened considerably in
1976 with the establishment of the Ministry of Culture, headed
by Armando Hart Davalos, replacing the more dogmatic and
bureaucratic agency that preceded it. In regards to music, one
may also detect in Cuba a progressive relaxation of the initial
circumspection with which the state regarded North American-
influenced *nueva trova* and jazz, to the extent that these
genres are now enthusiastically supported by the
government.[28] As in Hungary, the criteria for acceptability of
art were gradually broadened to include humanistic, essentially
apolitical art. This relaxation was made explicit in the 1988
Congress of the Union of Cuban Writers and Artists (UNEAC),
where Cuban Vice-President Carlos Rafael Rodríguez clarified
that Fidel's oft-reiterated but ambiguous dictum -- "Within the
Revolution, everything; against the Revolution, nothing" --

---

[28]The state has even embraced the *lambada*, a Brazilian-derived
dance promoted by the French and American pop music industries in
the late 1980s; in 1990, Cuban youth were exhorted to attend a patriotic
demonstration and dance the *lambada*.

should be interpreted to mean, in effect, "If you are not against us, you are with us." The official Cuban tolerance of animistic Afro-Cuban cults, and the contradictions that their existence implies, also invites analogy with the Hungarian official quoted by Haraszti: "Socialism does not involve a world without contradictions and conflicts, but it is a society of resolvable, reasonably reconcilable contradictions."[29]

Musical policy in Cuba, of course, has never been as repressive and totalitarian as that under Stalin, or the Chinese Cultural Revolution. Modern Cuban painters and filmmakers have also felt quite free to explore all manner of avant-garde styles, synthesizing, in some cases, contemporary Western trends with stylizations of Afro-Cuban art. And as we have seen, since the mid-1970s, imported genres like rock and, for that matter, European art music have not been regarded as subversive vehicles for nihilistic or reactionary values. Rather, as León and others have argued, the meaning of these art forms changes in the context of Cuban socialism. Haraszti, writing from a Hungarian perspective, argues that the superficial tolerance of socialist countries in the post-Stalinist period masked a deeper stagnation and mediocrity, and that the "autonomous spirit" of the imported Western art was "permanently detained at the customs gate." He concludes, "It is the integrating capacity of state culture and not authentic pluralism that conquers."[30]

Modern Cuban commentators like art historian Gerardo Mosquera would counter that a cosmopolitan, hybrid *mestizaje* has always been and remains a fundamental rather than contrived feature of Cuban culture. In a similar vein, the comments of journalist Coco Fusco in reference to the Cuban visual arts scene may offer a more balanced perspective than Haraszti's, and one which is more representative of Cuban viewpoints as well as the reality of Cuban culture:

---

[29]*The Velvet Prison*, p. 148.
[30]*Ibid.*, p. 113.

Rather than locating an essential Cuban identity in a past indigenous culture or a homogenized future one, the most sophisticated commentary and artwork now focuses on the syncretic, synthesizing procedures by which Cubans make the foreign their own. To understand the present, they suggest, is to understand how the material conditions of Cuban socialism force this "recontextualization" to become a part of everyday life. The latest chapter in this procedure is the importation of what some Cuban artists perceive as a "postmodern attitude" -- which conveniently removes the stigma of dependence from the act of appropriation, celebrates eclecticism and skeptically disavows the rhetoric of authenticity.[31]

It is difficult to assess objectively the true vitality of Cuban artistic culture, and the extent to which the apparent pluralism of cultural policy masks a deeper one-dimensionality. Most Cubans as well as foreign observers, however, would probably tend to agree that it is in the realm of music that Cuba's artistic creativity and activity are the most dynamic. One factor, as we have suggested, is that the state, recognizing the international renown of Cuban music, gives special support and license to musicians in order to retain the island's musical fame.

Another factor, also discussed above, is the official policy of not only recognizing, but embracing the country's rich Afro-Cuban heritage -- especially music and dance. The strength of Afro-Cubanism as a cultural movement extends well beyond the support for folkloric groups (and indeed, it explains much of the public support for Cuba's defense of Angola against South African aggression). Afro-Cubanism plays an important role in the official and public enthusiasm for popular musics like *son* and *rumba*, and even informs art

---

[31]Coco Fusco, "Drawing New Lines," in *The Nation*, 10/24/88, p. 400.

music insofar as modern composers like Caturla, and Roldán have turned to Afro-Cuban rhythms for inspiration.

Thus, Cuban scholars like León, noting the healthy nationalistic and proletarian ethos of Afro-Cuban music, would not deny the significance of extra-musical values and associations. At the same time, they would insist that the *context* of Cuban socialism -- with its progress in combatting poverty, racism, illiteracy, and machismo -- strips imported or archaic musics of the negative values which they might promote in other social contexts. Thus, the argument runs, animistic cult music loses much of its associations with violence, chauvinism, and obscurantist superstition in the context of an educated, progressive society. Meanwhile, esoteric art music promotes arrogant elitism only in a hierarchic class society. And finally, objectification of women (or of men) is pernicious and destructive primarily in the context of a generally sexist community, not in a society of relative equals. Cuban Marxists, then, could be said to aspire to the condition envisioned by Adorno, in which "liberated mankind would be able to inherit its historical legacy free of all guilt."[32]

Content, Context, and Multiple Readings

We are now in a position to articulate more clearly the apparent contradiction between this belief in the omnipotence of context, on the one hand, and the notion that art works embody values in themselves, somewhat independently of the audience's context. In suggesting that the meaning of music and art depend almost entirely on the context in which they are perceived, the prevailing Cuban Marxist ideology and its related cultural policy would seem to be in opposition to the view that musical form and style iconically reflect and embody the social and ideological structures of their parent societies. Certainly, the evident pluralism of Cuban cultural policy toward music could be seen as the somewhat disingen-

---

[32]Adorno, *op. cit.*, p. 60.

uous rationalization of circumstances beyond the control of
state cultural policy -- that is, it is possible that Afro-Cuban
cult music is tolerated because the state is unable to eliminate
the cults, that clubs like the Tropicana flourish because of the
need for tourist revenue, and that the radio stations broadcast rock for fear of losing their audience to Miami stations.

Indeed, there is no doubt that Cuban Marxism, rather than
evolving in an ideological vacuum, has been shaped by such
objective external conditions.   Its ideology, however, has long
since taken on a life of its own, with its own consistency, coherence, and effects.   As such, its pluralistic attitude toward
musics associated with diverse social bacgrounds revives the
familiar question posed by Karl Marx: Why do we still like
Greek art when its foundations are a dead mode of production?   There are two factors involved in the answer to this
question.   The first depends on the recognition that a work of
art (or any "text") may be subject to multiple interpretations,
especially if it is complex and rich. Hence the ability of, for
example, Mozart's music to acquire new ideological readings
in the Cuban context.   The second key to addressing the paradox lies in the realization that artistic meaning is not imma-
nent in the text, but only in its interpretation.   That is, strictly
speaking, there is nothing *in the notes* that expresses iconic-
ity or social values (or for that matter, beauty); it is only
when it is humanly perceived that music acquires ideology
and meaning.   Thus, we may assume that a listening audience
must have some considerable familiarity and exposure to the
aesthetic and value system of a given society in order to ap-
prehend the ideological character of a music from that society.   In this sense, modern Cuba can be said to lie in an ambiguous grey area, in the sense that Cuban society has considerable affinites with the cultures that produced, for example,
19th century Western art music, or African cult music; the
extent to which the socialist Cuban context can overcome
"inherent" values in the case of such traditional, yet familiar
musics may be genuinely arguable.

This article has attempted to raise such philosophical questions by looking at the apparent contradictions in Cuban musical culture. At the same time, it has explored these questions in order to understand the meaning of Cuban musical pluralism itself. An assessment of the integrity of this pluralism involves the degree to which musics in Cuba promote authentic, dynamic, and progressive values, as opposed to negative, alienating ones. And the degree to which they do so itself depends upon the nature of Cuban society as a whole, and the extent to which it constitutes an environment conducive to spontaneity, authenticity, and self-realization in general. This evaluation thereby becomes incomparably broader and more subjective, and thus well beyond the scope of a short article, or, for that matter, the perspective of any single observer.

Glossary

abakuá -- Afro-Cuban cult of Carabalí derivation; syn. *ñañigo*
abwe -- scraper used in *lucumí* (Yoruba-derived) music
aplití -- *arará* drum
arará -- Afro-Cuban cult associated with descendants, known by the same term, of Dahomeyan Fon and Ewe
asajún -- *arará* drum

bacú -- archaic conical drum used in *comparsas* and *misas espirituales* in Oriente
bajo -- lit., bass; *iyesá* drum played with hands
bandola -- Spanish-derived mandolin-like instrument
bandurria -- Spanish-derived mandolin-like instrument
batá -- double-headed drum used in *lucumí* ceremonies
bembé -- (1) in Cuba, a type of *lucumí* ceremony, using drums and rhythms by the same name, where possession may occur, but wherein the drums are not consecrated as they would be in a standard *santería* ceremony; regarded as "a party for the gods"; (2) in Cuba, staved barrel drums, with the skin affixed by pegs, used in the above; (3) the standard 12/8 rhythm used in the above; (4) in New York City, a term used loosely to designate a *santería* ceremony, using either *batá* drums or "drum and *güiro*"
biankomé -- *abakuá* drum
bokú -- eastern Cuban drum played with bare hands
bolero -- sentimental, danceable song in slow quadratic meter, with a characteristic bass pattern (when bass is present) of a half-note followed by two quarter-notes
bombo -- Spanish drum used in military bands
bonkó echemiyá -- largest drum in the *abakuá* ensemble
botija -- jug, whose mouth is blown over to produce a bass note, in *son, punto* ensembles, etc.
briyumba -- Bantu-derived Afro-Cuban society
bulá -- medium-sized supporting drum in the *tumba francesa* ensemble

cabildo -- Afro-Cuban mutual aid society

cachimbo -- smallest drum in the *yuka* ensemble

caja -- (1) lit., box; (2) largest drum in the *arará* and *yuka* ensembles

campesino -- lit., peasant, though generally used in Cuba to denote peasant of European descent

canción -- lit., song, especially a through-composed, sentimental slow song not associated with dance

carabalí -- descendent of the Calabar region (presently in coastal Nigeria)

catá -- log played idiophonically, especially in *lucumí* music and *tumba francesa* ensembles

cha-chá -- uncovered baskets played idiophonically in Santiago de Cuba *comparsas*

chachachá -- popular dance and music genre in medium-tempo quadratic meter, originating in the 1950s, archetypically played by a *charanga* ensemble

chambelona -- in Cuba: (1) lollipop; (2) a popular processional song/genre, used to promote political campaigns in Cuba from 1917 on

changüí -- song genre of eastern Cuba, resembling the *son*

charanga -- dance ensemble typically consisting of flute, two violins, piano, bass, percussion, and vocals

cinquillo -- rhythmic ostinato recurring in the *danzón*: ♩♫‿♫♩

clave -- (1) lit., key (esp., metaphorically); (2) one of a pair of hard wooden sticks struck together idiophonically; (3) the characteristic ostinato played on the above; (4) a 19th- and early 20th-century urban genre in 6/8 meter, sung archetypically by strolling working-class choruses of blacks, accompanied on assorted instruments (*coros de clave*)

columbia -- one of the three main types of rumba, danced by a solo male, in what could be regarded as 12/8 meter

comparsa -- street procession, associated with Carnival, incorporating music and mimetic dance (especially *conga*)

composé -- lead singer in *tumba francesa* ensemble

conga -- (1) single-headed drum used in dance ensembles; (2) song and dance genre, characteristically used in *comparsa* processions (italicized in this volume)

conjunto -- standard dance ensemble consisting of rhythm section, two to four horns, keyboard, and vocals

contradanza -- 19th century salon dance genre, known more commonly abroad as *habanera* (from *contradanza habanera*, or Havana-style *contradanza*)

controversia -- *punto* in the form of a duel between two singers

criolla -- early twentieth-century urban genre in syncopated 6/8 meter, resembling the *clave*, although more sophisticated, and with texts idealizing rural campesino life

cuatro -- Puerto Rican guitar-like lute with four double or triple courses

cumbia -- secular dance and song genre of Columbia

danza -- (1) Puerto Rican genre closely resembling the *danzón*; (2) a mid-19th c. Cuban predecessor to the *danzón*

danzón -- salon music and dance genre popular from late 19th through early 20th centuries

décima -- text form of ten-line stanzas, with rhyme scheme of *abbccbbddb*, sung in Cuba in the textual-melodic form called *punto*

dengue -- (1) a kind of fever; (2) a 19th c. creole salon dance

diablito -- *abakuá* supernatural personage, represented by masked dancer in ceremonies

ekón -- cowbell used by *abakuá* performers

ekué -- sacred *abakuá* drum which may not be seen

ekueñón -- *abakuá* drum, used for ceremonial signals rather than for music

empego -- *abakuá* drum, as above

enkríkamo -- drum, as above

frente -- lit., (f.) forehead, (m.) front; final section of *yubá* dance in *tumba francesa*

galerón -- Spanish-derived song and dance genre of Venezuela

guajeo -- repeated melodic ostinato played in montuno section of *son, guaracha*, etc

316

guajira -- (1) a female Cuban peasant (i.e., fem. of *guajiro*); (2) a type of predominantly urban popular song, imitative of Cuban peasant music (from *música guajira*)
guajiro -- a Cuban peasant
guaguancó -- the most popular kind of rumba
guapachá -- commercial popular song and dance genre of the 1950s
guaracha -- a secular dance song popular in Cuba from the nineteenth century, bearing affinities to the *son*
guayo -- tin rasp
güegüé -- *arará* drum
güiro -- a serrated gourd used idiophonically as a scraper

habanera -- alternate term for *contradanza* (from *contradanza habanera*)

itótole -- medium-sized *batá* drum
iyá -- largest *batá* drum
iyesá -- Afro-Cuban Yoruba-derived religious sect, closely related to *santería*, having its own characteristic ceremonial songs and drum patterns

kinfuiti -- small, archaic Afro-Cuban drum
kuchí yeremá -- *abakuá* drum

laúd -- Spanish-derived mandolin-like instrument used in *punto*
lucumí -- Afro-Cuban of Yoruba derivation or descendence
malombe -- see *mayombe*
makuta -- Bantu-derived barrel drum, ancestor of the modern conga drum
mambo -- up-tempo, predominantly instrumental commercial genre, popularized in the 1940s, featuring antiphonal sectional writing for horn and reed sections
maracas -- pair of gourd shakers
marimbula -- box, with plucked metal keys, used as a bass instrument; an enlarged version of African "thumb-pianos" like the *mbira*

317

masón -- dance in *tumba francesa*
mayombe -- society of Bantu-derived Cubans
merengue -- predominant secular dance and song genre of the Dominican Republic, also popular in eastern Cuba
mongolés -- ephemeral pop genre of the 1960s
montuno -- (1) the final, and often longest, part of a rumba or *son*, employing call-and-response vocals over a rhythmic and harmonic ostinato; (2) the recurring pattern played, for example, on the piano, in the *montuno* of a *son*
mozambique -- a kind of *comparsa* rhythm, and dance song using that rhythm, popular in Cuba in the 1960s
mula -- medium-sized drum used in *yuka* ensemble

ñañigo -- *abakuá*
ñonajo -- *arará* drum
ñonufó -- *arará* drum
ngoma -- Bantu-derived cylindrical drum

obi-apá -- *abakuá* drum
okónkolo -- smallest *batá* drum
olokum -- archaic drum used in *lucumí* music
ombligada -- Afro-Brazilian dance wherein the partners touch navels
orquesta típica -- in the 19th century, an ensemble, primarily playing *danzón* and *habanera*, consisting of cornet, trombone, *figle, bombardino* (saxhorn), two clarinets, two or more violins, contrabass, *timbales*, and *güiro*
oyó -- West African dialect, elements of which occasionally appear in *lucumí* chants

pa-cá -- ephemeral pop genre of the mid-twentieth century
pachanga -- a sub-genre of dance song popular in Cuba in the 1950-60s, generally featuring the bass ostinato: ♩ ♪ ♩ ♩
pie forzado -- lit., forced foot; in *punto*, a given line upon which the singer or singers are obliged to improvise *décimas*
pilón -- colonial salon dance, incorporating some mimetic movements

plantilla -- in Cuba, the arrangement by which an established professional musician is paid a regular salary by the state
pregón -- (1) lit., call; (2) street-vendor's call; (3) a sub-genre of the *son* (i.e., *son pregón*) whose texts imitate such calls
premier -- largest drum in *tumba francesa* ensemble, used for improvisations, leading introductions, etc
punto -- in Cuba, the musical setting of a *décima*
puya -- song sung by *lucumí* devotees to provoke a deity into descending

quijada -- the jawbone of a donkey, used as a scraper
quimbisa -- Bantu-derived Afro-Cuban mutual aid society
quinto -- higher-pitched conga drum

redoblante -- Spanish drum used in military bands
regla -- generic term for Afro-Cuban society
requinto -- fife, in military band
rigodón -- nineteenth-century salon dance
rumba -- traditional secular music and dance genre, rendered by vocals with percussion, or later, in its commercialized form, by standard dance-band ensemble

salsa -- Cuban-style popular dance music, as performed by Latino communities in New York, Puerto Rican, and elsewhere outside of Cuba
santería -- Yoruba-derived Afro-Cuban religion
segón -- supporting drum in the tumba francesa ensemble
son -- the single most popular dance music genre of 20th century Cuba
sucu-sucu -- song and dance genre, resembling the *son*, of the Isle of Pines

tambor -- lit., drum; in New York City, one of the terms used to designate a *santería* ceremony with *batá* drums
tambora -- two-headed drum used in *masón* dance of the *tumba francesa*

timbales -- pair of single-headed drums, played with sticks, standard in 20th century popular dance ensembles (*charanga, conjunto,* etc.)
típico -- lit., typical, but more broadly connoting "traditional"
tiple -- Spanish-derived guitar-like instrument
tonada -- lit., tune, song; melody, in *punto*
toque -- (1) lit., touch, ringing, sounding, beating; (2) Afro-Cuban socio-religious event with dance, singing, *batá* drumming, and, often, possession (in New York City, roughly synonymous, in this sense, with *tambor*); (3) designation for any one of a set of specific *batá* rhythmic "salute" patterns
tres -- lit., three; Cuban guitar-like instrument with three double or triple courses
trova -- folk and popular music category, comprising in particular the bolero and *canción*
trovador -- lit., "troubador"
tumba -- drums used in *tumba francesa (premier, bulá, segón)*
tumbadora -- lowest-pitched conga drum
tumba francesa -- (1) mutual aid and social recreation society of Franco-Haitian immigrants to eastern Cuba; (2) dance and song genre performed by the latter

vacunao -- a pelvic thrust performed by the male rumba dancer symbolizing his conquest of his partner
vallenato -- accordion-dominated folk and popular ensemble, and associated genres, of northeastern Columbia
vals tropical -- archaic Cubanized version of the waltz

yambú -- one of the three major types of traditional rumba, resembling the *guaguancó*, but in slower tempo
yubá -- archaic *tumba francesa* dance
yuka -- (1) secular, Congo-derived dance and music genre, believed to be the ancestor of the rumba; (2) drums used in that genre
zapateado -- in Spanish music: (1) rhythmic stamping of the feet; (2) a dance and music genre featuring the latter
zapateo -- Spanish-derived rural dance
zarzuela -- Spanish light opera, also cultivated in Cuba

Index

EGREM, 189ff, 235-38
ekón, 315
ekué, 9, 315
ekueñón, 9, 315
empego, 9, 315
enkríkamo, 315
erikunde, 9

Fajardo, José, 119
Faílde, Miguel, 19-20
fandango, 11
Fania Records, 160, 165-67, 175-76
filin, 22, 188
flamenco, 98n
flute, 123
frente, 303
Fuentes Matons, Laureano, 12

gaditano, 11
galerón, 97, 100, 315
gayumbas, 13
guajeo, 315; in charanga, 122
guajira, 3, 16-17, 294
guajiro, 316
guaguancó, 6, 13-14, 49-73, 316
guapachá, 6, 316
guaracha, 3, 11, 18, 19, 125, 160, 316
guayo, 12, 110, 316
güegüé, 41, 316
Guevara, Ché, 217, 283
Guillén, Nicolás, 25, 68-69, 2862 278-80, 294
güiro, 4, 8, 99, 110, 121, 139n, 316
gurujú, 13

habanera, 3, 316 (see contradanza)
Haraszti, Miklos, 305ff
Hauser, Arnold, 301

About the Editor

Peter Manuel is the author of *Popular Musics of the Non-Western World, Thumri in Historical and Stylistic Perspectives,* and several articles on traditional and popular musics in India, Cuba, Spain, and elsewhere. He currently teaches ethnomusicology at Columbia University in New York.